MTV

THE MAKING OF A REVOLUTION

TOM McGRATH

RUNNING PRESS

PHILADELPHIA · LONDON

In memory of my grandfather,

Jerry Walker—a journalist and a gentleman

Photographs courtesy of the following:
AP/ Wide World Photos: p.196
© Janette Beckman/Retna Ltd.: p. 174 (left)
Cablevision magazine: pp. 14, 15, 17, 24, 34,
     122, 157
Capitol Records/Brian Aris, photographer: p. 95
Epic Records: p. 108
Everett Collection: pp. 55, 71, 87, 102, 109, 116,
     128, 129, 149, 167, 174 (right), 183,
          186, 200 (MTV logo), 202, 203
Les Garland: p. 77
© Jonathan Levine: p. 146
MTV Europe: p. 178
Bob McGroarty: p. 25
Lee Masters: p. 160
© Frank Micelotta/Retna Ltd.: p.189
NASA: pp. 20, 176 (composites), 200 (background), 201

Personality Photos, Inc.: p. 150
© Charlie Pizzarello/Retna Ltd.: p. 166
Dale Pon: p. 80
Reuters/Bettmann: p. 192
© Ebet Roberts: p. 52

Background patterns and textures by Stephen Mullen:
pp. 1, 6–7, 10 (background), 30–31, 44–45, 66–67, 87, 109,
128, 174, 184

9   8   7   6   5   4   3   2   1
Digit on the right indicates the number of this printing.

Library of Congress Cataloging-in-Publication Number
95–70676.
ISBN 1–56138–703–7

Designed by Nancy Loggins Gonzalez and Paul Kepple
Photoshop collages by Paul Kepple
Photo research by Susan Oyama and Tom McGrath
Printed in the United States of America

This book may be ordered by mail from the publisher.
Please add $2.50 for postage and handling.
But try your bookstore first!

Running Press Book Publishers
125 South Twenty-second Street
Philadelphia, Pennsylvania 19103–4399

CONTENTS

acknowledgments

ACKNOWLEDGMENTS
ACKNOWLEDGMENTS
ACKNOWLEDGMENTS

My goal in writing this book was simple—to chronicle how MTV grew into a successful and influential pop culture institution, and to capture what it was like to be part of that growth. Doing that wouldn't have been possible without the help of many people.

First, my thanks to the numerous MTV employees (both past and present) and other entertainment industry executives who spoke with me at length about MTV. Their memories, observations, and insights are the bedrock of this book.

I'm also indebted to the other journalists who've previously written about MTV. The abundance of newspaper and magazine articles on the subject provided me with a wonderful road map for researching this story. In addition, a number of books were helpful, among them: *American Express* by Peter Z. Grossman; *The Fifties* by David Halberstam; *Hit Men* by Frederic Dannen; *Master of the Game* by Connie Bruck; *In All His Glory* by Sally Bedell Smith; *The Rolling Stone Book of Rock Video* by Michael Shore; *Three Blind Mice* by Ken Auletta; and *To the End of Time* by Richard Clurman.

Others I'd like to thank are Carole Robinson and her staff at MTV; Craig Leddy at *Cablevision* magazine; Emily Bestler; Lou Harry; Ginny Moles; Kate Rindfleisch; my agent, Jeremy Solomon; my editors, David Borgenicht and Mary McGuire; my friends and family; and, of course, Harry and the Ghost Who Walks, to whom I owe everything.

MTV Time Line

September 1979
Warner American Express Satellite Entertainment Company (WASEC) founded

January 1981
Warner Communications and American Express approve creation of music video channel

August 1, 1981
MTV debuts at 12:01 A.M., playing Buggles's "Video Killed the Radio Star"

October 1981
MTV runs first contest—"One Night Stand with Journey"

December 31, 1981
MTV hosts first New Year's Eve Rock and Roll Ball.

Summer 1982
"I Want My MTV!" television ad campaign begins

September 1982
MTV debuts in Manhattan and Los Angeles

Fall 1982
Kraft becomes first major advertiser to make a commercial specifically for MTV

March 1983
Michael Jackson's "Billie Jean" and "Beat It" premiere on MTV

Summer 1983
Night Tracks debuts on TBS; *Friday Night Videos* debuts on NBC

October 1983
MTV featured on cover of *People* magazine

December 1983
Michael Jackson's "Thriller" premieres on MTV

December 31, 1983
MTV completes first profitable quarter

February 1984
WASEC changes name to MTV Networks

August 1984
MTV Networks stock goes public

September 1984
Dan Aykroyd and Bette Midler host first MTV Video Music Awards

Fall 1984
With visual style inspired by MTV, *Miami Vice* debuts on NBC

October 1984
Ted Turner launches Cable Music Channel

November 1984
National Coalition on Television Violence releases report critical of MTV

December 1984
Ted Turner pulls plug on Cable Music Channel

January 1985
VH-1 launched

June 1985
American Express announces its intention to sell its share of MTV Networks

August 1985
Leveraged buyout fails; Viacom purchases MTV Networks

February 1986
MTV begins airing episodes of *The Monkees*

March 1986
MTV airs first broadcast from Florida during Spring Break

June 1986
J. J. Jackson and Nina Blackwood are first of original veejays to leave MTV

August 1986
Chief Executive Officer Bob Pittman announces his departure from MTV Networks

February 1987
Sumner Redstone purchases controlling interest in Viacom

August 1987
MTV Europe launched; first video is Dire Straits's "Money for Nothing"

August 1987
Club MTV debuts on MTV

Fall 1987
The Week in Rock and *Remote Control* debut on MTV

July 1988
MTV declines to play Neil Young's "This Note's for You" video

August 1988
Yo! MTV Raps debuts

November 1989
MTV goes on the air in East Berlin; forty-eight hours later, Berlin Wall falls

January 1990
MTV Unplugged premieres, hosted by Jules Shear; Syd Straw and Squeeze are guests

November 1990
MTV declines to play Madonna's "Justify My Love"

September 1991
MTV Asia launched

Spring 1992
Real World debuts on MTV

February 1992
MTV begins coverage of 1992 Presidential campaign

June 1992
Bill Clinton appears in MTV *Choose or Lose* forum

Fall 1992
Beavis and Butt-head debuts on MTV

January 20, 1993
MTV Inaugural Ball, Washington, D.C.

Summer 1993
MTV Productions created

Fall 1993
MTV Latino launched

Summer 1994
MTV teams with America Online to create on-line presence

Fall 1994
MTV Interactive created to develop video games, CD-ROM products, and interactive TV services

Spring 1995
MTV Mandarin launched

Summer 1995
MTV launches a page on the Internet

THE BALL

They'd arrived.

Standing onstage inside the Washington Convention Center, the bright TV lights shining down on him, comedian Dennis Miller looked at the note he'd just been handed, read for himself the big news, and started to grin.

"Oh, wow," he said, gazing out at the hundreds of young, formally clad bodies who filled the audi-torium on this cold January night. "Somebody really important just showed up." Miller, the emcee for the evening's festivities—MTV's Inaugural Ball—paused for a beat, and then smirked.

"Kurt Loder," he said smartly.

The crowd laughed.

"No," Miller continued, "Tabitha will tell you who it is."

It was just past nine, only a few minutes after Miller and Tabitha Soren, the MTV news reporter, had officially gotten this event underway, and inside the cavernous convention center the crowd began to buzz. Everyone knew precisely who'd shown up. The rumor mill had been dropping hints for weeks. But even if it was no surprise, it was a thrill.

For MTV, a network that had known many big nights, this was arguably its biggest ever. Not that they really needed another big night. The network was already one of the most phenomenal success stories in the history of television. Eleven and a half years after going on the air, MTV had become a lucrative business with a solid reputation on Madison Avenue and Wall Street. The previous year had been a record setter for the company, with MTV and its sister networks, VH-1 and Nickelodeon, pulling in gross revenues of more than $500 million. Moreover, MTV was now truly an international phenomenon. Over the past several years, it had become the first true global television network;

it reached more than 200 million homes in seventy countries around the world.

Maybe most impressive of all was the impact the channel had made on popular culture over the past decade. Since first going on the air in August of 1981, MTV had transformed the music, television, and film industries. Indeed, the term "MTV-like"—a synonym for fast-moving images set to loud music—had entered the language. Some even argued that the channel and its visual style had started to change the very way young people's minds worked. Whether all of this influence was good or bad was debatable—and over the years many people had debated it—but you couldn't deny that the influence was great. As the *Washington Post* had put it in a story about the 1980s, MTV was "perhaps the most influential single cultural product of the decade."

Still, for all the attention they'd received and success they'd achieved over the past eleven and a half years, until this night, the people behind MTV had never received the kind of acceptance that now awaited them. The guest list confirmed the grandeur of the occasion. Most of the place was filled with young people—the crowd was so fresh-faced that the event looked almost like a high school prom, with slinkier dresses and a cash bar. But in the back of the auditorium, cordoned off from the masses, were some of the world's biggest celebrities. By the end of the night, Jack Nicholson, Barbra Streisand, Peter Jennings, Christie Brinkley, and dozens more luminaries had stopped by for a quick drink or just to be seen. And why not? On a night when Washington was filled with big, glamorous parties, this was the biggest and most glamorous of the bunch.

Inside the hall everyone's attention shifted to the right side of the stage, where redheaded Tabitha Soren, dressed in a strapless black evening gown and funky black boots, stood holding a microphone. If this was a big night for MTV, it was almost incredible for the twenty-five-year-old reporter. Just eighteen months ago she had been a cub reporter for a tiny TV station in Vermont. And now? Thanks to her coverage of the presidential campaign for MTV, she was practically a celebrity herself.

With the crowd buzzing in anticipation, Soren looked into the camera in front of her and finally made the official introduction. "Ladies and gentlemen," she said earnestly, "the President of the United States and the First Lady, Hillary Rodham Clinton."

The band started playing "Don't Stop," the Fleetwood Mac tune that Bill Clinton and his running mate, Al Gore, had adopted as their campaign theme song. Then the youthful-looking new president and his wife walked out from behind the curtain. They greeted Soren and moved to the front of the stage, holding hands and smiling as the audience screamed.

With the crowd cheering, Bill Clinton tried to talk.

"Hello, thank you, thank you," he said, smiling as the ovation started to die down. Just then, out from behind the curtain walked the Clintons' daughter, Chelsea, and the group began to chant her name.

"Don't my wife and daughter look beautiful tonight?" Bill Clinton asked, as the crowd erupted again. Finally, they quieted down and the president turned more serious.

"Now, I think everybody here knows," he said, his Arkansas drawl echoing throughout the hall, "MTV had a lot to do with the Clinton-Gore victory."

He paused for a moment, letting the crowd acknowledge the remark, and then continued. "And Tab, you know, brought me on to the show and let all the young people ask me questions, a lot of tough questions. And it was a fascinating experience. And I began to do it more and more. And one of the things that I'm proudest of is that so many young voters turned out in record numbers. I want you to know that I still believe in Rock the Vote. And we're going to have Motor Voter registration now. Thank you."

The band kicked in again, the crowd cheered, and the First Family left the stage. Bill and Hillary went to visit the other eleven balls taking place in their honor that night. Chelsea stayed.

Inside the convention center, the party continued with some of the biggest acts in music—Don Henley, En Vogue, 10,000 Maniacs, and an impromptu group consisting of members of U2 and REM. Later, Al and Tipper Gore showed up. Finally, at nearly 1:00 A.M., Don Henley sang the Bob Dylan anthem "The Times They Are A-Changin'," and the show was over.

It was an extraordinary night, and for a handful of people in the room that evening, it was especially so. They were middle-aged now, a bit grayer and a bit heavier than when they'd first met. As they looked at what had happened over the past decade, not only to MTV, but also to cable television and to rock and roll—and to themselves—they couldn't help but be amazed. Most of them could still remember the days when the idea of being embraced by anyone in a suit, let alone the president of the United States, was laughable.

Among this group, no one had a longer memory of MTV than one who'd long since left the network: John Lack. At forty-seven, he was as effervescent as he'd ever been. And who could blame him?

After all, this whole thing had really started with him, back in Columbus.

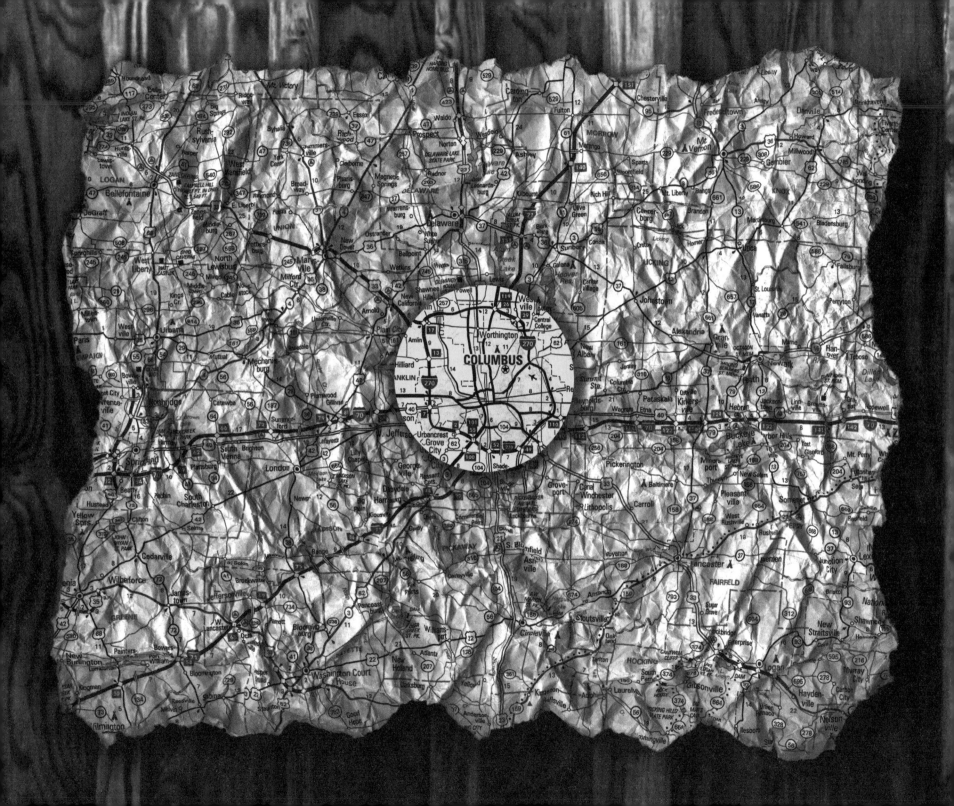

ONE

COLUMBUS

WINTER 1979 — SUMMER 1979

In the decades that followed World War II, an unusual thing happened to Columbus, Ohio: It became the most ordinary place in America.

Everything about this city seemed to mirror what America was, or at least believed itself to be, in those years. Columbus sat in the middle of Ohio, a state that was itself situated in Middle America. What's more, Columbus looked like an American city was supposed to look, with wide, tree-lined streets, stately old homes, and a river, the Scioto, running quietly along its western edge.

Then there were its people. By the late 1970s, more than a half a million people were living in Columbus—people who represented ordinary, mainstream America; people who made it corporate America's favorite testing ground for new products. Throughout the sixties and seventies, numerous companies came to town to try out their newest wares. The logic was simple: If you could sell your new product to the heartland of America, you could sell it anywhere.

All of which was why John Lack had absolutely no desire to go to Columbus, a fact that undoubtedly crossed his mind when his plane touched down on the runway at Port Columbus International Airport on a cold day in January 1979. Though Lack wasn't opposed to any of that heartland stuff, he just wasn't a very ordinary Joe. A well-built thirty-three-year-old, with thick black hair, a dark brow, and deep-set blue eyes, Lack had grown up in a well-to-do family in New York and could appreciate and afford the finer things in life.

There was nothing ordinary about his personality, either. Though he could be moody and brooding, and would occasionally flash a fiery temper, most of the time John Lack was generous, charismatic, and boyishly enthusiastic. He also had an uncommon ability to sell you on whatever notion he happened to be talking about. He'd always start out softly, his deep baritone voice quietly gaining your attention. Then slowly, carefully, almost rhythmically, he'd lure you in. He'd talk, and you'd listen. Gradually he'd become louder, more impassioned, then—bam!—suddenly, as though he'd taken you by the hand, you'd go wherever Lack took you, just because he made it all sound like so much fun.

All of these qualities had served John Lack well in his job over the past eight years as an executive with CBS Radio in New York. Though some questioned his maturity, Lack had done well at CBS with his engaging personality and polish. Starting as an account executive in the company's radio division in 1970, he quickly climbed the CBS ladder. By the time he was thirty-two, he was general manager of WCBS-AM, News Radio 88, the network's flagship radio station.

For those interested in broadcasting, there was no finer place to be than CBS. By early 1979, the broadcast networks were at the height of their power, and though CBS no longer dominated as it once did, it was still the preeminent network. Founded in 1927, at thedawn of the radio age, the company had become under its legendary chairman, Bill Paley, the most successful and highly regarded broadcasting company in the world. In fact, it became known as the Tiffany Network.

CBS executives were reputed to be the best and brightest in the business. It wasn't only that they were smarter, more savvy, and more ambitious than anybody else—they seemed to have more style. Taking their cue from Bill Paley, CBS executives dined in the best restaurants and smoked the best cigars. Jack Schneider, the executive who headed the company's broadcasting division through most of the sixties and seventies, embodied all that a CBS executive should be in those days: He was handsome, stylish, glib, marvelously successful—and for all those reasons, young John Lack idolized him.

So, in almost every single way, John Lack seemed to be too large a character for the very nice but very normal Columbus, Ohio. After all, who in his right mind would leave the Tiffany of CBS to go work in the Wal-Mart of Columbus? But several months earlier, an executive with Warner Communications, Ted Ashley, had approached Lack about a Warner's project in Columbus. Initially, Lack wasn't interested. Ashley persisted, taking Lack to meet the men in charge of the project, offering to nearly triple his CBS salary, and promising that he could still be based in New York and would only have to spend a couple of days a week in Columbus. Finally, at the end of 1978, John Lack did the unthinkable: He left CBS.

Lack drove onto Olentangy River Road, a few miles from the airport, and a moment later he pulled up in front of a large cinder-block building that looked very much like the warehouse it had been only a couple of years earlier. Though it might have seemed crazy to leave a cushy job at the most powerful broadcast network in the world, there inside the Warner Cable building they were doing something that the slick suits at CBS could never have done—something even more attractive to John Lack than the secure luxury of the Tiffany Network. They were working to create the future of television. They were working to create cable TV.

To be sure, cable had really started three decades earlier, in a place significantly smaller and even less glamorous than Columbus.

In the can-do years after World War II, a burly young man named John Walson opened an appliance store in the tiny town of Mahanoy City, in the eastern part of Pennsylvania. Anxious to cash in on what everybody seemed sure was the next big fad, Walson had begun to sell television sets. Or, more accurately, he had begun trying to sell television sets. The problem was that the nearest TV stations were almost ninety miles away in Philadelphia. With the mountains that surrounded Mahanoy City blocking the already-weak signals, reception in town was practically nonexistent—as were sales of TV sets. But Walson wasn't one to give up. To spur sales, he built an antenna on top of nearby New Boston Mountain and drove potential buyers there to witness the miracle of television. He soon concluded that it would be better to bring the miracle to the people, so Walson, who'd worked as a lineman for the local electric company, strung some wire through the trees and down to his appliance warehouse on the edge of town. The next year he built a larger antenna, added some amplifiers, and persuaded local authorities to let him run lines along the power poles all the way to his shop. Along the way, Walson fed the lines into the homes of some of his neighbors, each of whom paid $100 for the hookup, plus $2 per month for the service. The cable TV industry was born.

Walson wasn't the only one to have this idea, and for years afterward there would be some question about who exactly had come up with it first. Across the country in Astoria, Oregon, an entrepreneur named Ed Parsons launched a similar service around the same time. Down the road from John Walson, in the town of Lansford,

Pennsylvania, Robert Tarleton created the Panther Valley Television Company in 1950. (The people of Lansford were so excited by the idea of finally being able to see TV that they declared a school holiday the day the system was turned on.)

Throughout the fifties and early sixties, cable TV systems sprang up in small communities all over America, as rugged self-starters such as Walson, Parsons, and Tarleton petitioned towns for the right to string wire along utility poles and into the homes of local citizens. For the residents of these towns cable was pure bliss. Like everyone else in America, they could come home after a hard day's work and, together with the kids, watch Huntley and Brinkley, and follow the exploits of Lucy and Ricky and Rob and Laura.

But the residents weren't the only ones excited by this new technology. As the technology improved and more cable systems began popping up in rural and suburban communities, a few experts began noticing that coaxial cable, the wire cable operators used, was a more effective way of transporting TV signals. Cable provided a clearer picture, was more reliable, and could carry more TV signals. Consequently, cable operators began adding to their systems channels from cities that were hundreds of miles away.

Though the industry itself remained dominated by entrepreneurial hardware types such as John Walson, by the mid-sixties everyone from sociologists to bureaucrats at the Federal Communications Commission (FCC) was chewing over the question of how America might best take advantage of the possibilities created by cable. After much thought, they came up with the only sensible answer: They would build Paradise.

At least that was what it sounded like when some of the

high-minded idealists talked about cable during the late sixties. Though most metropolitan areas weren't yet receiving cable, when they did, some predicted, America would become the "Wired Nation." This was to be a land in which every home and office was connected to every other home and office by coaxial cable, over which would flow not merely the three major broadcast networks that catered to the lowest common denominator, but also dozens of channels offering culture and information.

The possibilities were staggering. When cable operators gathered in 1968 for the National Cable Television Association (NCTA) convention, they saw a prototype of a home communications center in which the user, by means of this coaxial cable, could enter into two-way exchanges with stores, or perhaps order different TV programs, or even have at his or her fingertips information housed in libraries across the country. And the exhibit was just the beginning of what this new technology would make possible. Because cable could carry so many channels, television would no longer be limited to broadcast professionals such as Walter Cronkite, Andy Griffith, or Johnny Carson. Instead, channels would be made available for average citizens to discuss the issues of the day, or to cover events happening in their neighborhoods, or maybe even to star in their own shows. As FCC chairman Kenneth Cox told the National Association of Broadcasters in 1968, "The potential of cable excites a good many social scientists, who envisage every little town as having its own outlet for self-expression, even though it is far too small to support a regular broadcast station in the foreseeable future."

It was incredibly liberating. No longer would TV be controlled by the cigar-smoking, martini-drinking network sharpies who'd force-fed the public shows like *My Favorite Martian* or *My Mother the Car*. With cable, America could have television of the people, by the people, and for the people.

But the dreams didn't come true. One of the biggest obstacles was that the broadcast networks saw cable as a lethal threat. The network brass knew that if each viewer could choose from dozens of channels, the chances that he or she would pick ABC, CBS, or NBC were significantly reduced. And that meant fewer viewers for network shows, falling ad rates, and less money for the networks. Consequently, the broadcasters did all they could to beat back cable's challenge, suing cable operators, lobbying the FCC, and testifying before Congress. (CBS's Jack Schneider was among those leading the fight, explaining to the Senate Commerce Committee how disastrous it would be if cable operators were allowed to show certain sporting events.) The result of all this campaigning came between 1968 and 1972, when the FCC imposed numerous regulations on what cable operators could show, mostly to protect the ground the three broadcast networks called their own.

For the charismatic John Lack, the excitement of the brave new world of cable was too much to pass up. A rock and roller in his soul, he saw endless programming possibilities for the emerging medium.

The regulations were loosened slightly in 1972, but by that point the cable industry seemed to be losing steam. Its biggest problem was getting city residents interested. With cable operators unable to offer city dwellers anything more than they were already getting for free, the march into the city had slowed significantly. In most of America's largest markets there wasn't even enough interest to get a system built. Equally troubling, at least to many of the pro-cable idealists, was that in the urban areas where cable systems had been built, the Wired Nation hadn't quite lived up to its advance billing. One problem was that cable system owners were forbidden from regulating the content of public access channels. On the Sterling Cable system in lower Manhattan, for instance, alongside the Boy Scout merit badge ceremonies and other heart-warming examples of civic pride were shows like *The Bath*, in which a man in a bathtub smoked marijuana and dis-

the next couple of years Hauser began whipping Warner Cable into shape, changing things at the company's money-losing operations, acquiring more systems, and recruiting bright young executives—professional managers unlike the rugged entrepreneurs who then dominated the cable business. Finally, Hauser and his team began pondering the question that obsessed nearly everyone in the cable community: How could cable crack the large and lucrative urban markets?

In early 1977, Warner unveiled its answer. It was a new programming service called Qube, and there had never been anything like it. To be tested on the Warner system in Columbus, the service would use thirty of the thirty-six channels that system could handle. Ten of them, what Warner called the "television channels," were to be regular broadcast stations from Columbus, Akron, and Cincinnati. Ten more, the "community

Hard-driving cable executive Gus Hauser. With Qube, he and his team were creating the future of television.

played the delights of bathing, and *Transsexuals*, in which a woman shed her girdle to display the results of her sex-change operation.

In 1973, seeing that his company's cable division was struggling, Steve Ross, the chief of Warner Communications, went searching for a savior. A warm, stylish forty-five-year-old who'd built Warner into an incredibly successful entertainment conglomerate, Ross eventually found who he was looking for. He turned to Gustave Hauser, a hard-driving forty-three-year-old lawyer. Though they were opposites in personality, the two men shared a belief in cable TV's potential. Over

channels," would be programmed and produced at a new Warner studio in Columbus. Each would focus on a particular subject—one showing religion-only programming, another kids-only programming, another listing prices in local grocery stores, another covering news and events in Columbus, and so on. Finally, there would be ten "premium channels," for which viewers would pay a fee—$3, say, for a new movie, maybe $2 for a sporting event, a play, or an adult film. Viewers would select programs by punching buttons on a black remote-control box they would receive when they signed up for

Qube. The black box would then send a signal over the cable to a computer at Qube headquarters, and the selected program would pop up on the viewer's screen. At the end of each month, viewers would get a bill showing which programs they'd ordered.

The black box made Qube truly revolutionary. In addition to allowing viewers to select individual programs, it also gave them a way to interact with the programs. By pushing one of five response buttons on the box, Qube viewers would theoretically be able to take part in polls, play games, participate in quiz shows, vote in town meetings, take college courses—anything, in short, that required talking back to their television sets.

Just like that, all the promise cable TV had in the 1960s was untethered. Not only did Qube have the potential to change what America watched—could you imagine, thirty channels?—but it would also change how they watched. Thanks to pay-per-view, each viewer could become a "station manager." Qube-ites wouldn't just watch TV, they'd take part in it, through the magic of that little black remote control.

Qube debuted in December 1977, and the array of programming it presented to its ten thousand charter subscribers was staggering compared with what the rest of television offered. That winter, in addition to regular broadcast channels, viewers could watch new movies such as *A Star Is Born*, taped performances of cultural events such as *Madame Butterfly* and Bach's *Christmas Oratorio*, and sporting events such as Cleveland Cavaliers basketball. Above all, there was a whole range of new, interactive programming—everything from games to an entire channel called Columbus Alive, which asked viewers for their opinions on various issues.

It was a new world, right there in the middle of Columbus, Ohio. *Newsweek* commented, "It hardly requires a science fiction mentality to sense how revolutionary Qube could be."

By the time John Lack arrived at Warner Cable thirteen months after Qube's launch, some of the initial revolutionary fervor had begun to wear off. Not that the project had been a bust—there was much about Qube that had been wonderfully successful. The kids' channel, Pinwheel, was a big hit with parents, and some of the interactive programming on the Columbus Alive channel demonstrated the potential the new media form had. Indeed, just a month after Qube's launch, a blizzard hit Columbus, and during the emergency the city's mayor had been able to "dialogue," as Qube-ites put it, with viewers.

"Artistic self-expression for the common man" had become a cable reality as well, although not in the way the social scientists of the 1960s had anticipated. *Talent Search*, a Qube version of *The Gong Show* in which home viewers decided whether or not acts should be allowed to continue, gave a forum to local Columbus talent such as Bo's Burping Band, a quartet of young boys who belched out tunes accompanied by a mouth harp.

The pay-per-view channels had turned out to be popular, too, though not in the way the idealists had hoped. It seemed that the average people of Columbus weren't very fond of Bach or Beethoven, but they loved the first-run movies, the Ohio State football games, and even the adult films that Qube offered. (Movies such as *Massage Parlor Hookers* and *Super Vixens* were the most profitable programming on the whole cable system.)

But despite pockets of success, Qube had enormous problems. Some customers had inadvertently run up huge pay-per-view bills that they couldn't afford to pay, and others had stolen the $200 black boxes when they moved out of town, mistakenly thinking they could use the new technology on other cable systems. But Qube's biggest problem was financial. While it was fascinating as a prototype, it was losing money—even more than Warner had anticipated.

John Lack had been hired to help correct such problems, and in those first few months of 1979 he spent two or three days a week in Columbus and worked with other Warner executives to revise Qube's marketing strategies and hone its programming, searching for ways to improve the bottom line.

But Qube wasn't Lack's only focus. As Warner Cable's new executive vice president of marketing and programming, he also oversaw the company's entry into a whole new area of cable, one that by early 1979, seemed to have even more promise than Qube: satellite distribution.

during the Kennedy administration, and in 1974 Western Union became the first company to launch its own satellite. Despite the $1 million per year it cost to lease a transponder, which sent the signal to a receiving dish on earth, satellites were still cheaper and more efficient than building microwave towers.

In 1975, HBO leased a transponder on America's second domestic satellite, RCA's Satcom I. HBO persuaded a few cable operators around the country to purchase receiving dishes, and began sending its signal out into the heavens. The effect on subscriptions was phenomenal. In one year, the number of people subscribing to HBO zoomed 500 percent, and by 1978, 1.5 million Americans were receiving the service. And much to the delight of cable operators, people around the country were signing up for cable just to get HBO.

Other programmers began to follow HBO's lead. In 1976, Ted Turner, the glib, fast-talking owner of a struggling

The inimitable Ted Turner. Was his Cable Music Channel a crusade against MTV's "sleazy" videos, or merely a way of helping out his buddies in the cable industry?

Home Box Office (HBO), the program service owned by Time Inc., was the first cable entity to realize the potential in satellites. Launched in 1972 on a single cable system in Wilkes-Barre, Pennsylvania, HBO struggled in its early years. Just as the broadcast networks did with their affiliates, HBO sent its signal to cable operators over a series of microwave dishes. However, this method was inefficient and expensive. Not surprisingly, distribution was dismal.

Around that time, the communications satellite business began heating up. The first satellite was launched by the U.S. government

UHF-TV station in Atlanta, put his channel's signal on a satellite and distributed it to cable operators as America's first "superstation." A couple of years later, Viacom put the signal from its HBO-like service, Showtime, on the satellite. Interest in satellites was so high that a dozen new services were being planned by the time John Lack went to work at Warner Cable in early 1979.

Warner itself had leased two transponders on Satcom I in the fall of 1978, and the following spring it dipped a toe in the satellite waters by putting two services on it. One was a nightly movie feature called Star Channel, which it sent out to its own cable systems across the country. The second service was Pinwheel, the children's programming block that was airing on Qube. Later renamed Nickelodeon, the channel was offered to any cable operator who was willing to pay for it.

By the summer of 1979, John Lack was enjoying his new job, content that he had made the right move in leaving CBS for the frontier of cable. He found Gus Hauser difficult to work for and found Columbus to be pretty dull, but he learned to cope. On the nights he spent in Columbus, he would often retreat to his apartment and watch something on Qube, amusing himself with the new world of television and dreaming of other ways to make it come alive.

That September, John and his wife, Karen, flew to Europe for a couple of weeks. One day while they were in Paris, they returned to their hotel and received a message that Bess Myerson, the former Miss America, had called. Myerson sat on the Warner board of directors, and she and Lack had been friends since his days at WCBS, when he hired her to do regular consumer reports for the station. Lack called her back.

"I just wanted to let you know," Myerson said, "that when you come home you're going to have a new owner."

"What are you talking about?" Lack asked.

"American Express just bought half your company."

Warner chief executive officer Steve Ross had been searching for a cable partner for months. Though cable was a small business compared to network broadcasting—fewer than 20 percent of Americans received cable—the cable industry had begun to heat up again, and it was clear that cable operators were preparing once again for an

assault on America's cities. But competing for franchises and constructing systems in large metropolitan areas would be extraordinarily expensive. Taking on a partner seemed to be the best way to raise the needed capital.

American Express (AMEX) was also searching for something: a "fourth leg," as AMEX executives put it, to complement the company's hugely successful insurance, banking, and travel-related services divisions. But though the companies had compatible needs, a partnership between Warner and AMEX was anything but natural. The personalities of the chief executive officers were different: Ross was free-wheeling and emotional, while AMEX chief executive officer James Robinson III was staid and conservative. What's more, the cultures of their companies were vastly different. Warner was filled with street-smart sharks who knew the entertainment business, AMEX with buttoned-down Ivy Leaguers who specialized in insurance, banking, and finance. But when investment banker Felix Rohatyn had brought Ross and Robinson together, the two men had managed to look past their differences and see in each other the potential perfect mates. AMEX had the financial stability and top-notch reputation Warner was looking for, while Warner Cable had both the growth potential and synergy that AMEX was after.

John Lack returned to New York a few days after the partnership deal was announced. On his first day back at Warner corporate headquarters in New York, he was summoned to see cable chief Gus Hauser. Hauser filled Lack in on the details of the deal and told him they'd decided to split the cable business—which would now be called Warner AMEX—into two divisions. One, Warner AMEX Cable Communications (WACC), which was being run by Hauser, would oversee

Qube, the company's hundreds of other cable systems, and the ultimate wiring of America's cities; the other, Warner AMEX Satellite Entertainment Company (WASEC), to be run by someone else, would develop satellite-delivered program services like the Star Channel and Nickelodeon. He asked Lack which one he preferred to be part of.

Lack barely hesitated. He wouldn't mind not working for Hauser anymore. More important, it was the business of programming that excited him, not the business of lobbying for franchises and stringing wire. Maybe they'd even put him in charge of this new operation. He told Hauser he wanted to be part of the programming venture.

"That's fine," Hauser said. "But, unfortunately, we can't make you CEO. I don't think you have enough gray hair. We can probably make you the number two man, though."

Lack was disappointed. He asked if they had someone in mind for the job.

"Yes, we do," said Hauser. "He's sitting in the office next door. Why don't you go say hello to him."

Lack got up and walked into the visitors' office next to Hauser's. When he saw who was behind the desk, puffing away on a cigar, he could hardly believe his eyes or his luck.

There, sharply dressed and looking very CBS, was none other than Lack's own idol, Jack Schneider.

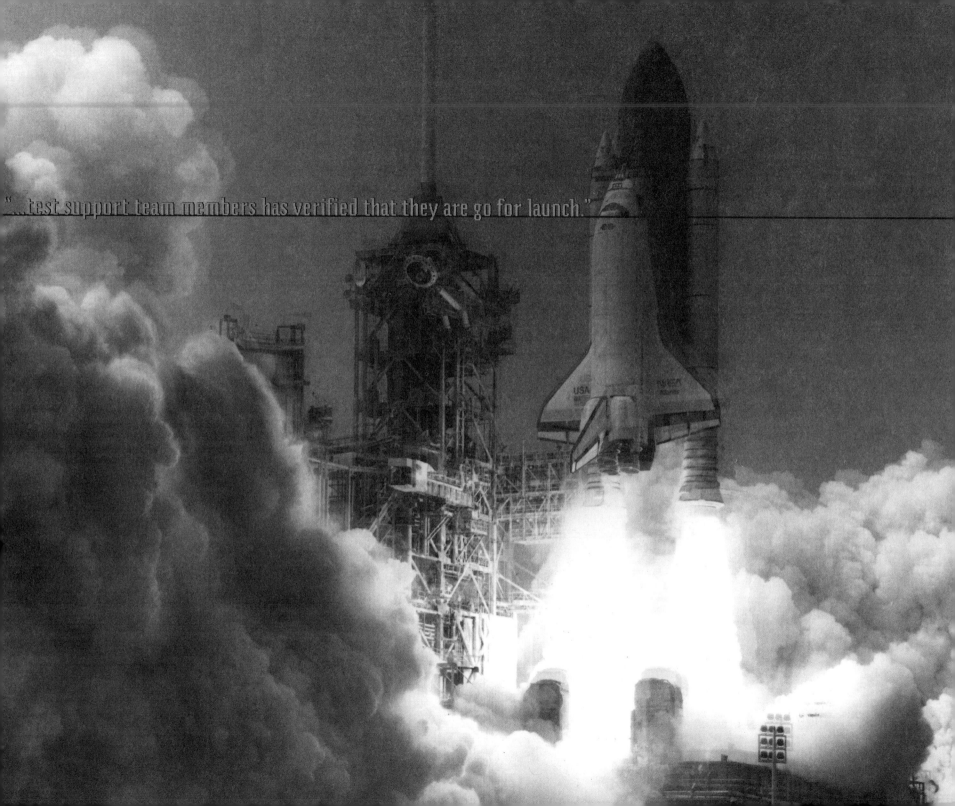

"...test support team members has verified that they are go for launch."

the PIONEERS

At fifty-two, Jack Schneider still had the look and style of the quintessential CBS executive, despite the fact that his jet-black hair was turning gray and his handsome face was beginning to show the effects of gravity. "A broadcasting poster boy," someone had once called him, and after more than thirty years in the business, he still conveyed that image.

Jack Schneider had joined CBS in 1949. A smart, slick, and ambitious Chicago native, he was the kind of guy for whom CBS, then on the cusp of the television revolution, was tailor-made, and he thrived there. Beginning his career as an ad salesman in the network's Chicago TV affiliate, by 1958 he'd worked his way up to general manager of WCAU, the CBS-owned-and-operated station in Philadelphia. Six years later he vaulted into the top job at WCBS in New York. Six months after that, he became president of the CBS Television Network, and then a year later, president of the CBS Broadcast Group. By age thirty-nine, he oversaw all television and radio operations at CBS, with only the president, Frank Stanton, and the chairman, Bill Paley, above him in the corporate hierarchy.

He was in a powerful position—the number three man at the number one television network in the world—at a time when network television was truly king. Didn't like the way a show was performing? Jack Schneider could cancel it. Unhappy with something CBS News was doing? Jack Schneider could change it. He was part of a small group of executives—Stanton, Paley, and their counterparts at ABC and NBC—who were the gatekeepers of the American airwaves in those days, the men who ultimately decided which programs would be beamed out into America's living rooms each night. It was the kind of power over people's lives that even the president of the United States didn't have—and don't think the president didn't know it. (At one point, Richard Nixon, angry with the way CBS News was treating him, reportedly put Jack Schneider on his infamous "enemies list," had the CBS executive's phone tapped.)

In 1969, Bill Paley and Frank Stanton promoted Jack Schneider to executive vice president of CBS Inc., placing all divisions of the company—including broadcasting, publishing, and records—under his leadership. Paley and Stanton were clearly grooming him to succeed them one day at the very center of the CBS eye. But it never happened. While Paley once thought highly of Schneider, the CBS chairman soon decided that his heir apparent might be too glib and smart-alecky for his own good. It became clear to everyone one day that their relationship had turned sour. The two men were in a meeting with a group of other executives when Paley began peppering Schneider with questions and complaints about the smallest things. After the meeting, Paley asked Schneider to wait for a moment, then apologized to him. But Schneider turned and walked out without accepting the apology.

The relationship between the two men deteriorated so much that, in 1971, Schneider asked to return to his old job as head of the broadcast group. By 1977, Schneider had completely lost patience with what he considered Paley's harebrained schemes, while Paley began to blame Schneider for the fact that CBS had slipped into second place in the ratings behind ABC. Finally, in the spring of that year, John Backe, former head of CBS Publishing, took over as chief executive officer of the company while Paley remained chairman. Backe realigned the corporation's management team, taking away much of

Schneider's power and giving him a new title, executive vice president. Six months later, with Paley's apparent blessing, Backe asked Schneider for his resignation.

What do you do for an encore after you've been the number three man at the number one television outfit in the world? Jack Schneider decided to go into business for himself, so he became a consultant, taking on clients like AT&T, Coca-Cola, and the Kennedy Center. In mid-1979, Warner chairman Steve Ross asked him if he'd like to join his company as an exclusive, full-time consultant. Ross had a habit of taking in stray but talented executives, offering them consulting deals, and keeping them around in case he needed them for various projects. Schneider said yes.

Jack Schneider had only been consulting for Warner for a few months when Ross and AMEX honcho Jim Robinson offered him the job running WASEC, their new programming division. In their eyes, Schneider was the ideal fellow to head this new outfit. Not only did he have tremendous experience as a programmer, but he also had the kind of class and credibility that were sure to be an asset to the new company, as well as to the cable industry. After all, if Jack Schneider—who'd once sat at the right hand of Bill Paley, and who was known as a cable basher—was involved in this venture, cable must be legitimate.

After nearly three decades at the greatest broadcasting company in the world, Schneider had no passionate desire to run a brand-new venture. Nor did he have any great belief in cable. Still, he was pleased to be offered the position, if only because it would free him from the consulting business, which he'd begun to loathe. He'd soon discovered that nobody ever did what he told them to do, and Schneider wasn't accustomed to that. Besides, at age fifty-two, he was hardly ready to be put out to pasture. He'd spent twenty-eight years with CBS, but he still felt that his programming and management skills were sharp. So with John Lack as his second in command, he took the job.

The reason for creating WASEC was simple: Television was about to change forever. At least that's what the top guns at Warner believed. With more and more cable systems being built, it was as though a whole new plumbing system were being installed in America. Before, with the broadcast networks monopolized programming, only a handful of choices flowed out of the broadcast pipeline. Sometimes it would be a cop show, sometimes a movie, and sometimes a children's program. With all of the channels cable would be able to handle, they could hook up dozens of pipelines to each home. Even more impressive, they could put a different type of programming into each one.

That was the vision that Schneider and Lack were to carry out in this new cable programming venture. By the time they were through, they wanted as many channels as they could get—each one dedicated to a different topic and targeted to a different audience.

Although both Schneider and Lack came from CBS, from the outset the idea was to make WASEC as different from CBS as possible. In fact, one of the reasons that the corporate parents had made WASEC separate from Gus Hauser's Warner AMEX Cable (in addition to the tax benefits) was to make its corporate culture unique. Unlike companies on the hardware side of the cable business, this new company needed to nurture creativity—and yet, unlike Warner's own creative outfits, their TV and film production units, it needed to be lean and entrepreneurial, with a hey-kids-let's-put-together-a-

company spirit. And lean it was. Located at 1211 Avenue of the Americas, right in the middle of midtown Manhattan, WASEC's digs were anything but plush. All the offices were small, even Jack Schneider's. Things were so raw, in fact, that on the autumn morning they arrived for work in their new corporate home, Schneider and Lack found themselves longing for one of those luxuries they'd grown accustomed to in their years at CBS—desks.

Though the operation was bare bones (furniture was delivered within a couple of days), it was exciting, especially for John Lack. With WASEC based in New York, he was no longer forced to endure long days and nights in Columbus, a development for which he was immensely thankful. Moreover, while he wasn't top dog at this new company, he was working side by side with a man he had long idolized. And Schneider had made it clear that Lack would be the one who handled the day-to-day running of the company; Schneider would be content to sit back and steer.

The two CBS alumni didn't waste much time in getting down to work. Within a month they had two new channels up and running. One was Nickelodeon, the kids' channel they'd inherited from Warner Cable. Both men believed that a quality children's channel would not only be popular, but it would be good for WASEC's image. The other service was also a hand-me-down from Warner, although Schneider and Lack revised it considerably—the Star Channel. Both men felt that a strong movie service could be the engine that drove the whole company. The success of HBO and its main competitor, Viacom's Showtime, had shown that people across the country would pay handsomely for the privilege of getting commercial-free movies in their homes. What was interesting to both Schneider and

Lack, though, was that neither existing service had taken full advantage of that fact. Both channels were only on during the evenings, and both mixed sports and specials with the films. In December, shortly after arriving in their spare little Manhattan offices at 1211, the two WASEC honchos took Warner's old Star Channel, renamed it The Movie Channel, and relaunched it as a twenty-four-hour-a-day, all-movie network.

Of course, while making those two channels operational as quickly as possible was an important job, both Schneider and Lack knew that the most crucial task they would face in those first couple of months was finding the right people to work in this company, the right people to carry out their vision. They already had one person on board—another CBS alum, Bob McGroarty.

A boyish thirty-four-year-old, who bore a resemblance to David Letterman, McGroarty grew up in

his pal Lack started talking to him about coming to Warner and trying his hand in the burgeoning cable industry, McGroarty resisted. But he had finally been persuaded and joined Warner Cable in the summer of 1979 as vice president of marketing. He and Lack talked often during those next few months about the future of cable and about possible new networks, so it was only natural that when WASEC was formed, McGroarty was the first person Schneider and Lack hired.

McGroarty was in place as the head of sales and marketing, the number three man in the company, but dozens of other people were obviously going to be needed—programmers and marketers and finance types and sales people. The question was: who? Very few people had experience in satellite-delivered cable TV networks.

So an interesting variety of people passed through the plain WASEC offices during those cold winter months, and one by one, an equally odd assortment

Suave, sophisticated WASEC president Jack Schneider. Once the number-three man at CBS, he was trekking out into the untamed world of the cable frontier.

Brooklyn as the son of a judge, graduated from the University of Scranton, and briefly went to law school before deciding what he really wanted to do was work in the media. After a short stint at *Life*, he jumped over to CBS in the early seventies, around the same time John Lack started there, and began his climb through the ranks. While he was a kind, soft-spoken man outside the office, one who lived a quiet suburban life in Connecticut, inside CBS McGroarty had a reputation as a demanding boss, and he eventually rose to become vice president of advertising sales in the company's radio division. So when

were hired. Several of them came over from CBS, NBC, PBS, and HBO, another came from a Madison Avenue ad agency, and another had owned an import/export company that operated in India and Afghanistan. About the only thing they seemed to have in common was their ages: Nearly all of them were under thirty-five.

Some came for the money, or the promise of it. While the salaries at WASEC weren't great, there was a sense that everyone was getting in on the ground floor of what might become a success.

Others were just frustrated in their old jobs. Jordan Rost, the new head of the company's research division, who'd come over from NBC, had developed some ideas about how to use audience research more effectively in sales and marketing. But when he presented his concepts to his NBC bosses, they didn't want to hear anything about it. NBC already had a way of doing things, and because the company was already making a couple of hundred million dollars a year, they weren't going to change things just because some uppity young kid thought he had a better way. Rost finally became so frustrated that he set up an interview with the guys at WASEC. They loved his ideas and hired him.

But money and job satisfaction weren't the only lures. What really seemed to attract this group to the cable industry in general and to WASEC in particular was some sort of half-formed desire—an instinct, really—to start something of their own. It wasn't usually talked about, nor was it even necessarily a conscious thought at the time. Nevertheless, years later almost all of them would admit to sharing it: an urge to create something and then be part of shaping and nurturing it.

That was the spirit at WASEC during those first months. It was quite a time. The company was still so tiny—just a couple of dozen people—that whenever new people were hired, they were immediately taken around and introduced to everyone else, just so they would know what each of their new co-workers did and where each of them thought WASEC was headed. And all of them were working their tails off, questioning this, suggesting that, and trying to figure out just what in the hell they were doing for a living.

John Lack, who'd been blessed with that special knack for exciting people, was the one who was most articulate on this last subject. Anyone who doubted the decision to leave the old world behind and join WASEC only had to find Lack and say, "Tell it again, John. Tell what it's gonna be like. Tell about the channels." And in his own marvelous way, Lack would lay it all out . . . about the channels they were going to create, the business they were going to build, and the dreams they were going to make come true.

Within a few months, they hired a staff, opened regional sales offices across the country, and did all the things you had to do to start a company. It was not unlike the early days of the broadcasting business decades earlier, or even what the American frontier was like for the pioneers who settled there. Obviously, the stakes were lower—the folks at WASEC didn't have their lives on the line, just their livelihoods. But it seemed to be just as exciting. And there weren't many places where they could get that kind of rush anymore; there wasn't any more land to explore, and the country wasn't at war. No, in 1980, if you were young, had gone to college, and wanted to wear the corporate uniform and be part of the business troops, the WASEC wagon train—with Schneider at the front and Lack riding shotgun—was one of the few places where you could find true adventure.

Like many other WASEC pioneers, senior vice president Bob McGroarty, a former CBS executive, was energized by the idea of launching a new company.

They weren't the only band of explorers out on the cable frontier. In the one year since John Lack had left CBS and gone to work for Warner, the cable industry had picked up an amazing amount of steam. With the demand for HBO and other cable services greater than ever, many of America's unwired cities had once again begun soliciting franchise bids, and the big cable operators, WACC included, were vigorously pursuing them. At the same time, lured by the promise of big dollars, more and more players were entering the cable programming business. A few months earlier, in September 1979, an out-of-work sports publicist named Bill Rasmussen had launched an all-sports network called ESPN. Meanwhile, Ted Turner was preparing to start an all-news channel called Cable News Network (CNN). And dozens of new networks were being planned—everything from a health channel to an arts channel to a channel aimed at folks over fifty. There were actually so many new specialized services being talked about that a few at WASEC started joking about simply putting a clock on the air and calling it the Time Channel.

All of these new channels were possible because of the wonders of satellite distribution. At the end of 1979, RCA had sent up its third satellite, Satcom III, much to the delight of several cable programmers, who were depending on the new satellite to carry their new networks. Though the launch went well, RCA technicians lost contact after a few minutes. The satellite simply vanished from their tracking screens. After a few hours of searching, from 22,000 miles away, they finally called on the North American Air Defense for help. But they couldn't find it, either. Eventually, RCA resolved that either its tracking device had malfunctioned or Satcom III

had blown up. RCA executives had to break the bad news to the cable programmers.

The disappearance of Satcom III notwithstanding, the proliferation of new networks was beginning to have an effect on the cable industry; it was changing the balance of power between cable system owners and cable programmers. For decades, the cable operators had been desperate for any and all programming. Now, little more than four years after the satellite-delivered networks had started, the tables were turning. Suddenly it was the programmers who were desperate. After all, what good would it do to launch an all-sports channel if no cable operator would carry it?

The fact that the cable operators had begun to amass so much power was certainly disconcerting to Jack Schneider. Being an old CBS hand, Schneider wasn't exactly on the best of terms with the old guard in the cable industry. The cable operators were suspicious of Schneider—after all, he was the walking symbol of the very industry that had tried to smother their baby a decade earlier—but in terms of style and background, the two sides could hardly have been more different. Schneider had retained all of his CBS panache, whereas most of the cable operators were cut from the same cloth as cable pioneer John Walson, the man who'd strung the first cable lines thirty years earlier in Mahanoy City. These were hard-working small businessmen, roll-up-your-sleeves kinda guys who had climbed poles and run cable throughout America.

History and style weren't the only things causing the rift—power came into play as well. With all the new networks, the cable operators were becoming gatekeepers, which was baffling to Schneider. What did these pole climbers know about programming, anyway?

Though things were icy between Schneider and the cable operators at first, it hardly seemed to be a problem. As chief executive officer, Schneider wasn't the only one who had to deal with them. This was the job of the young pioneers—the affiliate sales group—Schneider, Lack, and McGroarty had shipped out to WASEC's regional offices. They were the ones who knocked on the doors of cable operators every day, trying to persuade them to put The Movie Channel and Nickelodeon on their systems. And in the early months of the company they seemed to be doing a fine job, particularly with The Movie Channel. Though it was only a few months old, the new network was already available to several hundred thousand homes, and both HBO and Showtime were beginning to get nervous.

By the spring of 1980, things were going so well that inside WASEC's Manhattan offices they'd started working on the next channel. There were a number of possibilities. An all-games channel was one option; a shopping network another; a talk show channel a third. John Lack liked all of those ideas, and hoped that one day WASEC would develop each of them. But for the next network he had something else in mind; something that was a little closer to his soul: music.

*   *   *   *   *   *

Although he was stylish and sophisticated on the outside, John Lack had a rebel spirit. Whether it came from his parents (Lack's father was a fun-loving, if irresponsible, playboy who was shot to death by a lover's husband in the early 1950s) or the era in which he grew up was hard to say. But it was there. As a teenager, Lack had been tossed out of prep school for underage drinking, and even when he went to work at CBS, he was known as a wild man. In fact, he even had his own trademark at the network: Whenever someone

who worked for him did something outstanding, Lack gave him or her a bottle of Dom Perignon. You only went around once, right?

Given his rambunctious nature, it was hardly surprising that Lack loved rock and roll. His fondest teenage memories were of sneaking off to the Brooklyn Paramount to hear the Coasters or Louie Lymon and the Teenchords. And that passion for music never left him. When he worked at CBS radio, Lack was envious of his buddies in the company who ran CBS's rock music stations.

All of which helps explain why he was so fascinated with the idea that Michael Nesmith proposed to him one day.

A tall, Texas-born musician, actor and producer, Nesmith was best known as one of the Monkees, a made-for-TV rock group popular in the mid-sixties. When the Monkees (both the show and the band) fell apart at the end of the sixties, Nesmith began a career as a solo performer, but without much success. So, in 1976, his European record distributor suggested that he shoot a promotional video clip for a new song he had just released, "Rio." Although they weren't well known in America, these clips—three- or four-minute visual interpretations of songs—were becoming increasingly popular in Europe. European radio didn't play as much rock music as American radio did, so television, particularly the weekly chart shows, was a prime source for hearing new music.

With the help of his friend Bill Dear, Nesmith made a promo clip for "Rio" that turned out to be terrific. While most of the clips being produced at the time were inexpensive and didn't do much more than feature an act lip-synching their song, Nesmith dropped $25,000 into "Rio" and came up with a colorful, surreal clip that had the look and feel of an old Busby Berkeley Hollywood musical. The clip was so imaginative that when Nesmith brought it over to London and showed it to a gathering of record company promotion people, they stood up and cheered. They weren't the only ones who liked it. Within a few weeks, the "Rio" video clip was being played on music shows all over Europe and Australia, and the record was becoming a hit.

With "Rio" a success, Nesmith went on tour in Australia, and while he was there he saw even more of these short films—what the Australians referred to as "pop clips." It occurred to the former Monkee that he really might be on to something. Over the previous year or two he had become fascinated by the home video technology—videocassette recorders and laser disc players—that was just then beginning to trickle onto the market. Nesmith believed that these new gadgets would ultimately allow viewers to program their own TV sets; in time, people would be able to put laser discs into their disc players just as they were then putting records on their stereo turntables. He believed that the pop clips that he'd seen so many of in Australia, and that he himself had started making, might become the pop records of the future. Just as they did with albums, music fans would buy these clips and take them home to play over and over.

More inspired than ever, Nesmith returned to Los Angeles and made another clip, this one for a song of his called "Cruisin'." Once again, those who saw it loved it. But Nesmith had a problem: There was no forum in America to show "Cruisin'" or "Rio." What few music shows there were in the United States generally preferred live performances. And as he thought more about it, Nesmith decided that was the biggest problem with his whole vision of pop clips.

To help solve that problem, Nesmith decided to put together a television show that played only these clips. With the support of

Jerry Perenchio, his one-time manager who was now head of a TV syndication company called Embassy Television, Nesmith and Bill Dear created a pilot for a program they called *Popclips*. Thirty minutes long, the show exclusively featured video clips, along with a host who introduced each clip and explained what exactly these little movies were. Unfortunately, broadcasters had little interest in the show. In early 1979, Embassy TV took the program to the National Association of Television Program Executives (NATPE) convention—the annual gathering at which producers and syndicators try to sell their creations to stations around the country—but they couldn't get enough takers to make producing *Popclips* worthwhile.

Nesmith didn't give up, though. He called his friend Jack Holtzman, an executive at Warner Records, and told him what he was up to. As Nesmith would later remember it, Holtzman suggested that Nesmith talk to this new hotshot they'd recently hired at Warner Cable, John Lack. Not only was Lack a creative, hip young guy who loved rock and roll, but Warner Cable had a satellite transponder that wasn't being used. Maybe Nesmith could commandeer it for his pop clips.

In the summer of 1979, Mike Nesmith flew to New York and met with John Lack, showing him "Rio" and the *Popclips* pilot and laying out an idea for what would essentially be a video radio station. As an old rock and roller himself, Lack was knocked out by what he saw. In fact, he told Nesmith that while he wasn't sure how Warner was going to use its extra transponder, he did think they could put *Popclips* on Nickelodeon, the kids' channel they'd just launched on one of their other satellite transponders. He asked Nesmith to make another episode of the show so that he could test it.

But the more he began to think about it, the more John Lack began to like the idea of a channel that played these clips—and the idea of a whole network dedicated to rock and roll. By the time the fall came around, and he and Jack Schneider had WASEC up and running, Lack was convinced it would work. To begin with, people loved the clips. When Nesmith delivered a new version of *Popclips* and they measured viewer reaction to it at Qube in Columbus, the good, ordinary folks there went crazy for it. What's more, the idea fit perfectly with the pipeline vision they all had for WASEC—an entire channel of nothing but rock and roll. Plus, it sounded like so much fun.

Lack gave Nesmith the go-ahead to make a whole batch of *Popclips* shows, and started discussing the idea of a music channel with various people. That November, he mentioned it at a *Billboard* magazine-sponsored music video convention. And as Lack, Schneider, and McGroarty were hiring people for WASEC during the fall and winter, Lack told each of these young pioneers what he was planning. Most of them loved the idea. Like Lack, they, too, had been raised on rock and roll.

Michael Nesmith delivered the *Popclips* shows in early 1980. Unfortunately, there were a few problems. Not only were some of the clips he featured in the show a little too sexy for a kids' channel, but Nesmith had used some zany comedians—among them Howie Mandel—to introduce the clips. Lack thought they took away from the music, and he suggested that real radio deejays would be better. Nesmith disagreed, but he nevertheless made the changes Lack wanted, and in early March *Popclips* debuted on Nickelodeon. Once again, the reaction in Columbus was positive.

In the spring of 1980, with both The Movie Channel and Nickelodeon off to strong starts, Michael Nesmith's *Popclips* a hit, and the rock and roll spirit burning stronger than ever in his soul, John Lack decided it was time to go ahead with the next WASEC service: a music channel. He called Nesmith, and the two of them met to talk about the idea. The way Lack saw it, they would feature these clips, along with concerts and music news.

Nesmith thought about it, and ultimately decided there were two reasons he didn't want to be involved. First, at the same time that he'd been putting together *Popclips*, he'd also been making more promotional videos of his own and was now close to completing a whole video album, which he was calling *Elephant Parts*. He didn't want to give that up. Second, and maybe more important, he believed his vision of this channel was very different from Lack's. It seemed to him that Lack was talking about running commercials for records. He, on the other hand, thought that music videos, as they were being called, were an art form all their own, one that people would go out and buy and then play at home on their disc players and VCRs. He wished John Lack and his colleagues at WASEC well, but he was going to pass.

Lack said fine. That Mike Nesmith wasn't going to be part of this project wasn't really a big deal to him. After all, he had a whole company of young pioneers who were passionate about this idea; one of whom seemed perfectly suited to putting together this new channel—WASEC's third pipeline.

That was precisely why Lack had hired him.

the keeper of the vision

Bob Pittman was tall and skinny. He had dark wavy hair, big brown glasses that dominated his boyish face, and a noticeable drawl that gave away his southern roots. Though he was only twenty-six when he came to WASEC, he seemed far older in manner—and thanks to a stunning career in radio, he was practically a legend in the broadcasting business by the time he arrived in December of 1980.

His success in the entertainment industry was rather unexpected, given his background. Born in 1953, in Jackson, Mississippi, he was the younger son of a Methodist minister and his wife. Being a preacher's kid in those days was a bit like being an army brat: every so often your daddy took a new assignment, and you'd pack up your belongings, say goodbye to your friends, and move to a new place—where you'd stay until your daddy took another new assignment, at which point you'd do the whole thing all over again.

Having moved around so much as a child, he had by an early age, mastered the art of fitting in. (Years later some would wonder aloud whether that was one of the reasons he was so good at sensing what radio audiences wanted to hear.) In other ways, he was different from the rest of the teens in that tiny southern town. To begin with, he had a glass eye (the result of being stepped on by a horse as a child), which made him something of a novelty wherever he went. Sometimes he had fun with it—especially in the classroom. Every so often he'd put a pin in the eraser end of a pencil and start tapping his eye until his teacher noticed that the Pittman boy was sticking a pin in his eyeball! Determined to prove that having only one eye wasn't a handicap, he was constantly picking up new hobbies—skeet shooting, fly fishing, photography—mastering one and then moving on to the next.

Restless with life in Mississippi, Bob Pittman decided early on that he wanted to get the hell out. Many were the nights that Pittman, who for years afterward would be slightly embarrassed about his Dixie roots, would sit up in his bedroom listening to the Doors or some other rock band, thinking of life beyond the nation's poorest state and dreaming of becoming rich and famous.

When he was fifteen, Pittman decided that he wanted to learn how to fly an airplane, and to pay for the lessons he went looking for a part-time job. After striking out at the local Piggly Wiggly, he walked into one of the town's radio stations, WCHJ-FM. They auditioned him as an announcer, gave him a job, and he was on his way to becoming one of the greatest programmers ever.

In some ways, the life of a deejay can be similar to that of a preacher. Like a minister, a deejay comes to a town, starts talking about this and that until, if he is any good, he gets an offer to move up to a slightly bigger town. At which point he picks up his belongings, says goodbye to his friends, and moves on to the new place, where he stays until he gets an offer in the next biggest town and does the whole thing all over again. If a deejay is talented enough, this routine can continue until he makes it all the way to one of the big markets, like Chicago, or Los Angeles, or even New York.

Such was the journey that Bob Pittman embarked on after graduating from Brookhaven High in 1971. His first stop was Jackson,

Mississippi's capital, two hours north of Brookhaven. There, while going to school at tiny Milsaps College, he worked as a deejay at a small, underground FM station in town. Such stations, which frequently featured long-haired hippie types playing albums instead of the day's hottest hits, had arisen in response to the tightly formatted Top 40 AM stations. Pittman used the FM experience as a stepping stone, and within a few months had moved up to the big Top 40 station in Jackson, WRBC, as both deejay and music director. For a seventeen-year-old kid, it was a tremendous opportunity—deciding which songs would be played on one of the largest stations in the entire state. He handled it the way you might expect a seventeen-year-old to handle it: He wrote down all the songs he liked, wrote down all the songs his friends liked, played them, and then watched as the station's ratings plummeted. While the setback didn't ruin his career—he was still a strong enough on-air presence that within a few months he took a new job as a deejay in Milwaukee—the WRBC experience did teach him a valuable lesson about radio: When it comes to programming, it's the *listeners'* tastes that are important.

His shot at programming redemption came a year later at a station in Detroit, where the deejay life led him after Milwaukee. Though radio was his passion, he continued with school, and in Detroit he enrolled at nearby Oakland University. A sociology major, Pittman wrote a research paper in the fall of 1972 on the effects of integration on the Pontiac, Michigan, school system. After doing surveys and interviews to determine people's attitudes about integration, it struck Pittman that he might be able to use these very same methods to determine people's attitudes about music. His boss at the radio station loved the idea, made him research director, and within a few months WDRQ had become the number one rock and roll station in Detroit.

The idea of using research to program a radio station was not novel. For decades programmers and deejays had relied on record-sales data to determine which songs to play and how often. But what Pittman (and, as it turned out, a handful of other young programmers around the country) did differently was attempt to survey the tastes of the entire listening audience, not just the small percentage who actually bought records. In many ways it was the ultimate method of avoiding the mistake Pittman had made a couple of years earlier in Jackson. Need to know what the people want to hear? Ask them.

Pittman stuck with this approach in his first program director's job, at Pittsburgh's WPEZ in 1973. The program director is to a radio station what an editor is to a newspaper or a movie director is to a film: the person who controls and shapes the creative content. In radio, this means supervising everything from the deejays to the music to the station's jingles and contests. It was a job at which Bob Pittman excelled. Using research to determine what audiences wanted to hear, and his own smarts to transform all that data into an actual radio format, in less than a year he led WPEZ from the back of the pack to third in its market in ratings. The station did so well that when Pittman's outgoing boss, named Charlie Warner, was offered a new job as general manager of WMAQ, the NBC-owned-and-operated station in Chicago, he asked his twenty-year-old program director to come with him. Thrilled with the chance to move up on the radio ladder, Bob Pittman packed his belongings, said goodbye to his friends in Pittsburgh, and moved to Chicago.

If Warner and Pittman were an effective team in Pittsburgh, they were unstoppable in the Windy City. They changed WMAQ's format to country music—despite the fact that Pittman himself couldn't stand the stuff. Applying the same research techniques that he'd used in Pittsburgh, Pittman created a format for the station, hired new deejays (including a young woman named Ellie Dylan), and put the new sound on the air. Within one ratings period, WMAQ went from fifteenth in the market to third and became the most listened to country music station in the nation. With WMAQ an unqualified success, the next year Warner and Pittman focused their attention on WMAQ's sister station, WKQX-FM, an all-news operation that had so few listeners it didn't even register in the ratings. Taking aim at WDAI, the top rock and roll station in Chicago, Warner and Pittman changed WKQX into an automated (meaning no deejays) rock station, and designed an ad and marketing campaign to promote it. The star of the ad campaign? Bob Pittman himself. "This station is going to be good because I'm programming it," the twenty-two-year-old program director said to all the other young rock and roll fans out there. And they believed him. Within thirty days after switching formats, WKQX became the number one rock station in Chicago.

Charlie Warner, who had once worked with the best in the business at CBS, knew he had something special in Pittman, and he wasn't alone. Though Pittman arrived at the station every morning looking like every other hip twenty-two-year-old of the time—with long hair, a full beard, wearing blue jeans, and with a gold chain around his neck—to those who worked with him it was clear that he was no typical kid. His mind was extraordinary. Not only was he analytical and able to cut to the heart of a problem, but he was also creative, full of strong ideas. Perhaps even more impressive, particularly for someone so young, was his ability to implement those ideas. Pittman rarely let his personal tastes interfere with his decisions, and he never let his emotions get the better of him. He seemed at all times to be in total control of himself and the situation.

Though his father kept urging him to put radio aside for a few years to return to college full-time and to really enjoy this time in his life, Pittman had little interest in traditional education and little desire to do anything other than what he was doing. Consumed by his job, he thrived on the process of sizing up a situation, creating a strategy to deal with it, and then making sure that his plans were carried out. As he would put it years later, he saw himself as "the keeper of the vision." He allowed for input from those who worked under him, but when it came time for a decision to be made, he made the call, and he took responsibility for getting things done.

At twenty-three, Bob Pittman was the hottest radio programmer in America—one who commanded a large salary, flew his own plane, and was fast becoming a legend in the broadcasting industry. In 1977 he won the album-rock program manager of the year award from *Billboard*, the trade magazine of the music industry, and was nominated as country program manager of the year—the first time in *Billboard*'s history that one person had been a finalist in two categories. Pittman's stock was so high that even the president of NBC, Herb Schlosser, had taken notice. Like almost everyone else who came in contact with the young program director, Schlosser was impressed with how bright and articulate this kid was, and he began telling Pittman that one day he could see him as head of programming for all of NBC.

Within weeks of arriving in New York, Warner and Pittman scrapped WNBC's format and fired the entire on-air

The Keeper of the Vision, Bob Pittman. At twenty-six, the Mississippi minister's son was already a legend in the radio business when he joined WASEC in late 1979.

Given their success in Chicago, it wasn't surprising that by early 1977 Bob Pittman and Charlie Warner had caught the attention of the top dogs at NBC radio, who were searching for someone to fix their struggling flagship station in New York, WNBC. For years the station had been trounced in the ratings by mighty WABC, and the heads of NBC wanted somebody to turn things around. Having completed their mission in Chicago, that summer Warner and Pittman packed their belongings, said goodbye to their friends, and moved to New York, the very top of the radio mountain.

staff, including the station's biggest star, morning guy Don Imus. Replacing Imus with Ellie Dylan, the young woman Pittman first hired in Chicago (and with whom he was now romantically involved), Pittman turned WNBC into a straight-ahead rock station, one designed to topple mighty WABC. Initially, things seemed to work wonderfully. The station jumped from thirteenth to eighth in Warner and Pittman's first ratings book. But after a few months WNBC began to slide backward again. The problem? Well, at least one of them was Dylan, whose all-important morning show was the station's lowest-ranked program. One day Charlie Warner finally called Pittman into his office and put it to him straight: "I'm going to fire Ellie," he said. "It's not working out, and you can't do it because you're emotionally involved." Pittman looked at him and, with tears in his eyes, simply thanked him.

Ellie Dylan wasn't the only problem, however. Just as WNBC was switching to a rock format, disco music was exploding in America, drawing listeners away from most rock and roll stations. And the radio landscape itself was shifting as well. By early 1978 the FM side of the dial, with its clearer signals and fuller sound, had evolved from an outlet for free-form radio into a collection of stations as tightly formatted and commercially successful as AM had ever been. When WABC, New York's top-rated station for sixteen straight years, was finally knocked out of the top spot in the fall of 1978, it was not by Charlie Warner and Bob Pittman's WNBC, but by all-disco WKTU, 95.7 on the FM dial.

As months went by and WNBC remained in the middle of the pack, Bob Pittman's political status at NBC began to suffer. In mid-1978, programming wizard Fred Silverman (the man who'd led ABC television to the No. 1 spot in the ratings with shows like *Three's Company* and *Charlie's Angels*) replaced Herb Schlosser as president of NBC. Just like that, one of Pittman's biggest boosters was gone, and with him Pittman's fast track to the top programming job at the network. In September, Bob Pittman and his new boss, Bob Sherman, re-hired WNBC's former morning deejay, Don Imus, and the station's ratings began to climb again.

But by the time Imus returned, Pittman had begun to lose his passion for both NBC and radio, and with Charlie Warner's help he began exploring opportunities in television. He already had some

TV experience: from December 1977 to June 1978, while still working as program director at WNBC radio, Pittman produced and co-hosted a show called *Album Tracks* that aired on NBC. A fifteen-minute program that was broadcast after *Saturday Night Live*, *Album Tracks* featured Pittman and a WNBC deejay, Lee Masters, reading the week's music news and showing the kind of promotional video clips that Michael Nesmith had become facinated with.

So with Pittman interested in doing more TV work, Charlie Warner sent his young protégé over to see some of the people at WCBS-TV in New York. They were impressed with Pittman, and offered him a job as head of broadcast operations at the station. There was no question that it would be a wonderful opportunity—it was a foot in the door at the Tiffany Network. But Pittman also found himself intrigued by one of the other people Charlie Warner had suggested he see—John Lack.

Charlie Warner and John Lack had worked together at CBS radio in the early seventies. When Charlie Warner called him late in the summer of 1978, just as WASEC was getting started, Lack told him he was looking for someone to program WASEC's soon-to-be-revamped movie service, The Movie Channel. Lack and Pittman got together a few times and hit it off. To Pittman, cable seemed like the perfect place to get hands-on television experience, and to Lack, Pittman looked like an ideal hire for this new company. He had an incredible set of radio credentials, so he clearly understood the idea of narrowcasting. And thanks to *Album Tracks*, he had as much experience as anyone in marrying music and television.

Lack was ready to offer Pittman the job as head of programming at WASEC. Unfortunately, WASEC chief Jack Schneider had other ideas.

After meeting with the young NBC programming whiz, Schneider told Lack there was just no way a twenty-five-year-old kid was going to run programming at any company of his. Maybe he could be the number two or number three man, but not number one. Lack wasn't about to give up, however. He had Pittman meet with Mike Dann, the former CBS programmer who was now a Warner consultant. Dann was impressed with Pittman, and told Schneider, who had been Dann's boss at CBS during the sixties, that this young guy really had what it took. Schneider finally gave in, and in December 1979, a decade after wandering into his first little radio station in Brookhaven, Mississippi, Bob Pittman packed up his belongings, said goodbye to his friends at NBC, and moved into one of those ordinary little offices at 1211 Avenue of the Americas—another pioneer on the cable frontier.

He and Lack made an interesting pair. When people saw them together in those days, Lack always seemed to be taking the lead, with Pittman a step behind, looking like a loyal underling. This wasn't surprising—Lack was exuberant and larger than life, while Pittman, nine years younger, was not only new to most of this television stuff, but was generally more reserved. And even though Pittman now looked very much the young executive, having cut his long hair, shaved his beard, and traded in his blue jeans for a closet full of sharp suits, when it came to style he was still no match for big, bold John Lack. Then again, not many people were.

*　　*　　*　　*　　*　　*

Though it was Michael Nesmith who had planted the music video seed in John Lack's brain, by early 1980, Nesmith was not the only one captivated by pop clips—nor was he the only one who believed they could bloom into something larger and more beautiful. It had become clear that somewhere, somebody was going to do something with these things.

The idea of putting pictures to music was not new. Not only had Hollywood been doing it for years in its musicals, but there had actually been music videos, more or less, for several decades. In the late 1940s, the Panoram Soundie, a jukebox with pictures, appeared in America, and for a couple of years some top singers created short film versions of their songs to be shown on it. While these "soundies," as they were called, enjoyed a brief period of popularity, by the early 1950s they'd died out, at least partly due to the advent of TV. A decade later, a French company came up with another video jukebox, called the Scopitone. Although it was popular for a while among European music fans and artists, not many American acts ever made Scopitone films, and the machine never caught on.

The true forerunners of the videos that Mike Nesmith and others were now so passionate about were the promotional films that record companies had started to make in the mid-1960s. After Beatlemania began in Britain in 1963 and America a year later, television executives on both sides of the Atlantic sensed that there was a demand for rock and roll music on TV, and several shows had debuted. In England, where the weekly chart countdown program *Top of the Pops* was already airing, shows like *Ready Steady Go!* and *Oh Boy* popped up, while in America, which already had *American Bandstand*, programs such as *Shindig!* and *Hullabaloo* debuted.

All the shows were similar in content: Each week a few of the most popular acts would go on and play their songs. The problem, of course, was that really popular bands like the Beatles, the Rolling

Stones, or the Who were frequently too busy or too far from the television studio to make a personal appearance. As a result, record companies had begun shooting simple little films and sending them to the shows when the bands couldn't (or chose not to) make a live appearance. Most of the promos were pretty simple—a band would just go to a sound stage somewhere and lip-synch their song as a camera crew caught the whole thing on film—but occasionally some of the clips were fairly creative. The Beatles, whose films *A Hard Day's Night* and *Help!* foreshadowed the frenetic style of later videos, did several promos—including ones for "We Can Work It Out," "Penny Lane," and "Strawberry Fields"—that went beyond the band-in-the-studio concept. The Who and the Stones also experimented with this new format. In the Who's "Happy Jack," the group played a band of bumbling burglars, and in their promo for "We Love You," the Rolling Stones spoofed the trial of Oscar Wilde—Mick Jagger as Wilde and Keith Richards as the Marquis of Queensberry.

Most of the shows that played the clips were happy to have them, and the record companies were even happier. After all, the promos meant more exposure for their acts, and that usually meant more record sales. Over the next decade, the clips (of which there were only a few) were used mostly to increase exposure around the world. The international divisions of record companies would send them to European and Australian pop music shows because it was difficult for many acts to tour there.

In the mid-1970s both the creativity and number of the clips started to increase. The turning point came in 1975, when the British band Queen hired a young director named Bruce Gowers to make a clip for their song "Bohemian Rhapsody." Taking his cue from the song's unusual vocal effects, Gowers filled the clip with all sorts of unusual visual effects. When the song reached No. 30 on the British charts, *Top of the Pops*, Britain's weekly chart show, started to play the clip, and people went crazy for it. After just one airing on *Top of the Pops*, the song leapt into Britain's Top 5 and stayed there for more than a dozen weeks.

With "Bohemian Rhapsody" as proof that a video could really give a jolt to a record's sales, a growing number of European acts made promo clips for their songs. By 1977, the same year that Michael Nesmith made his hit clip "Rio," *Top of the Pops* was playing clips more than ever, and a small music video industry had actually started to form in London. Among the leaders of this new business were Bruce Gowers, who was making clips for acts like Genesis and Rod Stewart; Russell Mulcahy, a young Australian filmmaker who'd been making clips there before moving to London; and Keefco, a company made up of a producer named John Weaver and an album cover artist named Keith McMillan. It was all fairly primitive. Most of the clips were shot on videotape in a single afternoon. Still, British music fans loved them, and by 1978 video was so popular there that a program called *The Kenny Everett Video Show* debuted on British TV. Hosted by Everett, a loony British comedian, and directed by David Mallet, former assistant director on ABC's *Shindig!* in the mid-sixties, the show featured in-studio performances as well as music videos.

In America, the music video scene was nowhere near as vital, but there were increasing signs of life. In 1977, *Billboard* started a division called Starstream, which supplied clubs and other outlets with these promo clips. What's more, some record labels—among them Warner Records, which started its own video department that same year—

began to recognize video's potential. Not only could these clips help promote an act, but with the rise of the VCR and the video disc, they might have some commercial potential of their own.

Probably the biggest pro-video push came from the artists themselves. The record companies were focused on the cash the clips could create, but several artists saw the creative possibilities videos offered. In addition to Mike Nesmith, musicians Todd Rundgren and David Bowie and the bands Devo and Blondie become involved in video early on. Rundgren was so convinced that music video was the art form of the future that he was constructing a multi-million-dollar video studio at his home in upstate New York.

By the fall of 1979, not long after Mike Nesmith had first pitched the idea of a music video network to John Lack, a music channel was actually on the air in Atlanta. Called Video Concert Hall, the network appeared on several cable systems in the South and featured many of these early videos. And deejay Casey Kasem had recently launched a half-hour syndicated video show called *America's Top Ten*.

Still, John Lack didn't view either outlet as competition. That fall, he and Nesmith went to *Billboard*'s first music video conference in Los Angeles. Addressing the several hundred producers, directors, and record company execs attending the three-day convention, Lack announced that his company was considering starting up a twenty-four-hour-a-day music service.

"We want to promote software," he told the crowd. "We want to be your radio station."

Jack Schneider wasn't so sure. Despite the excitement in the burgeoning music video industry and the enthusiasm of all the young pioneers on the WASEC staff, Schneider was skeptical about the idea

of a rock and roll channel, and who could blame him? With a few exceptions, television and rock and roll had never had a great relationship. The reason was partly fear. If network television was a great mirror reflecting the way life was in America (or at least the way Americans wished it were), then rock and roll was the stone that seemed capable of smashing it all into a million pieces. That was why so many adults had initially found rock and roll so distasteful, and why, as teenagers, people such as John Lack and later Bob Pittman were so invigorated by it. In the best rock and roll music, every single note, every single beat, every single lyric is a rebellion, and network television didn't know how to handle that. In 1956, when Elvis Presley had become popular enough that TV could no longer ignore him, comedian Steve Allen booked him on his Sunday night TV show. But to make sure that this pelvis-swivelling, long-haired hick didn't offend any of the viewers, the producers put Presley in some dopey skit with comedienne Imogene Coca and actor Andy Griffith. Later in the show, Elvis performed his hit "Hound Dog"— wearing a tuxedo and singing to a basset hound. Ed Sullivan was just as stifling. Three weeks before Elvis went on the Allen show, Sullivan proclaimed that the scandalous singer would never appear on his program. But once he saw the ratings Allen got, Sullivan quickly changed his mind and signed the King of Rock and Roll to a three-show, $50,000 contract. He did, however, take precautions: Elvis was only shown from the waist up.

By the mid-sixties, the networks were more at ease with rock music, and rock and roll musicians regularly appeared on Sullivan's show, as well as shows such as *Shindig!*, *Hullabaloo*, and *Bandstand*. But the truce didn't last. By the early 1970s Ed Sullivan has died, *Shindig!*

and *Hullabaloo* had long been canceled, and *Bandstand*, though still on the air, had lost its cutting-edge credibility with young people. By the middle of the "Me" decade, about the only place to find real rock on American TV was on late-night weekend shows such as NBC's *Midnight Special* or *Saturday Night Live*, or the syndicated *Don Kirschner's Rock Concert*. By then it wasn't fear that relegated rock to the TV nether world as much as money. It was the mission of the broadcast networks to program for mass audiences, and rock and roll, despite the passion young people might feel for it, only appealed to a small group. When you got down to it, Led Zeppelin just couldn't pull the same kind of ratings as Lucille Ball.

This was why John Lack, programming guru Bob Pittman, and WASEC senior vice president Bob McGroarty knew they were going to have a hell of a time convincing Jack Schneider to let them go ahead with this rock and roll channel. Luckily for them and the rest of the pioneers who were so charged up about this network, they did have some ammunition. First of all—and this was very important given the bare-bones, entrepreneurial spirit they were trying to foster at WASEC—they were almost certain they could get these video clips for free from the record companies. Radio had set this precedent. For years the record labels had provided stations with records free of charge, knowing that exposure on radio was the best sales tool they had. Because a music channel on TV would, theoretically, be at least equally effective in helping sales, it only made sense that the labels would be just as giving when it came to the video clips.

In early 1980, the record industry needed the help. The previous year had been disastrous for most labels. For the first time since rock and roll became popular in the mid 1950s, industry revenues had declined from the previous year. During 1977 and 1978, disco music was at its peak, and the entire industry made an incredible amount of money. Suddenly, though, the American public treated disco like a bad joke, and in 1979 revenues plummeted. Radio wasn't doing much to help matters. For years the record industry had relied on radio to provide exposure for new artists and help the recording industry keep regenerating itself. By the late 1970s, competition among radio stations was so fierce (and the research championed by Bob Pittman and others so prevalent) that radio played far less new music than it used to. Thanks to such conservatism, a whole musical movement— punk and New Wave, which exploded in England in the second half of the seventies—was all but ignored by American radio, and it was the record companies that felt that disdain the most.

And so, with the music industry ready to support a new music venture, this new cable channel would at least be cheap to produce. But that was just the first reason that Lack, McGroarty, and Pittman gave to Jack Schneider for supporting the creation of a rock and roll channel. Another was the flip side of the equation: how much money advertisers would pour into a rock and roll channel.

Thanks to the country's economic prosperity in the years after World War II, the first real and distinct youth market had arisen in America. Generations of young people who grew up before the war had taken what little money they had saved and either contributed it to their families or used it to pay for their own educations. But youngsters who came of age after the war knew few such restrictions. One survey found that the average teen in 1956 had a weekly income of $10.55—equal to the disposable income of an entire family just fifteen years earlier. And the pot only sweetened through the sixties and seventies. The only problem was that when it came to advertising, young people were difficult to reach. They read fewer newspapers, subscribed to fewer magazines, and even watched less television than other demographic groups. If you were an advertiser and wanted to use TV to reach this age group, probably the best place to go was *Saturday Night Live*—and even that wasn't a very efficient buy, since a sizable portion of that show's viewers were over age thirty-five.

Clearly advertisers needed a way to reach young people, and this new music channel could be it. Jack Schneider listened to the reasons that his young subordinates gave him, and finally, by the summer of 1980, with the two other WASEC services, The Movie Channel and Nickelodeon, both thriving, Schneider was convinced that the idea had merit. He and Lack gave Bob Pittman, who was going to oversee the new channel's programming, the go-ahead to hire a development team.

Pittman immediately encountered the same problem that Schneider, Lack, and McGroarty had encountered the previous fall and winter: who to hire? There just weren't any people with experience in satellite-delivered rock and roll cable channels aimed at America's ever-growing youth market. But it didn't bother Pittman. He preferred hiring people who'd never done the job they were being hired for. Not only did such folks bring a fresh perspective and new ideas to their jobs, but at the same time it was easier for Pittman, the Keeper of the Vision, to ensure that they all had a similar concept of what this channel was going to be like.

He ended up with a diverse bunch. Sue Steinberg, executive producer, had worked at both Qube and Nickelodeon; Steve Casey,

40

music programmer, had been a radio program director in Phoenix; Fred Seibert, on-air promo head, and Tom Freston, marketing chief, had each come over from The Movie Channel; and Carolyn Baker, talent and acquisitions director, and John Sykes, promotions director, had each worked in the record industry.

It was Sykes, who'd been with CBS Records, who best represented the spirit of this new endeavor. Only twenty-four years old, he grew up in Schenectady, New York—a typical kid in a typical American town doing typical things like watching TV and playing the drums in a local rock band. A slender, handsome young man with curly brown hair, a Pepsodent smile, and an air of easygoing innocence, Sykes graduated from high school in Schenectady, then went down the road to attend Syracuse University, dreaming of one day becoming a big television executive like Fred Silverman. While in college, he took a job as a campus promotional representative for CBS Records, and after graduating from Syracuse he went to work for the company full-time, promoting CBS acts all over the Midwest.

During the summer of 1980, Sykes heard from someone at a radio station in Chicago that Bob Pittman, the hotshot radio programmer, was starting up a music video network on cable. To Sykes, it was the dream job. Not only did it combine his two loves, TV and rock and roll, but for months he had been working with music videos, trying to get some of CBS Records's clips played in Chicago movie theaters. He wrote to Pittman, and for weeks afterward badgered him with phone calls until finally Pittman agreed to an interview. Two weeks later, he quit his job at CBS, gave away his plants, moved to Manhattan, and was walking around the WASEC offices, ready to put rock and roll on television.

In their own ways, all the people on the development team had done something similar—given away their plants and given up their old lives. They were drawn to the idea of creating something new, of being a pioneer on this WASEC wagon train. But for this group it wasn't only that; it was also the intoxicating spirit of rock and roll that attracted them. In one way or another, every single one of them had been deeply touched by the music. Fred Seibert's life had been changed by the Beatles; Sue Steinberg had spent a year on tour with the band Foreigner; Steve Casey had been programming rock and roll radio stations since he was a teenager; Carolyn Baker had worked several years for Warner Records; and both Tom Freston and John Sykes had spent countless hours listening to records and reading liner notes. For all of them, the idea of putting rock and roll on television, and getting paid for it, was almost unspeakably alluring.

If only because of this passion and the era in which they'd grown up, they were also confident that this new channel would work, confident in a way that Jack Schneider, who was old enough to be a father to any of them and for whom rock and roll was just loud stuff that kids listened to, could never be.

"You know that this is a rather unnatural marriage," Schneider said one day to Steve Casey and Carolyn Baker, talking about rock and TV.

"I'm not really worried about it," Casey replied.

Schneider looked at him. "Well, you ought to be!" he said.

But none of them were. Throughout the fall of 1980 they crammed into their single tiny office at 1211 and talked and dreamed about what this new channel would be like.

Most days, WASEC was a terrific place to be, but one day early on, the optimism of the young staffers was temporarily dampened and the mood got a bit surly. It seemed that when Bob Pittman hired some of them, he neglected to mention that no one at AMEX or Warner had actually given them the money for it yet.

* * * * * *

As plans for the new music channel took shape, Jack Schneider and John Lack tried to keep their parent companies informed. At Warner, a man named David Horowitz—a member of the company's four-person office of the president and the programming liaison between Warner and WASEC—loved the idea of a music channel. Not only did it fit in with Warner's concept of narrowcasting, but it was sure to help out the company's record labels, which Horowitz also oversaw.

His counterpart at American Express, Sandra Meyer, was initially less enthusiastic. A sophisticated woman who headed the publishing arm of American Express and who also sat on the board of New York's Metropolitan Opera, Meyer was invited by Schneider and Lack over to 1211 one day to hear about the new channel. As she sat listening to their presentation, she didn't know quite how to tell them that this was just about the stupidest idea she'd ever heard. A music channel? All music, all the time? This is ridiculous, she thought to herself. How could these guys possibly believe that any significant number of people were going to turn on their television sets to hear the likes of Mozart and Bach and Beethoven and— Then John Lack said something about rock and roll, and Sandra Meyer started breathing a little easier.

Meyer ultimately came to love the idea of a music channel, but neither she nor David Horowitz nor even the Warner AMEX board of directors could give the final approval. Because both WASEC and its sister company, Warner AMEX Cable, were legal partnerships between Warner and American Express, all the major decisions—such as whether to spend $25 million to start up a new music channel—were made by Warner chief executive officer Steve Ross and American Express chief executive officer Jim Robinson.

Everyone involved thought Ross would be a cinch to persuade. As David Horowitz had seen, this new channel seemed a perfect investment for Warner. Persuading Robinson, on the other hand, was a more difficult job. American Express was filled with buttoned-down conservatives, and maybe the most conservative of the bunch was Robinson. Whereas Ross was a street-smart soul who'd scraped and scratched his way to the top, Robinson was a flag carrier for the Establishment—the Harvard-educated son of a wealthy Atlanta banker. Despite the fact that Robinson was seven years younger than Ross, Robinson was the one with the more traditional attitude and style.

What made persuading Jim Robinson even trickier was the fact that in the year since the start of the Warner AMEX partnership, the cable industry had picked up momentum. More channels were being launched—even CBS had a cable network planned—and more cities were being wired. While this was precisely what everyone in the cable business had hoped for, it did present problems. Specifically, there was now so much competition for franchises that the cost of winning them had become astronomical, as cities demanded more sophisticated systems before granting exclusive rights to their particular areas. In Pittsburgh, where WACC, Gus Hauser's division of Warner AMEX, won the bidding, it was projected that building the system would cost $50 million. The situation was similar in other places. While Jim Robinson and his lieutenants weren't looking to get

out of the business, the financial realities were harsher than they'd ever anticipated.

Jack Schneider arranged a meeting with Ross, Robinson, and the Warner AMEX board for the middle of January 1981, and as the day came closer the troops readied themselves. John Lack and senior vice president Bob McGroarty polished the new channel's business plan, while on the programming side, Bob Pittman had John Sykes and Fred Seibert put together a reel of music videos to show everyone. Because Jim Robinson was clearly not a rock and roll guy, Pittman told them to make sure everything was as G-rated as possible. A couple of days before the presentation, Seibert and Sykes stayed up all night putting the reel together, finally finishing some time after the sun had come up. They gave the tape to Pittman and went home to bed. An hour later, Seibert's phone rang. It was Pittman—John Lack wanted some changes made in the tape; so Seibert got up, went back to the editing booth, and once again stayed up all night long. This time Lack was happy.

The presentation, with Schneider, Lack, McGroarty, and Pittman performing for WASEC, took place in Warner Communications's ornate boardroom inside 75 Rockefeller Plaza. The Warner AMEX board was there, as were some of the people from Warner's record labels, and Steve Ross and Jim Robinson. Jack Schneider introduced his young WASEC team, then turned it over to Lack.

Summoning up all the salesmanship and exuberance he had inside, Lack summarized the strategic reasons why the channel would work—the free videos from the record companies and the vast but untapped youth market. Pittman got up next and showed the reel of videos that Seibert and Sykes had put together. There was a cut from

Michael Nesmith's "Rio," another from a clip by Dire Straits, "Skate-away," and even a cut from a disco clip by Cher in which she roller-skated while wearing a leotard. Finally, Bob McGroarty presented the business plan, telling Ross and Robinson that they would probably have to spend about $25 million before the channel turned a profit in its second year.

All together it took less than an hour, and when it was over Ross turned to Robinson.

"Well," the silver-haired Warner chairman said, "I think I know where I stand on this. Why don't you go first?"

Robinson agreed. He double-checked the fact that the videos were likely to be free, and hearing that they would be, he looked pleased. He then turned to Jack Schneider and said, "Jack, if you were spending your own personal money, would you go ahead with this?"

John Lack looked over at his idol. *Don't let me down*, he thought to himself. *Say yes, damn it, or I'm going to jab you in the leg with my pen.*

Schneider considered the question. He hated rock and roll, and it had never really succeeded on mainstream American television before. Yet he did believe that there were sound business reasons for why this would work. He said yes, and then added, "Actually, if you'd let me, I'd like to put some of my own money in."

Schneider knew they'd never go for such a thing, but still, a little CBS swagger couldn't hurt.

"Obviously, this is not our kind of material," Jim Robinson said finally. "But we're very impressed with the presentation, and I've talked to Sandra Meyer about this, and we think it makes sense. We're prepared to put up our share."

Well, there it was. Robinson had said yes. Lack could hardly believe it. He was finally going to get his chance to rock and roll and—

Wait a minute. What the hell was Steve Ross saying now?

"I'm not so sure, Jim," the Warner chairman said. Lack looked at him. He wasn't joking. "I've been thinking about this for a while. Promoting music would obviously be a wonderful thing for our record companies. But I have a lot of questions about this thing."

Lack wanted to slide under the table. How could it be Ross who was blowing them out of the water? This was just too much.

Ross and his lieutenants started discussing things, firing questions at the WASEC guys about who owned the rights to these videos and about cable operators and about advertisers and about whether kids would actually want to watch these clips over and over again, the way they listened to records. Finally, after what seemed to Lack to be forever, Ross said, "You know, last night I had a long talk with my daughter about this.

"And she said to me, 'Dad, this is going to be the hottest thing that ever happened. Kids need their own channel for rock and roll. You've got to be behind this thing.'" Ross looked out at the people in the room. "So we're in."

That was it. There were hurrahs and handshakes and pats on the back, and then the WASEC team went off to celebrate. Was that whole episode some kind of game Ross was playing to avoid looking overly anxious? After all, Warner record companies stood to benefit greatly from the channel. Regardless, John Lack was ecstatic. His dream was coming true, and he had Steve Ross's daughter to thank for it.

FOUR

WAR

W I N T E R   1 9 8 1 — S U M M E R   1 9 8 1

It was war. That was the only way to describe the atmosphere during those next few months, as the pioneers scrambled and scratched and scraped to put this channel together. They'd gone to battle. That was how it felt.

Who was the enemy? Partly it was time itself; they only had about six months to create an entire television network. The reason for this mad dash was simple: competition. It was early 1981, and a quickly growing number of people were starting to see the potential of these video clips. Not only were video shows beginning to pop up here and there—HBO had *Video Jukebox*, USA network carried *Night Flight*—but a couple of other video networks, including one in which Todd Rundgren was involved, were in the planning stages. Though none of them had the money, manpower, or prestige of AMEX and Warner behind them, nobody at WASEC wanted to delay the project and risk having one of these smaller players get a toehold in the market—or having some big cable hotshot like HBO or Ted Turner steal the idea and beat them to it. And so Schneider, Lack, and the rest gave themselves slightly more than six months—until 12:01 A.M. on August 1—to get their channel operational.

So much had to be done. To begin with, there were all the technical details involved in launching a new network, which were being overseen by a young pioneer named Andy Setos. An affable, roly-poly young man with dark curly hair and glasses, Setos had joined WASEC the previous spring after several years at the public broadcasting outlet in New York City. He had a bear of a job to accomplish in the next six months. For starters, the new channel was going to be the first in history to be telecast in stereo—something that Bob Pittman in particular thought was very important. Not only would stereo make the channel more attractive to cable operators by allowing them to earn a few extra dollars per month selling special hookups to their customers, but it also helped the channel's image. You couldn't have great rock and roll without great sound, could you? But as difficult and complicated as developing stereo was, it was a lay-up compared to the other big technological challenge Setos faced: supervising the construction of a new "uplink" that transmitted the channel's signal to a satellite. WASEC already had an uplink that it was using for Nickelodeon and The Movie Channel, but it was pretty primitive. Not only was it located hundreds of miles away in Buffalo, New York, but part of it was actually housed inside a burned-out tire factory. The company had been able to make do with it for the first two channels, but there was no way the Buffalo facility would work for the technically more complex music service. Schneider and Setos

had persuaded Warner and AMEX to shell out several million bucks for a new uplink to be built on Long Island. The only problem now was that Setos had just six months to get it built, and these things usually took nearly a year.

As hectic as things were for Setos, the rest of the pioneers who were putting together this new network—John Lack, Bob McGroarty, Bob Pittman—had just as much to do. And time wasn't their only enemy; they also had to fight the status quo.

The programming of this new channel was being overseen by Bob Pittman, whose past year had certainly been an exciting one. First, though he had little TV experience before signing on at WASEC, he was doing very well at the company. The Movie Channel, which he was programming, was a hit, and WASEC boss Jack Schneider, despite his initial misgivings about hiring someone so young, was clearly pleased.

Pittman's personal life was on the upswing as well. His relationship with Ellie Dylan had ended while he was at WNBC, but in the early part of 1980, not long after joining WASEC, he had boarded a plane headed for Los Angeles and sat next to a pretty, chic fashion editor, Sandy Hill. The two struck up a conversation, hit it off, and when their flight was rerouted from Los Angeles to San Francisco, they ended up spending the night at Sandy's parents' house in northern California before driving down to Los Angeles the next day. Several months later, after a whirlwind romance (Bob sent so many roses that Sandy would later say her apartment looked like a funeral home), they were married.

In the early months of 1981, Pittman was focused on launching this new network and determining what this new music channel was going to show. In certain ways the choice was obvious: It would show the videos that everyone was becoming so hot and bothered about. However, as Pittman was well aware, there was far more to it than simply acquiring a bunch of clips and throwing them on the air. Ever since he'd failed so miserably as a teenage music director in Jackson, he had focused intently on giving the audience what it wanted. He had come to see himself not so much as a programmer, but as a marketer, creating and selling products that provided "benefits," as business types put it, for the consumer. Using research to determine people's tastes was part of that, and by the time the channel was on the air, WASEC would do four separate surveys, polling potential viewers about everything from what kind of music the channel should play to what the on-air personalities should be like to what the new service's name should be.

While such surveys were important, Bob Pittman also believed in looking deeper and trying to understand what forces were affecting the tastes and attitudes of the people he was trying to reach—which was why, as he designed this new channel's programming, he began to focus on just what it meant to be a young person.

Pittman knew that the period of adolescence and young adulthood is an unusual time in a person's life—most teenagers are trying to take some control over their lives and define who they are and how they're different from their parents. This was why pop music had long been so important to young people, and why rock and roll in particular was so appealing. In its words and, just as important, in its sound and its beat, rock and roll spoke to the feelings that most young people seemed to have. There was just something in the grooves of a great rock and roll record that burrowed its way into your central nervous system and commanded you to rebel, to be

free, to unshackle yourself from all those rules and ideas and attitudes that the previous generation had tried to lock you into, whether they were about sex or politics or careers or even just the way you wore your hair. No wonder Ed Sullivan was so scared of Elvis.

As he pondered just what to pour down this new musical pipeline, Bob Pittman decided that if this rock and roll channel was going to be successful it would have to be part of young people's culture in the same way the music itself was. It would have to speak to the audience in the same way the music did. It would have to break the rules the way rock and roll itself always had. In short, it would have to be more than just rock and roll on television; it would really have to be rock and roll television.

How? For starters, the channel's format was going to be different. Unlike most television programming, this network would have no separate programs, with the exception of a Saturday night concert, a Sunday night movie, and the occasional rock-star documentary. It would simply feature one song after another, the way radio stations did. It is hard to overstate what a radical notion this was, given that television, from the day it started, had consisted almost exclusively of regularly scheduled thirty- and sixty- and ninety-minute shows. Such a setup made life simpler for everyone involved. The idea of regular and predictable time slots had become the standard on American television, the thing audiences had come to expect. Certainly Jack Schneider believed that.

"There is a compact with the viewer," he said to Lack and Pittman when they first broached the idea of a channel with no shows. "And the compact says you will have programs."

But ultimately, even Schneider accepted the idea of doing away with scheduled shows. To begin with, there were still so few videos out there that the idea of grouping them into separate programs—*The Rolling Stones Hour*, for instance—was simply unreasonable. Beyond that, Bob Pittman persuaded him that the audience they were going after—twelve- to thirty-four-year-olds—would accept a channel that had no beginning, middle, or end, that was really nothing more than a constant stream of sounds and images. This was a group of people who'd grown up with television—"TV babies," Pittman called them—and they had an attitude toward TV far different from their parents. While their parents and Jack Schneider's generation had been raised on newspapers and radio and saw television almost as a luxury, TV babies took the tube for granted; to them it was as familiar and lovable as the family dog, and as a result, they tended to use it differently and expect different things from it. Bob Pittman believed that their brains functioned differently because of it. He theorized that the older generation's minds worked linearly, like print; but TV babies had brains that were non-linear, like TV. People who were Jack Schneider's age tended to do one thing at a time: They watched TV, and then they read a book, and then they talked on the telephone. TV babies, on the other hand, frequently did all those things at the same time. Somehow, all those hours of *Hawaii Five-O* and *Mr. Ed* made them able to take little fragments of information—some from here, some from there, none of it really connected—and make sense of it.

Pittman believed that this music channel needed to be different not only in form, but also in attitude. Like the young people it was trying to reach, it had to have a rock and roll attitude, to be irreverent—to poke a finger in the eye of television itself. And what better place to start than with the name? To get that feeling of youthful arrogance across, the Keeper of the Vision decided he wanted to call this channel TV-1. Unfortunately, not only did most of the other people at WASEC not like the name, but another company had already trademarked it. And so, during the early part of 1981, the name TV-1 had evolved into TV-M—M standing for Music. One day, however, as a few of them sat in a meeting, Steve Casey, the radio expert Pittman had brought in to work on programming the videos, started writing the letters TVM on a pad in front of him. As the others in the room babbled on about something or other, it began dawning on Casey that the letters themselves just didn't look very good together; they were clunky and out of balance. Casey was hardly an artistic type— his forte as a programmer was analyzing data from a computer—but still, as he continued staring at the letters, they just looked ugly to him. Finally, he decided the whole thing would be much more attractive if the T were in the middle, rather than at the beginning. He told the rest of the group his idea (although he never told them why), they kicked it around for a while, and the next thing you knew this music channel officially had its handle: MTV.

Though he'd lost out on his choice for a name, Bob Pittman was hardly upset. After all, there were plenty of other ways to convey the proper rock and roll spirit. And luckily, Pittman had just the guy who could help him do it.

* * * * * *

In the long history of corporate America, it's hard to imagine there had ever been anyone quite like Fred Seibert. Tall and gangly, with dark hair, a prominent nose, and glasses, Seibert, twenty-nine, was an incredibly unlikely candidate for a corporate career. He seemed to have little interest in money and no talent for numbers; he had no stomach for (and consequently was horrible at) the politicking that is necessary to get ahead in a company, and he made no secret of his disdain for many of the ideas and attitudes put forward by most corporate types. In fact, he was such a free thinker that he hadn't even had a real job until he was in his late twenties. And yet, there was some part of his personality that made him more than happy to show up at 1211 each day in a nice tie, shiny shoes, and a starched shirt and toil away for two corporate powerhouses like AMEX and Warner. He was precisely what WASEC needed to get this rock channel rolling: a subversive in a suit.

Seibert grew up on Long Island, a bright kid who loved music and art but who saw himself headed for a more traditional field, like medicine. After high school he went to Columbia University and majored in chemistry. But one day while sitting in a science class, he had a revelation: It dawned on him that he was far more passionate about the Beatles than he was about beetles; that he was far more turned on by music than he was by science. And so he began devoting most of his time to a small record label that he and a friend had started.

The plan for the label was simple, although in its own way revolutionary: Seibert and his partner wanted to put out jazz and blues albums that were as popular as rock and roll records, and they truly believed the world would be a better place if they could do it. They couldn't, as it turned out, and the label eventually went out of business. Afterward, Seibert became an independent jazz-record producer and eventually stumbled into the radio industry, first in Los Angeles, then in New York, mainly doing what was called on-air

promotion—producing the jingles and IDs that radio stations play between songs.

He and WASEC's Bob Pittman were brought together in the spring of 1980 by Dale Pon, an advertising and radio-promotion specialist Pittman had worked with at WNBC and Seibert had worked with at another station in New York. Pon had become a mentor to Seibert, trying to ingrain in him that when he was doing on-air promotion, he was actually communicating to the audience what the radio station was all about, what its personality was. As a result, when Bob Pittman, then working to get The Movie Channel up on its feet, told Pon he was searching for someone to oversee on-air promotion at the network, Pon had recommended Seibert. The two met, and though Seibert wasn't sure he wanted to work in TV—at that point he still dreamed of being a record producer—Bob Pittman, the Keeper of the Vision, impressed him, and he signed on.

At most TV networks and stations, on-air promotion usually meant putting together the short spots that urged viewers to watch upcoming programs. Is someone out to kill Joe Mannix? Tune in tonight at nine. . . . Who shot J.R.? Find out on the thrilling season premiere of *Dallas*! At The Movie Channel, however, Seibert and Pittman felt they needed a different approach, one much more like radio than conventional television. Because, thanks to cable, the number of channels people had available to them was increasing so rapidly, the two believed the most important thing was not promoting particular films, but rather telling viewers what the channel itself was all about. In the past, the broadcast networks were able to assume that viewers knew who they were and what they did, but out here on the frontier narrowly focused cable networks had no such luxury; they had to tell viewers who they were and why they were there.

Just a few months after Fred Seibert joined WASEC and began churning out spots for The Movie Channel, Bob Pittman got the go-ahead to hire the development team for the new music channel, and Seibert volunteered for the mission, mostly because he wanted to stick close to Pittman. Seibert's mentor, Pon, had taught him that if you find a good boss, you should attach yourself to him like gum to a shoe, so that's what Seibert did. And Fred Seibert ultimately proved to be a perfect fit for this new channel. The minute he heard Pittman's vision of what the programming would be like—the rock and roll attitude, the need to break the rules of traditional TV—the subversive in a suit got it.

Seibert's official title in those days was Director of On-Air Promotion for MTV (he continued his work at The Movie Channel as well), but that didn't even come close to defining what he did. In fact, by the time serious work on the channel began in early 1981, his real mission—the one Pittman himself had implicitly given Seibert—was to ensure that everything about this channel had the proper attitude; that it had, as Seibert himself would put it, the beat. If Bob Pittman was the Keeper of the Vision at this new channel, Fred Seibert was the Keeper of the Grooviness.

In those early months of 1981, one of Seibert's first assignments was to commission a logo for the new channel, and to do the design work he called on some friends at a studio called Manhattan Design. Since, at that point, the name MTV hadn't officially been decided on, Seibert suggested that they create some kind of nonverbal symbol that would illustrate what this channel was all about. So the crew at

Manhattan Design came up with a drawing of a musical note being squeezed by a white-gloved hand. While Seibert liked it, there was a problem: When the channel finally got a name and they tried to fit the letters "MTV" into it, it just didn't work.

Seibert sent them back to the drawing board, where after what seemed like hundreds of attempts the folks at Manhattan Design came up with a new logo: a large block "M" that looked like it was made out of bricks, with a small "TV" that looked like it was spray-painted onto it. The instant he saw it, Fred Seibert knew it was the one. Not only did it look like nothing else on television, it also unleashed a world of possibilities in Seibert's head. Sure, sometimes it could be bricks and spray paint, but other times it could have different coverings—wooden strips or zebra stripes or polka dots. It was perfect.

Seibert took the new design back to WASEC, where most people just hated it. Hated it. This was particularly true of the guys on the sales and marketing side of the business. One day, one of them said to Seibert, "You think this is good, huh? You think it's gonna last as long as the CBS eye?" All Seibert could do was roll his own eyes.

As bad as that was, even harsher was the reaction at Ogilvy & Mather, WASEC's ad agency. One day Seibert took it over to show them, and the instant one of the Ogilvy & Mather guys saw it he rushed out of the meeting and came back with a sheet of paper, on which were listed Ogilvy & Mather's company guidelines for logo design. It seemed the big "M" and the little "TV" broke practically every one of them.

While it caused a bit of a stir inside the company, Seibert, with Bob Pittman's backing, finally won out in the logo debate. John Lack agreed that the design basically conveyed the right attitude and, after a couple of minor changes, approved it.

The logo conflict wasn't the only time Fred Seibert clashed with the boys on the business side of WASEC, for whom he had increasingly little patience. One day that winter, Seibert and Alan Goodman, his partner at WASEC and someone Seibert had known since his Columbia days, were asked to put together a tape to be used at the official announcement of this new channel. It was going to be shown at the Cable Television Administration and Marketing (CTAM) convention at the New York Hilton in March. Unfortunately, when the two of them read some of the information the sales and marketing types wanted to include in the tape, they were disgusted. It was all just a bunch of bogus hype, it seemed to them. How were they ever going to get across the proper rock and roll spirit amid all this bullshit about the new channel? They decided to approach the tape as if it were a rock and roll record.

In rock and roll, the words never make much of a difference as long as the beat is right. All you had to do was listen to an early rock record like Little Richard's "Tutti Frutti" to understand that. The lyrics in the song were just gibberish, but somehow, the way the music leapt out of the speakers and the way Little Richard sang it, you knew exactly what the song was about—sex. And so Seibert and Goodman decided to take what Seibert would later call their own corporate white-guy version of that approach. Alan Goodman wrote a script with all the necessary information, but when the two of them went to the studio to record it, they did it in stereo, with the first line coming out of the right channel, the second out of the left, the third out of the right, and so on. They then added some music, and

finally matched the whole thing up with some video clips. The idea was simple: They wanted to do everything possible to make people feel the renegade spirit of this project—and to ignore the words.

The announcement was to come at the end of the convention's last session, which was dedicated to new programming services. One by one the other cable programmers got up and talked about their new channels, using the tiny TV monitors to demonstrate the kind of programming they'd have. Finally, it was WASEC's turn. To ensure that their tape had the maximum impact, Seibert and Goodman had WASEC engineering chief Andy Setos set up a huge TV screen in the room, along with two monstrous speakers. When it was time, WASEC sales and marketing head Bob McGroarty stood at the front of the room and said very officially: "Warner AMEX Satellite Entertainment Company announced today, to our over fifteen hundred Nickelodeon and Movie Channel affiliates, our third cable television service—MTV: The Music Channel."

The big screen flicked on, the speakers kicked in, and they rolled the tape. Nobody could believe what they were seeing or hearing. It was overwhelming—sound came from everywhere, one image blending into another, one song dovetailing another song. For a few minutes it was an all-out assault on the senses, and few people in the room seemed to know what hit them. When it was over they stood up and cheered.

Bob McGroarty delivered a short speech about the new channel, and at the end he invited everyone to a champagne reception WASEC was hosting upstairs in one of the suites. It was quite a scene. The room was so crowded you could hardly move. People were climbing over each other trying to hand their business cards to all the WASEC people. Call me, will you? . . . Hey, let's get together for lunch! . . . Count me in on this thing, okay?

As he stood in the room watching all the chaos, Fred Seibert just smiled. He never told anyone why he and Goodman had made the tape the way they did. He figured that if he had, somebody on the business side probably would have tried to get them fired.

After all, those other guys wore suits and meant it.

By the time spring rolled around, the pace had started to pick up, particularly in programming. Strategies were being planned, systems were being set up and people—more young pioneers anxious for adventure—were being hired. There were so many people joining the company so quickly that there wasn't enough space for all of them at WASEC headquarters, and the company had to rent rooms for people to work in at the New York Sheraton, over on Seventh Avenue. The place was a

CBS Records whom Bob Pittman had hired to oversee contests and promotions, was trying to put together an MTV poster with pictures of various rock stars on it, among them Mick Jagger. Because he needed Jagger's permission to use the photo, Sykes called a friend of his who knew the Rolling Stones and explained to her what he wanted to do. She phoned someone with the Stones, and told Sykes it was all set up; Mick was going to call Sykes to talk about it. The problem was that she never said exactly when Mick was going to call. So for a couple of months, every time Sykes was on the phone and he heard another call coming in, he always said the same thing: "I gotta run. I think I got Mick Jagger calling on the other line." But nobody really complained much; they were too busy for that.

No one was working harder than Bob Pittman. To begin with, he and music programmer Steve Casey were trying to finalize the channel's musical format. By

Young, smart and ambitious, John Sykes was typical of the pioneers at WASEC in its early days. Like many of his colleagues, Sykes thrived in the just-get-it-done atmosphere that dominated in the months before MTV's launch.

dump—old and stuffy, with walls the color of pea soup. Even worse, everyone was so busy that they always had to have lunch brought in from the deli around the corner, and before long all the rooms began to smell like corned beef.

The whole operation was incredibly raw—the space MTV was using over at WASEC headquarters didn't even have a phone system with multiple lines. If another call came in while you were on the phone, you heard a beep and had to hang up to answer it. This could get a bit annoying. One time, John Sykes, the curly-haired guy from

now, the spring of 1981, pop music had splintered into several different forms. There was straight pop, urban, adult contemporary, rock. Which route should they follow? For a number of reasons, the decision was made that the new network would most closely resemble an album-oriented rock (AOR) radio station, although they also hoped to feature many more new and New Wave artists than the majority of AOR stations did. The main reason for that programming choice was that those were the only videos that were out there. Most clips had been made for the British market, and AOR was the music the Brits liked. But there were other advantages to this format. AOR was the music most white suburban kids preferred, and since cable TV was still largely a suburban and rural phenomenon, that's clearly who their audience was going to be. What's more, conservative radio had turned a cold shoulder to the New Wave artists so playing such acts was bound to endear MTV to the record industry.

The commitment to playing new artists wasn't the only overture MTV made to the record industry. Pittman and others spent a lot of time in those first months meeting with label executives, trying to persuade them to let the channel use their videos for free. The industry's cooperation was vital—without it there simply wasn't going to be any music channel. As a result, Pittman, along with Carolyn Baker, MTV's talent and acquisitions director, and Ben Begun, from WASEC's business affairs area, spent weeks meeting with people at the labels, laying out for them how this new channel was going to look and how much it was going to help record sales. A few companies grasped the idea immediately and agreed to supply their videos, but others were more hesitant. It was tough economic times in the music industry. Because cash was tight, many labels simply didn't want to spend money making videos, and if they did, they certainly didn't want to give them away for free. Many in the record business thought a huge mistake had been made with radio all those years ago in giving the stations free records, and they didn't want to see history repeat itself.

Equally troublesome in getting the labels' cooperation was the very nature of the music industry. Though from the outside the record business always seemed like the hippest thing going, it could be conservative. People in the business just didn't like change. "I already have a big network of radio promotion people set up to hype my artists," they would argue to the WASEC crew. "Why should I throw money into something new?"

While Pittman and Baker tried to get the record companies on board, the rest of the young pioneers at the channel were working their butts off, too. MTV's executive producer, former Qube staffer Sue Steinberg, had begun the search for the channel's on-air hosts. These hosts—video jockeys, or veejays, they'd started to call them—were to be the human face of the network, the people who would guide viewers through the music, much as deejays do on radio. In addition to announcing the clips, the veejays were to read the latest music news a couple of times an hour and also do occasional interviews with artists. Once again, the question came down to: Who were they going to hire?

To aid her in the search, Steinberg brought in an old friend of hers named Robert Morton, with whom she'd worked on *Talent Search*, Qube's version of *The Gong Show*. Working out of the rooms at the New York Sheraton, they supervised a nationwide veejay hunt, placing ads in industry trade newspapers, calling agents, networking with friends and colleagues. The response was overwhelming. More than fifteen hundred people called or wrote or sent photos—everyone from actors and comedians to deejays and TV professionals to record company executives. For Steinberg and Morton, the whole thing felt a lot like *Talent Search*—about the only thing missing was Bo's Burping Band. It was funny, too, because if you called to inquire about the job, you weren't really certain that this operation was, uh, legitimate. "We don't really have offices at the moment," Steinberg or

Morton would tell potential candidates. "We're in room 2118 at the Sheraton. Make sure you bring a picture and—"

Click.

The veejay auditions took place in several cities around the country—New York, Chicago, Los Angeles, San Francisco—and had two parts. First, Steinberg and Morton would videotape candidates reading music news off cue cards. If a candidate performed well, he or she would advance to the second round, an on-camera interview with musician Billy Joel. Actually, it was an on-camera interview with Robert Morton pretending to be Billy Joel. Morton had a merciless sense of humor, and as the veejay-wannabes sat there asking "Billy" about his latest album and upcoming tour, Morton would do all sorts of odd things. Sometimes he'd act annoyed and sometimes he'd simply grunt, and sometimes he'd reach over and start playing with the poor interviewer's tie. Morton figured it was all fair game, though. After all, you never knew how a rock star was going to behave.

Hundreds of people auditioned that spring, but few candidates seemed capable of handling the job. Many of the deejays who auditioned had trouble dealing with the camera, while many of the actors couldn't ad-lib, many of the comics knew nothing about music, and many of the TV professionals came across like Phil Donahue or a game show host.

Finally, by mid-June, they'd found five people who not only seemed capable of handling the job, but who were also diverse enough when it came to sex and race and overall look. There was Mark Goodman, a handsome, dark-haired deejay from New York's WPLJ; J. J. Jackson, a black deejay who'd spent over a decade working in FM radio, most recently in Los Angeles; Meg Griffin, an attractive young woman

who'd been working at WNEW-FM in New York; Nina Blackwood, a blonde actress and professional harpist who was living in Los Angeles; and Alan Hunter, an all-American-looking actor who hailed from Mississippi.

Hunter literally stumbled onto the job. One day that spring he and his wife were in New York's Central Park, attending a picnic for Mississippi natives, when they ran into Bob Pittman. As it turned out, Pittman and Hunter's wife already knew each other. (Coincidentally, both of their fathers were ministers.) Pittman filled the Hunters in on this new music channel he was working on and suggested that Alan, who was looking for work as an actor, try out. He did, and a few weeks later got the job.

Not surprisingly, all five of the veejays were rather unsure about signing on. Who really knew whether or not this channel was going to succeed? Nina Blackwood was particularly hesitant because her acting career was picking up, and she had a regular gig playing the harp at the Hyatt Hotel in Los Angeles. Did she really want to forfeit that and move to Manhattan for some cable channel that, as far as she knew, might not last more than a couple of months? To persuade her, Sue Steinberg and Robert Morton flew Blackwood to New York, where they showed her the WASEC offices, introduced her to the staff and took her to lunch at Tavern on the Green, the famous Central Park restaurant. When they got there, they sat down at the table and started talking and nibbling on some rolls, when suddenly, a big, dry lump of bread lodged in Nina's throat. She tried to swallow a couple of times, but that didn't work, so then she looked around for some water. Unfortunately, there wasn't any on the table yet. By now, she was beginning to gasp for air, and so she looked across the table

Alan Hunter, Martha Quinn, Mark Goodman, Nina Blackwood, and J. J. Jackson in an early publicity shot. These original veejays had thousands of fans across the country.

at Morton and Steinberg for help, who stared back with expressions of panic. Finally, as their veejay candidate started turning blue, Sue Steinberg yelled, "Do something!"

Morton stood up. "Uh, Nina," he said, "need a little Heimlich?"

At which point he clutched her around the mid-section, pushed in and up, and a big piece of roll popped out of her windpipe and onto the table.

As she sat there in Tavern on the Green, trying to catch her breath and thanking the Lord and Robert Morton that she would live to play the harp once again, Nina Blackwood figured she didn't really have much choice in the matter anymore. She was taking this job.

*　　*　　*　　*　　*　　*

Those on the programming side weren't the only ones at MTV engaged in battle. As they worked to get this new channel on the air, those on the business side of WASEC were also under the gun.

By the spring of 1981, more than a year and a half after WASEC was up and running, the business types—particularly the sales and marketing group, those pioneers out in the regional offices—had turned into a sharp organization, thanks in large part to senior vice president Bob McGroarty. While he didn't have Jack Schneider's background or John Lack's larger-than-life style, McGroarty was respected and liked by those who worked for him and quite effective at what he did. With Schneider and Lack largely involved in setting the course for WASEC, it was McGroarty who handled most of the day-to-day details of running MTV.

The staff responded to their leadership. Though most of them were still young, they began to develop a slick, aggressive style, one reminiscent of CBS. They wore sharp suits, made great presentations,

and possessed so much confidence that they sometimes came off as arrogant. Not surprisingly, they were all totally enamored of WASEC boss Jack Schneider. That spring Schneider and many of them had gone to the annual NCTA convention in Los Angeles. One night while they were there, Schneider hosted a dinner for them all at one of the old-guard Hollywood restaurants. After they'd finished eating, the waiters brought out humidors filled with cigars, and Schneider, as was his custom, selected one and lit up. You would have thought it was a sign from above. As the humidors made their way around the room, almost every single one of the young pioneers took a cigar and lit up, despite the fact that most of them, still in their twenties, had probably never smoked more than two cigars in their lives—it just wasn't what their generation did. (A joint would have been a different story, of course.) It was quite a sight: Schneider looking suave and elegant as he puffed away on his Macanudo, and all the kids turning green as they gagged on theirs.

Though they were a little raw, they had done a fine job in getting both The Movie Channel and Nickelodeon onto cable systems all over the country. The Movie Channel was doing so well that in response, both of its competitors, HBO and Showtime, had switched to around-the-clock programming. And everyone on the business side saw little reason why they couldn't be equally effective when it came to MTV.

They'd received a rousing send-off as they went into battle. One afternoon, John Lack gathered some of the business pioneers together for lunch at the Russian Tea Room in Manhattan. They all sat at one long table, and lined up in front of each person were several shots of vodka. Toasts were made and they all drank the shots and then Lack rose to his feet to say a few words.

"Have you ever seen a surfer get in a curl and ride a wave?" Lack asked them. "It's like a high. Well, you're all about to get on a wave, and it's going to be one of the great rides of your life. But to stay inside that curl you're going to need balance, and you're going to need strength, and you're going to need speed. Because people are going to tell you you're full of shit. But once you're in that curl, it's going to be a high. You're not even going to need drugs."

Lack continued talking for a few more minutes, and the instant he was through every single one of the young pioneers stood up and cheered. It was better than Knute Rockne's "Win One for the Gipper" speech. They were pumped up beyond belief. They were ready to make this thing huge! They were ready to rock and roll!

And then they went out and had doors slammed in their faces.

But this was through no fault of MTV's new ad sales department. Lack and McGroarty had hired Larry Divney, a warm, fun-loving guy with a radio background, to oversee it. Divney, in turn, hired several more ad sales people and placed them in various offices around the country. Unfortunately, despite the crazed reaction they'd gotten at the CTAM convention in March, as those first few months went by they were not only having trouble selling ads, they were having trouble even getting people to take their phone calls. "You're from M-what?" was the typical response.

Why the cold shoulder? Why weren't American companies ready to kill each other for the opportunity to send their commercials down this musical pipeline and into the homes, hearts, and minds of the country's youth? Partly it was because of the ad community's attitude toward cable. Not only did cable still reach a limited number of people—by the spring of 1981 fewer than 25 percent of the country's homes had cable—but more than that, the ad community, like the broadcast networks and the record industry, simply didn't like change. Ad agencies needed to get results for their clients, and consequently, weren't likely to take a chance on an experiment—which was what cable was to them. True, Budweiser had recently signed a big deal with all-sports ESPN, and a few other ad-supported cable networks had made some progress, but for the most part Madison Avenue remained leery of the whole idea of the Wired Nation. In the previous year, 1980, advertisers had spent only $58 million on cable advertising, a fraction of what they spent on broadcast TV.

What made things more difficult for Larry Divney and his group was that they were trying to sell a rock and roll network. Although it had been twenty-five years since Elvis went on Ed Sullivan, and although rock and roll itself was now big business, the music and the lifestyle that went with it were still viewed as dangerous and outside the mainstream, particularly by the forty-something and fifty-something businessmen who usually decided where the ad dollars went. Spend my client's money on a rock and roll cable network that's not even on the air yet? Try me again in a few years, pal.

The affiliate sales team was having just as hard a time, for several reasons. First, with the increasing number of networks, there was a scarcity of channel space, especially on the old twelve-channel systems that were still common throughout the country. Putting MTV on meant taking something else off, and until cable operators could see for themselves what this channel was going to be like, that was a lot to ask. What's more, many cable operators still saw WASEC as a bunch of network guys who'd come over to cable, an impression that was only reinforced at cable conventions when WASEC execs such as John Lack pulled up in limos. Finally, and perhaps most important, there were questions about the product itself. A lot of cable operators just couldn't comprehend it. A young WASEC pioneer would show up at some cable system and spend an hour telling the operator all about this exciting marriage of TV and music, sometimes going so far as to hook up a tape player and actually show him a music video. And after all that the cable operator would just sit there with a blank look on his face. An all-sports channel like ESPN cable operators could understand, and an all-news channel like CNN they could appreciate, but a channel that featured rock music videos only? You couldn't really blame the cable operators. Most of them just weren't rock and roll guys; they were hard-working entrepreneurs who in some cases had spent decades climbing poles and drilling holes and stringing wire, not doing the Twist or the Frug or the Watusi or trying to figure out the lyrics to "Louie Louie."

MTV was such a tough sell that very few people at WASEC's sister company, Warner AMEX Cable, saw the appeal of the channel at first. Not long after the music service was announced, Jack Schneider and Andy Orgel from sales and marketing attended a meeting of Warner AMEX system operators at The Greenbrier, a resort in West Virginia. The two got up and made a presentation about WASEC and MTV. When they were finished the cable guys all but laughed them out of the room. Judging from their reactions, this was just about the dumbest idea for a network they'd ever heard.

There were a couple of guys in the room who grasped what Schneider and Orgel were talking about, but even they had some suggestions about how to improve the concept. "I think this idea of mixing music and TV is fine," one fellow said. "But wouldn't it be better if you did it with country and western music?"

Maybe Schneider was right. Maybe these were just a bunch of pole climbers.

As the summer wore on and launch day approached, things became even more hectic, especially in programming. There was still so much to do that they all began working horribly long hours. Every day they would drag themselves out of bed after only a few hours sleep, hustle over to the office, get their marching orders, and do whatever it took to get the mission accomplished. *Just get it done.* That was the philosophy that drove them. Nobody cared that you weren't getting enough sleep or that you hadn't seen your loved ones in ages. Just get it done. Young John Sykes took this credo to heart: He finally stopped waiting for Mick Jagger's phone call and just put the lead Stone's picture on the MTV promotional poster anyway.

The individual who oversaw all that was getting done was Bob Pittman, and he was thriving. It was as if a whole new side of his personality had appeared. In the battle against time and the status quo, he wasn't merely the Keeper of the Vision, he was also the Battlefield Commander. That was how he approached the launch of this new network—like a twenty-seven-year-old George Patton driving the troops across the rugged terrain of cable start-ups. He was always ordering this and deciding that.

Everyone at MTV was being driven hard, but it was exhilarating. In fact, there was much to be happy about that summer. To begin with, the programming crew had finally been freed from the Sheraton's ugly green walls and the smell of corned beef—they now had real offices at 1133 Sixth Avenue, just down the street from 1211.

What's more, after months of negotiations and arm twisting, all but two of the twelve major record companies had agreed to give MTV their videos for free; the lone holdouts were MCA and PolyGram. Getting record industry execs to come around hadn't been easy. Most of the labels were still skeptical about this whole venture, and a couple of them had agreed to hand over their clips only as a personal favor to Bob Pittman, who in his radio days had helped promote a few of their artists.

Unfortunately, even though the channel finally had the rights to air the clips, the MTV engineering staff still had a ton of work to do on each one before it could be played. First, they actually had to get their hands on the videos—no easy task, given that many of the labels had, until now, paid so little attention to video that they often didn't even know what they had. Sometimes, when WASEC engineering chief Andy Setos or somebody else from MTV walked into a record company to ask for the clips, somebody would point to a storeroom and say, "Uh, I think they might be in there. Go help yourself." Somehow you just knew this wasn't how CBS got their shows.

Once they actually obtained the videos, the job was only beginning. Each clip had to be cleaned up visually—any scratches had to be taken out and often the colors had to be brightened. Next, each clip had to be transformed from mono to stereo, a process that involved getting a duplicate of the original recording and synchronizing it with the video. After that, each one had to be put onto a small cartridge so that it could be played on the tape machines Setos wanted to use. Finally, at the beginning and end of each video, the MTV guys had to superimpose an identification (ID) label that listed the name of the song, artist, album, and record company. Bob Pittman had agreed to

this last bit of business as a way of getting the labels to cooperate. From their standpoint, these clips were basically commercials, and they wanted the products they were promoting identified as clearly as possible.

As the head of operations, Andy Setos had other duties besides being a video gopher. In addition to overseeing the preparation of the clips and the construction of WASEC's new uplink on Long Island, officially known as the Network Operations Center, he also had to figure out how, from a technical standpoint, this new channel was going to work. Ultimately, Setos decided that since radio was the model for MTV's programming, it would also be the model for how the channel would be operated. The guts of the operation were two tape machines to be located inside the uplink. Used by most TV stations to play commercials, the machines had been modified for stereo, and Setos planned to utilize them for all MTV's programming. Each machine could hold up to twenty-four video cartridges at a time, and the idea was that an engineer inside the uplink would switch between them the way radio deejays switched between turntables. When one clip came to an end, the engineer would fade out of that and into a new video playing on the other machine. As in radio, the engineer would also insert commercials, promos, and station IDs at the appropriate times. About the only real differences from radio was the veejay spots. Unlike deejays, who usually broadcast live, the MTV veejays would be on tape. Everyone figured this would not only give them greater control over the segments, but it would also save money, since having a camera crew on hand twenty-four hours a day, as would be necessary for this twenty-four-hour-a-day channel, would be prohibitively expensive. The plan was that a week's worth of veejay segments would be shot over five days at a studio in Manhattan. Then the spots, along with a log of which videos were to be played in which order, would be couriered out to the Network Operations Center on Long Island.

The production studio they chose, Telectronics, was on the Lower West Side of Manhattan, and by early July executive producer Sue Steinberg and her staff (now minus Robert Morton, who'd gone to work on the new *Late Night with David Letterman* program) were there rehearsing and constructing the set where the veejay segments would be shot. The set looked like a New York loft, although whether this was supposed to look like a loft that somebody lived in or worked in was never clear. The idea was simply to have a place that looked cool, that people watching the channel would want to hang out in.

In addition to rehearsing, the veejays were also trying to stockpile band interviews. One day, Meg Griffin, the young woman Pittman and Steinberg had hired from WNEW-FM, did a segment with a band called the Equators. The conversation part of the interview went fine, but Sue Steinberg thought it all looked a little lifeless. So she suggested that as Griffin was introducing the Equators' video, she should get up and boogie a bit with the band. Unfortunately, Griffin didn't look comfortable doing it. This wasn't surprising—after all, she had spent her whole career camped out in a radio studio where nobody ever saw her. They tried it a couple more times, but it just never looked right.

Griffin and one of the other veejays, Mark Goodman, shared a cab uptown after work, and she was clearly upset. "I'm not sure this is right for me," she kept saying. "I don't know if I can do this." Good-

man tried to calm her down—by this point he had convinced himself the thing was going to work—but it didn't seem to help.

The next day Griffin didn't show up. Sue Steinberg called her at home, and her husband answered. "Um, I'm not really sure she wants to do this anymore," he said.

No one could believe it. Less than two weeks before they were supposed to launch, they were suddenly in need of a replacement. Panic set in, and Steinberg and her crew began going through old audition tapes, but nobody seemed right, and for a while it looked like they might have to launch with four veejays rather than five.

A couple of days later, Bob Pittman received a call from an old friend Buzz Brindle. The two had worked together years earlier in Pittsburgh—had been roommates, in fact—and now Brindle was the program director at Pittman's old station in New York, WNBC. There was an intern at the station who wanted to audition, Brindle said. Was she too late? Pittman said she had to get over to Telectronics immediately. When she got there, Julian Goldberg, one of the production staff, went out to meet her in the lobby. He told her he was sorry, she was too late—they weren't auditioning people anymore. Goldberg stood there looking at her, thinking *this girl couldn't be more than seventeen*, when all of a sudden he could see tears welling up in her eyes. She was crying, right there in the middle of the lobby. He felt so bad for her that Goldberg told her he'd put her on tape, and so he brought her into the studio, told her to read some lines off the TelePrompTer, and they started rolling. She was terrific. She was so smooth that it sounded as if she'd written the lines herself. When she finished, Goldberg said to her, "You were great. Why don't you have your father call me tomorrow."

"My father?" she said. "What for? I'm twenty-two."

"Yeah, sure," Goldberg said. "Have your daddy call me."

When she was gone, Goldberg went and showed her tape to Sue Steinberg and Bob Pittman, who agreed she was perfect. The next day Goldberg got a phone call.

"Hello, this is Martha Quinn's father," a voice said. "I just wanted to let you know that my daughter really is twenty-two."

They hired her.

As insane as things were in both production and operations, nowhere was it crazier in those last couple of weeks than in Fred Seibert's department, on-air promotion. Until early July, they hadn't really produced anything, so now, with just a couple of weeks to go, they were scrambling to put together promos and station IDs and contest spots.

Part of the reason they had fallen so far behind was that the record companies had been late in supplying the channel with videos. How were you supposed to create promo spots for a music video channel when you didn't have any music videos to work with? Equally important was the nature and personalities of the people in the department. Like Fred Seibert himself, the on-air promo staff—practically all iconoclastic, artistic types—really believed in the rebellion this channel stood for, and they spent months theorizing about how they could make this channel different from regular television. That was the conceit that energized all of them: Television will never be the same again. We're changing it.

That rule-breaking attitude came through when they finally did get down to work. Using as much public domain footage as possible since their budget was small, they started putting together spots that not only looked and sounded different from everything else on television, but that, indeed, mocked television itself. The best example was the concept that Fred Seibert came up with to launch the channel. To Seibert, the biggest event in television history was Apollo 11 landing on the moon a dozen years earlier. He and his family were on vacation in Eastern Europe the summer it happened, and years later he would still remember people rushing home to sit in front of their television sets and watch Neil Armstrong take those first historic steps.

Seibert decided that the really rock and roll thing to do would be to steal the whole event.

NASA had public domain footage available, and Seibert and his staff got hold of some of the Apollo footage, called up an animator in New York named Buzz Potamkin, and asked him to make the spot. A few days later Potamkin came back with exactly what Seibert was looking for. It began with a shot of a rocket lifting off, then cut to a shot of the Apollo 11 lunar module on the moon, then to a shot of astronaut Neil Armstrong standing on the moon's surface. Finally, as Armstrong said those immortal words—"That's one small step for man, one giant leap for mankind"—there was a shot of him standing next to the American flag he had implanted in the moon's gray soil. Except it wasn't the American flag anymore; it was a flag with the MTV logo on it.

Everybody at the channel loved the spot, although WASEC lawyers said that if they were going to use Armstrong's voice, they would have to get his permission. So they sent him a letter saying that if they didn't hear from him, they would assume he had no problem with what they were doing. Days went by and they heard nothing. Finally, on July 30, less than forty-eight hours before MTV's launch, word came from Armstrong's lawyer: The former astronaut was not pleased with his voice being used on a rock and roll channel; he was not giving them permission. Fred Seibert spent the whole night removing Armstrong's voice from the spot and replacing it with loud guitar music.

It was a hell of a six months. Looking back on it later, they would all wonder how they survived. Many of them had the kind of experience that a young staffer named Marci Brafman had one Sunday morning. It was about 5 A.M., and Brafman, an associate producer in the on-air promo department, had been working for something like seventy-two hours straight, putting together promo spots and so forth. As she rode up Sixth Avenue alone in a taxi, the lunacy of it all started to hit her. What am I doing here? Have I lost my mind? I'm giving my entire life over to this thing. The thoughts kept running through her head as the taxi headed uptown, until finally she decided she had only two options: She could quit and go back to some sort of normal, nine-to-five life, or she could relax, give herself over to all this insanity, and see where it led her.

Riding up Sixth Avenue, watching the sun rise slowly over the Manhattan skyline, Marci Brafman made a decision almost all of them made at some point. It was crazy, but she decided to stay on this wagon train and see where it was going.

Back in the winter, John Lack and Bob McGroarty made a deal with each other: McGroarty would make the official announcement about MTV at the CTAM convention, while Lack would be the one who actually signed the channel on the air. A day or two before MTV's launch, Lack went into Telectronics and recorded the official sign-on. Jack Schneider couldn't fathom Lack's need to do this; in fact, to him it seemed like a silly, immature stunt. Why couldn't the channel just

start? Why did Lack have to make such a fuss over this thing? There was probably no way Schneider could ever understand why this was so important to Lack. After all, Schneider had never sat in the Brooklyn Paramount listening to Louie Lymon and the Teenchords.

As launch day arrived, both ad sales and affiliate sales were still not looking as strong as everyone had hoped. On that first night, they would have only thirteen advertisers and be connected to only 800,000 homes across the country. While the latter number wasn't terrible by new-cable-network standards, it paled next to the tens of millions of viewers the broadcast networks reached every night, and was even short of the total the WASEC folks themselves had hoped for. Particularly upsetting was the fact that they weren't being carried in many of America's largest markets, including the five boroughs of New York. This lack of distribution in Gotham meant the following: First, few ad agency people would see the channel, something that was not going to help the anemic ad sales situation; second, few record company people would get to see the channel, either, which meant they wouldn't be able to witness first-hand all of the exposure that their artists were getting; and perhaps most disturbing, the young MTV pioneers themselves wouldn't be able to see the channel, at least not at WASEC headquarters or in their offices on Sixth Avenue. And because the network couldn't be seen anywhere in New York, how were they even supposed to have a proper launch party?

John Lack dispatched young affiliate-relations guy Andy Orgel to deal with this last problem. Orgel figured out that the nearest cable system carrying MTV was in Fort Lee, New Jersey, just across the Hudson River. After scouting the area, Orgel finally came across The

Loft, a small restaurant/bar on the edge of town. While it was tiny and dark and somehow seemed more suited to a bowling league banquet than the kickoff of a TV network, it did have a private party room downstairs and did have cable TV. He booked it.

The party began around ten o'clock Friday night, two hours before MTV was scheduled to premiere. Most of the WASEC staff met in Manhattan and rode over to New Jersey in a bus the company had chartered for the occasion. John Lack and Bob McGroarty and their wives arrived in a limo. Jack Schneider, who'd decided this was a party for the kids, spent the night at his home in Connecticut.

Out at the uplink on Long Island, there was absolute chaos, and it only grew worse as the hour got later. First of all, the uplink wasn't even finished yet, so they were all hunkered down in a facility that was little more than four walls, a roof, and a couple of tape machines. What's more, the program log and tape reel with the first veejay segments on it were late arriving, and Andy Setos and his staff were frantically attempting to put the damn ID labels on the clips that were going to be played in the first hour, as well as put all the programming onto plastic cartridges.

Back at The Loft, which had been outfitted with a number of TV sets, the crowd grew to about eighty people. In the room were a few local cable operators, a couple of advertising clients, and one journalist, Robert Hilburn from the *Los Angeles Times*. Mostly it was just the pioneers themselves. They were hardly in the best shape, either. All of them had been working so hard they were near collapse.

The crowd kept drinking and talking and waiting, until finally, several minutes before midnight, onto the TV screens in the room popped a shot of NASA's Mission Control in Houston. Fred Seibert and the on-air promo people had really taken this "launch" business literally, obtaining from NASA countdown footage from a recent space shuttle mission. As the screen showed shots of a rocket on the pad, you could hear the voice of a NASA official squawking away.

"This is launch control at T-minus eleven minutes, forty-five seconds and counting. Everything going very smoothly in the countdown at this point. The booster test conductor ordered the gaseous nitrogen purge of the solid rocket booster; the chase aircrafts have been ordered to start their engines; and a check with the test support team members has verified that they are go for launch."

With midnight drawing near, they all gathered closer to the TV sets. As the minutes went by, the screen kept flashing shots of the rocket, and the NASA announcer kept on talking.

"T-minus two minutes, mark, and counting. The liquid hydrogen vent valve has been closed and flight pressurization is underway. T-minus one minute, fifty seconds and counting."

A buzz began to fill the room now, and it only got stronger as they moved under one minute in the countdown, then to under thirty seconds.

"T-minus fifteen second," the voice said. ". . . ten, nine, eight, seven, six, five, four . . . we've gone for main engine start." A loud screech came through the speakers. "We have main engine start."

The screen turned white for a moment, and then there was a shot of a rocket lifting off, followed by a shot of the Apollo 11 lunar module sitting on the moon. John Lack's deep baritone, recorded earlier, came next.

"Ladies and gentlemen," he said assuredly, "rock and roll . . ."

They cut to a shot of Neil Armstrong standing on the moon, and then, as the music kicked in, an extended closeup of the MTV flag planted in the moon. They were on the air.

Choosing the very first video was a bit of a no-brainer. One of the clips they had gotten their hands on was "Video Killed the Radio Star," by a British band called Buggles. How could they not make it the first clip? As it came on, the room exploded with absolute joy. During those first few minutes everyone was shaking hands and hugging each other, toasting with champagne. Veejays Mark Goodman and Nina Blackwood started to cry. Ad sales chief Larry Divney actually got goose bumps on his face.

During those first few minutes, all of them were beaming; all of them except for one—Bob Pittman. As the second video, Pat Benatar's "You Better Run," came to an end, the Keeper of the Vision looked up and couldn't believe what he was seeing on the screen. What was supposed to come on next was a promo spot, followed by a veejay spot with Mark Goodman, followed by each of the veejays introducing themselves. Well, the promo spot came on just as scheduled, but right after that was . . .

"Hi, I'm Alan Hunter. I'll be with you right after Mark," he said. Wait a minute. Mark who? Goodman hadn't even been on yet. "We'll be covering the latest in music news coast to coast here on MTV: Music Television," Hunter continued.

Pittman couldn't believe it. Obviously some putz out at the Network Operations Center had put the tapes on in the wrong order, because then came Martha and then J. J. and then Nina and then, finally, Mark Goodman.

"This . . . is . . . it," Goodman said. "Welcome to MTV: Music Television, the world's first twenty-four-hour, stereo music-video channel. Now, just moments ago all the veejays and the crew here at MTV collectively hit our executive producer, Sue Steinberg, over the head with a bottle of champagne, and behold—a new concept was born. The best of TV combined with the best of radio. Your favorite tunes are never too far away any time you tune in. I'm Mark Goodman, and I'll be here this time every weeknight with the latest concert information and music news. Starting right now, you'll never look at music the same way again. We'll be right back to introduce the other veejays and other folks who are going to be with us on MTV."

But, of course, the other veejays had already introduced themselves, and after the commercials—the first was for a three-ring binder called the Bulk, the second for the new movie *Superman II*, and the third for Dolby Noise Reduction—Goodman was back.

"Are those guys the best?" he asked, meaning, of course, the other veejays—although nobody watching at home knew that. "We all are so excited about this concept in TV."

One screw-up might not have been so bad, but over the next couple of minutes it only got worse. At a few points there was nothing but white lines across the screen for a good ten seconds; apparently the engineers hadn't quite gotten the hang of switching between the two tape machines. Then one of the promo spots didn't have any sound. And then the cartridges got all out of order again, so that poor videotaped Mark Goodman looked like an idiot as he announced all the wrong songs.

As the mistakes kept coming, Bob Pittman started going completely crazy. As everyone else walked around the bar in a daze over what they'd created, Pittman ordered music programmer Steve Casey to call the uplink. Casey got Andy Setos on the line.

"It's all screwed up," Casey said. "Everything's out of order."

Setos paused for a moment. "Steve," he said finally, "is it on?"

It was, and though the programming was a mess, and though probably no more than a few thousand people were watching, and though the pioneers themselves were standing in some low-rent bar in Fort Lee, New Jersey, the fact that this channel was actually on was the important thing. That was all John Lack cared about that night: Two and a half years after leaving CBS, his new baby was finally here.

As he glided around The Loft, grinning from ear to ear and taking pride in the war they'd fought, Lack had no way of knowing that for him, this night was really the beginning of the end.

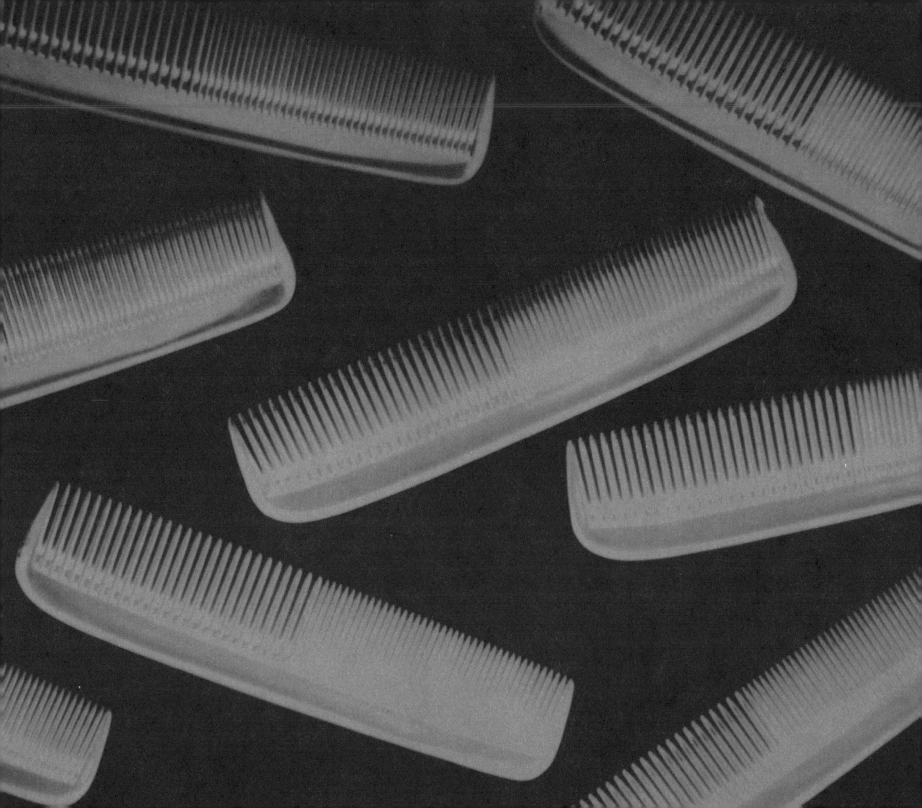

FIVE

hairdos
in the heartland

The third WASEC channel was finally reaching into homes all across America, but all was not well with the company. The biggest problem was The Movie Channel. Though it had started off well—sucking in 1.8 million subscribers its first year—its growth had stalled over the last six months, and now, a little more than a year and a half into its life, it was losing money. One reason was that the channel was no longer unique in the marketplace. Not only had both HBO and Showtime followed The Movie Channel's lead by going to twenty-four-hour-a-day programming, but HBO had even started another all-movie service, Cinemax. On top of that, because the video cassette recorder was now becoming more and more popular, video rental stores were popping up all over America, draining customers from all cable's movie channels. Finally, WASEC's relationship with the cable operators was deteriorating. Back in the spring, the company was forced to raise the price operators had to pay to carry The Movie Channel. That, along with the fact that the system owners never much liked the CBS-style WASEC guys anyway, meant that The Movie Channel wasn't getting a great deal of support in the cable industry.

Despite this, Jack Schneider, John Lack, and Bob McGroarty weren't worried about the future of the channel. Nor were they concerned about the viability of their multi-pipeline vision of WASEC. After all, the cable boom that had started in the second half of the seventies with the development of Qube and the launching of satellite services, such as HBO, was still going strong. Though cable was a long way from being in every household, the percentage of wired homes was growing every day.

What's more, new programming services continued to appear. Even CBS had finally sent a group of scouts out to the cable frontier with a cultural service channel called CBS Cable. Slated to debut that October, the new channel was to be more Tiffany-like than anything the network had done before. All its shows were to be first-class, and the channel's graphics were the best money could buy. But while CBS Cable may have been the most eagerly anticipated new service, it was hardly the only one. There were so many channels on the frontier at that point that one day a staff member walked into WASEC and announced that somebody was starting the Weather Channel—nothing but weather, twenty-four hours a day. Everyone laughed, remembering those old jokes about the Time Channel—that is, until the staffer looked at them soberly and said, "I'm serious."

If a channel featuring nothing but barometric pressure readings and nimbostratus clouds could get off the ground, curing whatever ailed The Movie Channel couldn't be so difficult. And John Lack saw no reason not to move boldly ahead with the other networks WASEC had been kicking around—a games channel, a shopping channel, and an all-talk channel. True, music was the service that stirred his soul, but with one pipeline already open, Lack was anxious to see more pipelines alongside it.

In those weeks and months after MTV's launch, Lack shifted much of his attention to developing WASEC's other channels, while McGroarty, Pittman, and the rest of the pioneers settled in to do the gritty work of running MTV. Within a couple of weeks they'd corrected most of the technical snafus that occurred on the show's debut. Not only were the engineers at the uplink keeping the cartridges in the right order; they'd also finally gotten the hang of

switching between the two tape machines, eliminating those dead air spots. And on-air promo group boss Fred Seibert and his staff had finally figured out why some of the promo spots didn't have any sound. Apparently, some wires had gotten crossed when they'd produced them, so the sound was out of phase. (On a stereo receiver such a miscue wouldn't cause a major problem—the sounds simply come out of the wrong channels—but in mono, which was what television sets are, what comes out is silence.)

Actually seeing the channel hadn't gotten any easier for the pioneers—MTV still wasn't being carried in Manhattan. So, Bob Pittman would occasionally hop into his car and drive across the George Washington Bridge to Fort Lee, eat lunch at The Loft and see the channel live—just the way the rest of America was seeing it. One day, after asking the bartender to tune in MTV on the big-screen television, Pittman once again couldn't believe what he was seeing: Now the picture was backward.

How could this be happening? he asked himself. He understood how the clips could be out of order, and he understood how there could be dead air, and he even understood how a promo spot could have no sound. But how in the hell did the picture end up backward? He immediately phoned the staff at the Network Operations Center on Long Island and, in his best Battlefield Commander voice, gave them the business. Of course, they insisted that it was impossible, even though Pittman told them that he'd seen it with his own eyes. But somehow, that wasn't even enough to convince them. When he got back to the office and told everyone what he had seen, his colleagues began to wonder if he was perhaps a little overworked. Fortunately for his reputation—and sanity—someone figured out that the Pittman had been watching a projection TV that wasn't being projected, so the picture really had been reversed.

Though the technical glitches had been worked out, Pittman and his crew still had plenty to keep them occupied. The veejay segments looked a little too stiff and scripted, too much like regular TV. Soon after the channel went on the air, the crew played around with the set and lighting to give it more of a rock and roll feel.

And then there was the ongoing process of deciding which clips the channel would play. Each week, the programming staff gathered to screen whatever new videos the record companies had sent over. This was by no means a long and grueling session; usually there were no more than a handful of new clips. And unless the song was totally wrong for MTV's rock and roll format or the clip itself was wretched, they put it on the air. How could they not? On launch night and during those first few months, they had no more than 250 videos to play (though years later, some veterans recalled the number being closer to seventy-five). And of the clips they did have, more than a handful were by Rod Stewart. Many of the other clips were by artists like Leo Sayer and Andrew Gold, two singers who didn't fit anyone's definition of rock.

The second part of the process was viewer research. As he had since his Detroit days, Pittman wanted to use research to determine which songs should be played most often. Every week researchers would phone people in MTV markets, searching for anyone who watched the channel. When they located a viewer, they'd play him or her sections of various songs, ask if the viewer had seen the song's video and how well he or she liked it. If a video was popular, it went into heavy rotation (six or seven plays per day). The less-popular videos went into either medium rotation (three or four plays per day) or light rotation (one or two plays per day).

But for all the time they were spending on music selection, Pittman believed that fostering relationships with the record companies was their primary job. For the launch, it had been vital for the channel to obtain whatever clips the labels had lying around in their storerooms, but MTV was only going to survive if the record industry, which was so lukewarm about the channel, committed itself to making new videos. One way to persuade them to do that was by helping the labels promote their artists. This was the job of the talent and acquisitions department, which was headed up by Warner Records refugee Carolyn Baker, along with Gale Sparrow, a sassy young woman who'd come over from CBS Records back in the spring. Baker and Sparrow not only secured the clips and the concert footage the channel ran weekly; they also worked with the labels to promote various acts, either setting up on-air interviews with the veejays, or putting information about them into MTV's music news segments.

Pittman knew that what would excite the record industry more than anything else were numbers. If he and the others could prove that exposure on MTV helped sell records, the labels were bound to make more videos—which was why, several weeks after MTV launched, Pittman sent John Sykes, MTV's head of promotions, and Tom Freston, the channel's chief of marketing, out to the small cities and towns of America's heartland to find proof that MTV was making a difference.

Their main job was to stir up interest in the channel among cable operators, advertisers, and viewers. However, Pittman figured that they also might be able to find some evidence that MTV was having an effect on record sales while they were there. (What he hoped to do was to create an ad for *Billboard* or *Radio & Records* or some other industry trade sheet saying, "Case Study: Tulsa, Oklahoma . . ." and listing underneath it examples of how MTV was helping to sell records there.) He wasn't particularly optimistic about what Sykes and Freston were going to find; the channel had only been on for a few weeks, and even Pittman assumed it might take up to a year before MTV started having much of an impact on sales. Consequently, when the two pioneers called him at home one night from the middle of Oklahoma, he wasn't quite prepared for what he heard.

"Man, you're not going to believe this," John Sykes said. "It's really happening."

And so it was. Sykes and Freston had spent the day visiting record stores and radio stations in Tulsa and made an amazing discovery: Magic was in the air. For seven months prior to MTV's launch, a local store called Peaches Records had fifteen Buggles albums sitting around collecting dust. But three weeks after the channel went on the air and started showing "Video Killed the Radio Star" several times a day, all fifteen copies were sold. It wasn't just Buggles, and it wasn't just at Peaches, either. Everyplace Sykes and Freston went in Tulsa they heard similar tales; people were asking about acts like Squeeze, the Tubes, Billy Squier, Talking Heads, and the Shoes—none of which was being played on local radio in Tulsa, but all of which was being shown on MTV. Even the local radio stations were besieged. "Hey, could you play that song 'Tempted' by Squeeze?" kids would call in and ask. "I just saw it on MTV."

As they would discover over the next several weeks, there was an equal amount of excitement in almost all of the markets where MTV was being carried—places like Wichita and Des Moines and Syracuse.

The response was incredible. Because not everyone in those places had cable, young people were going over to friends' houses to get a glimpse of MTV, just as people had done in the earliest days of television. Moreover, the channel seemed to be influencing everything from the records kids bought and what they talked about at school to how they looked. One barber in Wichita reported to Tom Freston that young guys kept coming in and asking to have their hair cut like that rock star, what was his name . . . Rod Stewart? The poor barber said he couldn't figure it out until one of the youngsters explained it to him: All the kids had seen Rod on MTV.

This sort of reaction was still limited. The channel was only being seen in a handful of cities and towns around America, after all. And some parents weren't exactly thrilled with what they saw and heard; this new channel could be awfully fresh. Yet among young people—among the target demographic—the response was passionate. It was as though someone had placed a virus that affected only young people in the drinking water of several mid-sized American cities. The only thing these kids wanted to do was watch MTV—and not just for a few minutes at a time or while they were doing something else, the way Bob Pittman had imagined when he'd first designed the channel's programming. They were spending whole afternoons and evenings staring bug-eyed at the TV, watching MTV's man-on-the-moon station ID come on at the top of every hour and then waiting to see what jumped out of the screen next. The kids were so captivated, in fact, that one day John Sykes suggested the channel make an addition to the line of promotional items it was hawking—the MTV drool cup.

Back in New York, inside the MTV offices, the rest of the pioneers got a glimpse of the viewer excitement about the channel a few

Rod is God. In places like Witchita, Kansas, MTV was so popular and influential that teenagers began asking barbers for "Rod Stewart" haircuts.

weeks later, during MTV's first contest. To build an audience, the top dogs at the channel decided to do viewer contests just like radio did, and Pittman placed John Sykes in charge. Since they didn't have large sums of money to give away, they decided to focus instead on access and fantasy: They would take young people places they could only dream about going and let them do things they could only dream about doing. The first contest Pittman and Sykes came up with was called a One-Night Stand with Journey. The winner and three friends would be flown in a private jet from their hometown to a Journey concert in either New York or Los Angeles, loaded down with gifts, taken backstage after the show to meet the band, and flown home—all in the same evening. More than forty thousand people sent in post cards to enter. The winner turned out to be an eighteen-year-old girl from Stevens Point, Wisconsin, Margaret Dobler. On the day of the concert John Sykes flew to Wisconsin, picked up Margaret and her friends, flew them back to New York for dinner at the trendy Maxwell's Plum on the Upper East Side, and then escorted them to the concert at the Nassau Coliseum on Long Island. When it was over, the winners were driven (via limo) back to the airport, where they boarded the plane and flew back to Wisconsin. To Margaret and her friends, the experience was just about the coolest thing ever.

What was causing this intensely positive reaction among young people? Part of it was the music MTV was playing. Mainstream radio had become so conservative that many album-oriented rock stations were playing up to 75 percent oldies—rock war-horses like "Stairway to Heaven" and "Freebird"—over and over again. The acts MTV featured—New Wave bands like Squeeze and the Shoes—seemed to quench this generation's thirst for new music.

Equally enticing were the videos themselves. They brought the musicians closer to the audience. Before this, the only way to get a closeup look at a rock star was to finagle a front-row seat at a concert or to pick up a magazine like *Rolling Stone* or *Tiger Beat*. But now, the most famous faces in music were right there next to the Ping-Pong table and the bean-bag chair in your paneled suburban basement, singing away while you and your friends drank Dr Pepper, ate Doritos, talked about the scuzzball teacher who gave you a D in chemistry. And the images in the videos themselves were unlike anything that had ever been on television before. They were so fast-paced and crazy and colorful that, by comparison, regular TV shows now looked like old, rumpled brown suits.

Television had never looked or sounded this way before. It had never talked to viewers this way. Indeed, the animated channel IDs and promo spots were often more entertaining than the videos themselves. One of the spots seemed to say it all: It started out with a shot of two formally dressed older people dancing to melancholy big-band music. Suddenly, the screen froze, a giant circle with a slash through it (the "no" sign) popped up, and an odd voice said: "Hey, you, don't watch that, watch this!" At which point videos by Talking Heads and Fleetwood Mac flashed onto the screen. "The first twenty-four-hour video music channel in full stereo sound," an announcer said. "Music television—MTV."

The spots the on-air promo crew were churning out were so successful that, as those first weeks and months passed, it became increasingly clear that Seibert and his group were the real rock and roll soul of this channel. Because Bob Pittman and executive producer Sue Steinberg occasionally clashed over the look and feel of the veejay spots, Pittman asked Fred Seibert to oversee production as well as on-air promotion, and to make sure he got that "screw you" spirit into the veejay spots as well.

*　*　*　*　*　*

Out in the heartland the kids were mesmerized by the new channel. And yet by late fall, the mood wasn't nearly as gleeful back in the New York offices and at the Telectronics production studio.

For those in Manhattan, it was as though the war they'd been fighting since the spring had never ended. Even after three months on the air, many of them were still crawling out of bed after only a few hours of sleep, dragging themselves over to the office or the studio, and staying until ten or eleven at night. Though most of them still believed in what this channel stood for, they were incredibly exhausted. For months they'd worked to get the channel up and running, but keeping this insatiable beast fed with new videos and veejay spots and promos was absolutely draining. Finally, near the end of the year, Sue Steinberg decided that she'd had enough and resigned. Julian Goldberg, who'd auditioned Martha Quinn over the summer, took her place as executive producer.

Even more troubling was the ongoing battle against the status quo. While the handful of kids who were actually seeing the channel seemed to love it, most of the adults with whom the pioneers came in contact each day couldn't have cared less about it. The music industry, despite MTV's help in selling records, still remained leery. For MTV's second contest, John Sykes wanted to do another One-Night Stand—this one with the Rolling Stones, who were then touring America. Unfortunately, when Sykes called the Stones' management to get tickets and backstage passes, they kept giving him the

brush-off. Nevertheless, in the just-get-it-done spirit, Sykes went ahead with the contest and took the winners to the Stones concert at the Superdome in New Orleans. When they all got there, Sykes excused himself, saying he had to go pick up their special-access passes. He walked a couple of hundred yards away, pulled out a roll of bills, and bought five tickets from a scalper. After the show, the group sneaked backstage and met one of the Stones' backup singers—before being tossed out on their ears. The kids didn't care; as far as they knew, the contest had gone off without a hitch.

The problems on the business side of the channel were even worse. Distribution was still below expectations; though the channel was now up to two million subscribers, they still weren't on the air in Manhattan or Los Angeles. The advertising department wasn't doing much better. By the end of the year, they had only half a million dollars in ad revenues (less than most medium-sized radio stations). To top things off, the ad sales chief, Larry Divney, announced he was leaving MTV to work for Viacom's new Cable Health Network.

Despite such difficulties, Schneider, Lack, and McGroarty still weren't panicking. After all, this was a brand-new operation, and glitches like these were to be expected. Moreover, by the time January rolled around, the problems looked like they were on their way to being solved. First, in hopes of increasing distribution, Schneider, Lack, and McGroarty decided to restructure the company's sales and marketing arm, and moved Andy Orgel from head of affiliate relations to a new job, head of WASEC's regional offices. To replace Orgel they turned to Sonya Suarez, the woman who'd been running creative services, the department responsible for all promotional and printed materials. To take Suarez's place, they brought over none other than the Keeper of the Grooviness himself, Fred Seibert. It made sense—no one understood MTV's look and attitude better than he did.

The other change they hoped would make a difference was in advertising sales. Back in the fall, CNN honcho Ted Turner had approached WASEC looking to make a deal to acquire facilities. Some months earlier, Westinghouse had announced it was going to start an all-news channel to compete with CNN, and in response Turner had drawn up plans to start a second service of his own, CNN2. It was a classic marketing strategy, one HBO had used when it created *Cinemax*, its answer to The Movie Channel. If a competitor goes after one of your products, create your own new product—a "fighting brand," as it was known. The hope was that the two new products would fight it out for shelf space and market share as the original product floated, untouched, above the fray. While Turner certainly had the manpower and facilities to launch CNN2 without much trouble, he didn't have a satellite transponder to put it on.

WASEC did. From the beginning Schneider, Lack, and McGroarty believed that because transponders were scarce, they were going to be a valuable commodity in this new business. The way they saw it, those who controlled the heavens were bound to control the whole cable frontier. Schneider had placed operations head Andy Setos in charge of WASEC's transponders, and the young engineer really took to the job, making up charts to show who owned what on which satellite, and acquiring transponders as though they were real estate in the sky. After all, the plan was for this company to start a magazine rack full of channels. They were obviously going to need as much satellite space as they could get. When Ted Turner approached them, WASEC not only had transponders for MTV,

The Movie Channel, and Nickelodeon, but for at least one extra channel as well.

The question was, what should they try to pry from Turner in return? Money was an obvious choice, but as Schneider, Lack, and McGroarty considered their situation, they decided that Turner might be able to help with MTV's struggling ad sales as well. Though Turner's CNN was hardly CBS when it came to revenue, it was doing better than MTV. And so they offered to give Turner one of their transponders if he'd let their ad staff sell CNN's advertising. Not only would WASEC collect a sales rep fee for each ad they sold, but being the rep for CNN was bound to open some doors for MTV's ad sales people. On paper it seemed as if WASEC would then have the demographic spectrum covered: MTV for those age twelve to thirty-four, CNN for those thirty-five and older.

The meeting to finalize the deal took place at the Ritz-Carlton in Boston during the CTAM convention that fall. Lack and McGroarty had dinner with Turner and one of his associates, and afterward Turner invited them all up to his suite.

After sharing a toast (or two) on behalf of the event, the chairman of Turner Broadcasting and the executive vice president of WASEC finalized their deal. Beginning in January, MTV would sell CNN's advertising.

The next day Lack and McGroarty were back in WASEC headquarters, and Schneider asked how everything went.

"We got the deal," Lack said.

"Was it tough?" Schneider asked.

Lack looked at his idol, and just smiled. "Don't ask," he said.

*   *   *   *   *   *

Despite the slow start on the business side, as those first months went by the MTV virus continued spreading quietly throughout America. By the end of December, some people were finally beginning to notice. *Fortune* magazine named MTV one of its ten products of the year, calling it "the purest example to date" of cable's ability to serve specific audiences.

Even more exciting was MTV's own New Year's Eve show. To ring in 1982 properly, Bob Pittman and the programming staff decided that MTV should telecast its own New Year's Eve ball, just as CBS had done all these years with Guy Lombardo and the Royal Canadians. To appeal to their audience, they knew they would have to make it as un-Guy Lombardo-ish as possible. So they booked three un-Guy Lombardo-like acts—singer Karla deVito, former New York Doll band member David Johansen, and New Wave band Bow Wow Wow. Then they found an un-Guy Lombardo-like venue, the Diplomat Hotel near Times Square in Manhattan. What a hellhole that was. It was so seedy, in fact, that to prevent partygoers from seeing the building's dingy lobby, the MTV folks erected a huge canvas tunnel between the door and the elevator.

Although they sent out a couple of thousand invitations, the day of the show John Sykes and Bob Pittman were struck by a horrifying notion: What if no one comes? After all, nobody in Manhattan had really seen the channel. Who would even know what this MTV thing was? To make sure they had enough guests, Sykes hit the streets during the afternoon, giving out hundreds more invitations to anybody who would take one. It turned out not to be necessary—that night about fifteen hundred people showed up. It was an incredible scene. In the pouring rain, people were lined up for blocks trying to get into

the Diplomat to see the show. They were ad execs and cable operators and even a few celebrities, including comic John Belushi. At one point, Sykes walked down the line pulling out VIPs and escorting them inside, where the scene was even crazier. Sometime long after midnight, the New York Fire Department came and shut them down.

The whole event illustrated the buzz MTV was starting to create. No one was benefiting from that buzz more than Bob Pittman. The unquestionable success of MTV's programming—not to mention Pittman's own style— was clearly raising his status inside WASEC. While he was a demanding boss, most of those who labored under him were incredibly loyal to him. And despite his youth—he had just turned twenty-eight—many of them saw Pittman as the brightest, most articulate person they'd ever met. What's more, though he was tough to get to know, most genuinely liked him, particularly when they got to see him outside the office, having a few drinks or hanging out inside a club.

Pittman was impressing his bosses too—not just Jack Schneider, but the top dogs at Warner as well. One of them, Spencer Harrison, had taken Pittman under his wing during the previous year, grooming him to run a big company someday. Though others had praised and encouraged him before this, none of them had made the impression that Harrison did. Maybe it was because Harrison really knew what it took to make it; he'd been the head of business affairs at CBS for years, and after that had run the Warner Brothers movie studio for Steve Ross.

By early 1982, Bob Pittman's star was rising quickly. With The Movie Channel continuing to struggle, Warner chairman Steve Ross and his lieutenants gave Pittman even more responsibility at the movie service, in addition to his work at MTV. That Pittman was getting so much recognition from those higher up did not sit well with everyone. There were those, particularly on the business side of the company, who found him just a little bit too calculating and political. In their eyes, he seemed only to be out to advance his own career, everyone else be damned.

As a result of Pittman's increased responsibilities at The Movie Channel, he needed someone to oversee programming at MTV on a day-to-day basis. Music programmer Steve Casey, the man who'd given MTV its name, was one possibility, although he didn't have any real management experience. The Keeper of the Grooviness, Fred Seibert, was another, although he seemed to lack the diplomacy necessary for schmoozing the record companies.

No, Bob Pittman decided to go outside the company and bring in a former radio programmer, Les Garland.

*   *   *   *   *   *

Like Fred Seibert, Les Garland was hardly what you might have called traditional executive material. If Seibert sometimes seemed as if he didn't belong in the same company as the buttoned-down Bob McGroarty, Garland sometimes seemed as if he didn't even belong on the same planet.

It wasn't that he was crude or abrasive. Rather, this tall, slim, handsome thirty-four-year-old appeared to have decided early in his life that he was put on this earth to enjoy himself. Like John Lack, Garland had a big personality.

And yet, where Lack was sophisticated, Garland was a lunatic. He could party longer and harder, tell wilder stories (often about himself), and do better with the ladies than most anyone else around. It

seemed that no matter what woman he happened to be standing next to, he'd invariably introduce her the same way: "Have you met my fiancée?" Still, if Garland was sometimes irresponsible and immature (and there were many who thought he was both), he was also endearing. For example, he had the charming habit of calling everybody he met "Bud."

Like Bob Pittman, Les Garland started his career in radio as a teenager, working at a station in his hometown of Aurora, Missouri. By age twenty-three, the deejay life led him to Tulsa, Oklahoma, where he became one of the hottest deejays in the market, doing evenings at station KELI and hosting his own dance show on local television. Despite his success on the air, Garland was increasingly attracted to the programming side of the business, and over the next several years he jumped from one station to the next, developing a reputation along the way as one of the top program directors in radio. Finally, in 1977, he ended up at KFRC in San Francisco. Known for years as one of the great AM rock and roll stations in America, KFRC had slipped to number five in the market by the time Garland arrived. He helped revive it, bringing it back to number one and earning himself *Billboard*'s program director of the year award in 1978. A couple of years later, figuring he had nothing left to prove in radio, he moved over to the record business, taking a position with Warner-owned Atlantic Records in Los Angeles.

Garland first heard about MTV from Pittman in the summer of 1981. The two had known each other since early in their radio days, and when Pittman was in Los Angeles that summer courting record companies, the two got together for dinner a couple of times. Garland loved the idea of a music video channel, and since MTV was not yet being shown in Los Angeles, he had a buddy of his in Tulsa tape a few hours of it each week and send it to him. He was so intrigued by what he saw that he started mailing Pittman memos about the channel—praising this, criticizing that, and making suggestions. Finally, Pittman offered him the job as vice president of programming. Not only did Garland have radio experience, but he also had terrific relationships with both artists and record label executives.

By the time Les Garland arrived at MTV in early 1982, most of the pioneers in programming had started to wilt, thanks to the grueling pace. Like original executive producer Sue Steinberg, another member of the channel's development team, Carolyn Baker, had grown weary of the lifestyle and left the channel early in the year. She was replaced by her assistant, Gale Sparrow. Luckily, Garland wasted no time in giving the staff a quick jolt of enthusiasm. Shortly after he arrived, Marci Brafman, the

up to her and said, "You know what, Bud? I like you. I'm gonna promote you tomorrow."

* * * * * *

Les Garland's large and loud presence at the channel didn't do anything to impede the advance of the all-powerful MTV virus. By the end of Garland's first few months, the excitement about MTV had spread to even more small cities and towns across America. Best of all, the channel now had actual numbers to back up some of the anecdotal evidence from the frontier. That spring, A. C. Nielsen, the television ratings company, did a telephone survey for MTV in three different markets—Palisades Park, New Jersey; Grand Rapids, Michigan; and San Jose, California. Seventy-five percent of those watching the channel rated it "good to excellent." What's more, MTV had the highest name recognition of any cable service.

Hey, Bud, it's Les Garland! Though his rambunctious personality and wild antics grated on some, the "Gar-man's" close relationships with the record industry were crucial to MTV's success.

young producer who'd recently taken over for Fred Seibert as head of the on-air promo department, invited Garland and his secretary, Joan Meyers, out for a "Welcome to MTV" dinner. In true Garland style, he and Meyers showed up about an hour and a half late, and immediately ordered a round of Manhattans for everyone at the table. And then another round. And then another. And another. By the end of the evening, Marci Brafman could hardly sign her name on the credit card slip when the check arrived. As they all left the restaurant and started flagging down cabs to go home, Garland came

The channel's programming was looking better and better. Not only were the videos getting more and more creative, but an increasing number of artists were starting to take note of the channel. Pete Townsend of the Who had recently done an interview, as had Chrissie Hynde of the Pretenders. At the same time, the network's rock and roll spirit seemed sharper than ever, thanks to the animated IDs, irreverent promo spots, and fantasy-fulfilling viewer promotions. The most recent contest was called the MTV House Party. John Sykes and company showed up at the home of the winner, sixteen-year-old Rob Kettleborough of Dearborn, Michigan, and threw a dream party, complete with thousands of dollars' worth of stereo equipment, food and drink for a hundred people, and actual coverage of the event on the channel.

Of all the people in programming, the ones who best understood the effect that all this programming was having on folks out there in America were the five veejays, who by now were developing a tight bond with one another. They were getting bushels of fan mail, and, to promote the channel, the five of them made frequent appearances in small and not-so-small towns across the country, signing autographs in record stores and having dinner with cable operators. It was an amazing experience for all of them. One day, Nina Blackwood was scheduled to go to a record store in some town out in the heartland. As she was driven up to the store, she saw a huge line of young people waiting outside, and she asked what was going on.

"They're all here to see you," she was told.

And so they were. It was ironic, because back in New York, inside MTV itself, all five veejays were viewed as small cogs in a large machine. Most of them believed that people like Bob Pittman saw them as merely talent, incapable of doing much else besides looking pretty and reading a TelePrompTer. And yet, out here in the heartland, where new music was selling and the MTV virus was spreading, the MTV veejays—Mark, J.J., Alan, Nina, and Martha—were stars. It made sense, because to the people watching, the veejays *were* MTV. As far as these kids knew, the veejays were the ones picking the music, creating the contests, and making those hysterical animated logos. Viewers began treating the veejays like celebrities.

★   ★   ★   ★   ★   ★

If only there had been such love and understanding inside the offices at 1211. Despite the passion kids across America had for MTV, WASEC's money problems continued, with all three program services struggling. They'd tried various tactics to jump-start The Movie Channel, but by the early summer of 1982 none had been very effective. Nickelodeon wasn't doing very well either. While its programming was hailed by critics and parents as first-rate, the kids weren't crazy about it, and the channel was still running in the red.

Finally, there was MTV. Despite the Ted Turner/CNN deal, ad sales, which were being overseen by former affiliate sales chief Gary Koester, remained dismal. Advertisers were still leery of both cable and a rock and roll channel. It seemed like the only good news in ad sales was the discovery of what would come to be called the Secret Army. A couple of months earlier, one of the ad sales people in the Atlanta office had finally gotten a contract with one client after months of trying. What closed the deal was a recommendation from the chief executive officer's son, who was a huge MTV fan. He told his dad he should advertise on it.

Despite the presence of this growing Secret Army of fans, times were tough at the channel, and making things even tougher were the significant changes taking place with WASEC's corporate parents. Over the past several years at Warner, much of the company's growth had been a result of the tremendous popularity of its Atari video games. In fact, in 1981 Atari accounted for nearly two-thirds of Warner's operating earnings. Unfortunately, there was now increasing competition within the video game industry, as well as a growing feeling that the video game market had peaked. As a result, Warner's stock went into a tailspin, dropping one-third in value in the first six months of 1982. Warner was in no position to bail out its financially struggling cable networks.

The bigger problem was that American Express was questioning its involvement in the cable business. While Gus Hauser's division of Warner AMEX had been successful in winning a number of big-city franchises, the wiring of America was costing much more than AMEX chief Jim Robinson, or anyone else at the company, had anticipated when they'd first gotten into the cable game in 1979. By the end of 1982, the whole Warner AMEX partnership (WASEC and WACC together) would be running in the red by more than $46 million.

Perhaps even more significant were the changes taking place within American Express itself. The previous summer, the company had merged with Wall Street's second-largest brokerage firm, Shearson Loeb Rhoades. The move made sense for both companies, but it changed American Express's strategic direction, positioning it clearly as a financial services company—one for which a cash-draining cable TV venture no longer made sense. At least that seemed to be the view held by the top executives at Shearson, including the firm's chief executive officer, Sandy Weill. Back in the winter, WASEC head Jack Schneider made a presentation about MTV at the annual American Express corporate retreat in Florida. He showed some videos and went over all the potential of the youth market. When Schneider was finished, Sandy Weill reportedly turned to one of his colleagues and said, "That was one of the biggest wastes of time I've ever sat through."

The effect of this parental attitude change was twofold. First, in the early part of the summer, Warner began talking to Hollywood movie studios MCA and Paramount about becoming partners in The Movie Channel. Both studios, along with Columbia and 20th Century-Fox,

had tried to start their own cable movie service a year earlier as a way of taking on pay-cable giant HBO. The Justice Department shot it down for anti-trust reasons, but the studios remained interested in cable, and with The Movie Channel in need of help, negotiations had begun.

Moreover, with money tight, with The Movie Channel, Nickelodeon, and MTV all still in the red, and with cable itself looking like it was finally starting to cool down after a five-year boom, there was little money or enthusiasm for some of the other channels John Lack had hoped to launch. Not only were tests for the company's shopping channel, ShopAmerica, being pushed back, but there were even some within WASEC starting to question the whole multi-pipeline vision.

*   *   *   *   *   *

Still, the financial situation wasn't without hope. MTV's best chance was a new ad agency they'd hired and a new ad campaign that was about to debut. Not long after the channel had launched the previous August, many in the company had started to believe that Ogilvy & Mather, WASEC's original ad agency, was botching the MTV account. In particular, the Keeper of the Grooviness, Fred Seibert, had little patience for the work they were producing: staid, low-key print ads that Seibert thought could just as easily have been for tires as for a rock and roll cable channel. Seibert had started to look at the Ogilvy & Mather team the same way he looked at many of the guys on the business side of WASEC: They just didn't have the rock and roll spirit. One day he told the folks at Ogilvy & Mather that they were fundamentally incapable of doing the advertising MTV needed.

But who was equipped to handle this task? Seibert and Bob Pittman agreed that the ideal person to do MTV's advertising was none other than the man who'd brought the two of them together two years earlier, Dale Pon. Not only was Pon a bit of a lunatic, but he also had a background in promoting the media. The son of Chinese immigrants, Pon had worked as a deejay for Radio Free America before getting into advertising and, later, broadcast promotion. Pon had recently left NBC radio and was now part of an ad agency with George Lois, a legend on Madison Avenue, and two other ad men, Bill Pitts and Dick Gershon. And so in January, after an agency review and much internal debate, LPG/Pon got the MTV account.

From the beginning, Pon and his partners believed that what MTV had to deal with was an old-fashioned, albeit serious, marketing problem. Simply put, unless they got more distribution, unless they persuaded more cable operators to carry the channel, they were going to shrivel up and die. To get across both to cable operators and potential advertisers just who was watching MTV, Dale Pon had quickly put together a campaign.

wrong message to cable operators. Some operators were even turning it back on the MTV affiliate sales crew: When the MTV guys showed up to pitch the cable companies on the channel, a few of the cable operators looked at these stylish, cocky young salespeople and said, "Hey, look, the cable brats are here!"

By summer, it was clear that a more radical marketing strategy was needed. Although distribution was growing—they were now reaching four million homes across the country—they were still below the number they'd projected, and they still weren't on in New York or Los Angeles. The cable companies were continuing to resist the idea of a rock and roll channel. Finally, it became clear to everyone at WASEC that if those white-shoe-wearing pole climbers wouldn't put on MTV of their own volition, they'd just have to get the cable brats themselves to demand they put it on.

Such was the genesis of the "I Want My MTV!" campaign.

"I Want My MTV!" campaign co-creator Dale Pon. A rock and roll guy doing rock and roll advertising for a rock and roll channel. Pon's ads were crucial in expanding MTV's reach.

"America is fast becoming a land of cable brats!" the ads proclaimed. "Who are the cable brats? They're that incorrigible generation out there and they're taking over America. They grew up with music. They grew up with television. So we put 'em together." The campaign's tag line summed up the attitude of these cable brats: "rock and roll wasn't enough for them—now they want their MTV."

The ads ran in the cable industry and ad industry trade press throughout the spring of 1982. Unfortunately, nobody at WASEC was very fond of them. The "cable brats" phrase seemed to send out the

Dale Pon and George Lois took the tag line from their "cable brats" ads and reworked it into an ad campaign aimed at consumers. The idea was simple. They would get rock stars to proclaim, "I want my MTV!" and then have them encourage kids to call up their cable companies and say the same thing.

Pon and Lois presented the idea to Schneider, Lack, and the rest of WASEC. The response was cool. To many, it had a strangely familiar ring to it—it sounded a lot like the "I Want My Maypo" ad campaign that ran back in the sixties (an account that Lois had overseen).

Seibert was incredulous. But after the presentation, when Seibert and Pon had lunch, Pon explained to him why "I Want My MTV!" was perfect. It captured the attitude of the channel—the instant-gratification spirit of rock and roll. Equally important, it played on what was truly unique about MTV: In a world where television networks had always tried to appeal to mass audiences, here was a channel that cared only about one specific audience. It's not their MTV, the ads told young people—it's yours.

The key to making the campaign work was persuading rock stars to do the spots. Once the idea was approved, they all began to call in favors to see who they could get. John Sykes, who'd first discovered the MTV virus out in Tulsa, called a friend who knew Pete Townsend, the lead guitarist of the Who, and the friend said he could probably get Townsend to do it. And so Sykes, Dale Pon, and a camera crew flew to London. Sykes went into Townsend's manager's office and explained who he was and what he wanted. Unfortunately, Pete wasn't going to be in that day. Sykes said he'd wait—which he did, for about the next six hours. Finally, Townsend showed up, Sykes explained why he was there, and Townsend agreed to give them half an hour. They all hustled across the street, where the crew was waiting, and Townsend did the spot.

Getting Mick Jagger was going to be tougher. Les Garland's secretary, Joan Meyers, had once worked for the Rolling Stones, so Garland asked her to make a couple of phone calls to see what she could do. She tracked down the Stones, who were on tour in Europe, and found out that Jagger would at least be willing to talk about doing it. In late June, Meyers, Garland, Dale Pon, and Fred Seibert's sidekick, Alan Goodman, flew to Paris to meet with Jagger. Garland went into Jagger's hotel room and explained what they wanted him to do, but Jagger started shaking his head.

"It's a commercial, man," he said. "I don't do commercials."

Jagger was correct; it was certainly a commercial, although Garland did his best to present it as more than that. If Mick did this spot, he said, it would be an endorsement of music video, and that could help create a whole new art form.

"I don't know, " Jagger said. "It sounds like a commercial to me."

Finally, Garland said to him, "Would you do it for money?"

"How much?"

Garland reached into his pocket and pulled out his wallet. "A buck," he said, slapping a dollar on the table.

Ultimately, Jagger agreed to do it and, in return, MTV agreed to broadcast a Stones concert on the tour and also to give Jagger final approval over the spot.

The campaign, which in addition to Townsend and Jagger featured rockers Adam Ant, Stevie Nicks, and Pat Benatar, debuted on New York TV stations during the third week of July. The spots turned out to be terrific. After each of the stars proclaimed, "I want my MTV!" there were lots of colorful, fast-paced graphics, and those watching were encouraged to call up their cable operators and demand their MTV.

No one at the network knew if the campaign would work. But they did know that, not everyone was a fan of this new form of television. In fact, the same month the "I Want My MTV!" commercials started running, the Institute for Living, a private mental hospital in Hartford, Connecticut, banned the channel. An official hospital memo put it succinctly: "We have observed ill effects on certain of our patients as a result of viewing MTV."

SIX
RISING STAR

A gloom had settled over WASEC. With a Movie Channel deal in the works, Warner and American Express reluctant to launch any new networks, and MTV struggling financially, all the camaraderie and anticipation the pioneers had felt when they'd first hopped aboard the WASEC wagon and listened to John Lack lay out where they were heading was now starting to fade. Two and a half years after the company had begun, everything was changing. The pioneers were even turning on one another.

It started at the very top, with WASEC president Jack Schneider and Warner chairman Steve Ross. The two men just didn't get along. Schneider was miffed that Ross and his lieutenants seemed to view WASEC as merely another division of Warner, instead of as a joint venture with American Express. Not long after the company had been launched, AMEX's Jim Robinson asked Schneider to look out for his company's interest in this venture. Robinson acknowledged that Warner was much better versed in the entertainment business, but half the cash in this partnership was still American Express's. So Schneider wasn't about to let Ross or any of his henchmen walk all over him. What strained his relationship with Ross even more was that the two of them were so dissimilar in style and personality. As an old CBS hand, Schneider was structured, polished, always courteous to those who worked for him, always concerned with doing things the right way, whereas Ross and his crew were more freewheeling, emotional, and less concerned with titles and protocol than with results.

Things weren't especially rosy between Schneider and John Lack, either. Schneider had grown increasingly impatient with Lack. He thought Lack's hefty expense account had become unconscionable (Lack was never shy about ordering a limo to get around), but more important, Schneider believed that Lack had simply stopped performing. At the same time, Lack was increasingly less enamored of Jack Schneider. In the early days of the company, Lack had been as enthusiastic as a puppy about the idea of working side by side with his idol. Now he was disappointed and angry with him for not fighting harder to stop the movie studios from getting a piece of The Movie Channel. Despite the channel's troubles, Lack truly believed it was on the verge of turning around.

Lack's relationship with Bob Pittman had changed as well. As Pittman's status within the company grew, some on the business side of WASEC warned Lack to watch his back. The Keeper of the Vision always denied that he was gunning for Lack's job, but Lack began to feel that Pittman was honing in on him. In many ways such charges merely reflected the split that had developed between sales and programming. Those in sales felt that programming ruled the company and that the sales department was being treated as an ugly stepchild.

Ironically, the mood among the pioneers in programming was far from cheery. Though they all remained passionate about the product, by this point they were also pretty burnt out—both from working hard and, thanks to Garland, playing hard. What made things worse was that few of them ever received much recognition. Out in America's suburbs and small cities, an increasing number of young people were going crazy for this new rule-breaking television. But in New York, few had a clue what MTV was. It really got to be frustrating trying to explain to their family and friends exactly what they did for a living.

As the channel's first anniversary approached, a few of the pioneers were determined to do something about the company's sagging morale. Case in point: Although MTV's first birthday would be celebrated on the air with a series of special events—concerts by the Go-Go's and Fleetwood Mac, a replay of the New Year's Eve show, a screening of the film *Reefer Madness*—no official company function was planned. Programming vice president Les Garland, artist relations head Gale Sparrow, and some of the other desperate souls in programming decided to take things into their own hands. Sitting in Garland's office, they called Bob Pittman to see if the company would spring for an employees-only birthday party. Pittman hemmed and hawed, and finally said they could go ahead with it—if they kept things extremely small and low-key. There just wasn't enough money for anything else. They immediately started pooling their funds.

"Well, I can probably squeeze a few thousand out of my budget," Sparrow said.

"Yeah, me, too," added somebody else.

"Why not?" said a third.

After a few minutes of this, it was clear that this function was going to be neither small nor low-key. Gale Sparrow and her assistant, Roberta Cruger, were in charge of organizing the affair, and they went all out. They hired a caterer, rented space in a Manhattan studio, and then threw themselves into decorating it. They gave each room a different theme. The main area had a soundstage, huge video screens, tables covered with pink cloth, and five hundred balloons suspended from the ceiling. In the second room, dubbed the Make-out Room, they put black lights and Indian wall hangings, and burned incense. They turned the third space into the Gambling Room, equipping it with roulette wheels and blackjack tables. When guests walked in the door they would be handed a couple of grand in fake money, and at the end of the evening the partygoer with the most cash would win a prize. And whose face did they put on these bills? None other than Les Garland's, Bud.

The turnout was great. Almost everyone from programming, production, and finance came, as did most of the engineers from out at the uplink on Long Island. It seemed as if all the frustration and tension they had built up over an entire year just detonated. There was live entertainment, too—Sparrow and Cruger performed as "The Pointless Sisters," and a couple of guys from finance went on stage as "The Black Books." Everybody danced a lot, ate too much, and drank far too many shots of tequila. A few even put some illegal substances into their systems. Finally, sometime after midnight, with many of them as out-to-lunch as they'd ever been in their lives, it was time to award the prizes. They had fabulous stuff to hand out, too, including some TV and stereo equipment that was supposed to be given away to MTV viewers but which the organizers had, well, appropriated for the party instead. Sparrow and Garland got up on stage and started making speeches and carrying on. Halfway through, the Keeper of the Vision appeared at the door.

He was standing there in a big, bulky sweater, and the look on his face was not a pleasant one. The man knew a small and low-key party when he saw it, and this was neither. Les Garland got off the stage and moved over to the other side of the room, but Pittman kept glaring at him, motioning for him to come over. Garland shook his head no, and so Pittman finally walked over to him. "Can't we do this on Monday?" Garland said.

Monday morning, Garland was waiting for the call. Finally, it came; It was Dwight Tierney, the head of personnel.

"Okay, Dwight," he rasped, "when do you want to do it?"

"Do what?" Tierney asked.

"I know I'm getting blown out of here."

"Listen to me, Les. The party never happened, right?"

Garland paused. "Uh, what party?"

"Good. Now, the only thing I need to know is who won the prizes. We have to report that stuff to the IRS."

* * * * * *

MTV's popularity continued to grow. By now enough young people across America had been exposed to the virus that the channel was actually starting to have an impact on the *Billboard* charts.

The British band A Flock of Seagulls was proof of that. A foursome from Liverpool, the Seagulls released their first American single, an echoey dance-rock track called "I Ran," in June, and then came to the States for a three-week club tour. Not that anyone, including their U.S. record label, Arista, was overly optimistic about their chances for success. Their synthesizer-heavy sound didn't really seem right for either album rock or Top-40 radio, and, frankly, the band wasn't even that popular in England. Still, they'd made an interesting video, one that Les Garland and the crew in programming liked, and so during the summer the clip was added to MTV's playlist. Within weeks "I Ran" began rising up the charts, and radio stations, most of which had initially ignored the song, were following MTV's lead and adding the song to their rotations. By the end of the summer, "I Ran" was in *Billboard*'s Top 10, the group's eponymous debut album was in the Top 20, and the Seagulls themselves were playing huge arenas around the country with the Go-Go's.

The Seagulls weren't the only new act that had taken flight with MTV's help. The Australian band Men at Work and the Long Island-based rockabilly band Stray Cats, two young groups that had been ignored by radio but played heavily over the summer by MTV, now had albums and singles moving up the charts as well. On their latest tour, the Stray Cats had decided to only play in markets where MTV was being carried—and they were selling out. To be sure, the music that all three of these bands were playing—somehow fresher and more vital than the power-chord rock that had dominated for the past few years—had much to do with their popularity. And yet, there was something else that fans couldn't help noticing: All three acts were visually interesting. While the biggest rock groups of the last couple of years, Journey and REO Speedwagon, hardly had any visual identity, each of these new bands was a spectacle. Mike Score, the former hairdresser who was the Seagulls's lead singer, had an odd-looking hairdo that made him appear appropriately birdlike. The Stray Cats looked to be straight from the 1950s, with their pompadours, T-shirts, and tattoos. And Men at Work, though lacking matinee idol looks, made up for it with loony antics in the video for their song "Who Can It Be Now?"

That MTV and music video were starting to make a huge impact certainly wasn't lost on the record labels. Several months earlier, PolyGram, one of two video holdouts a year earlier, acknowledged

the boost MTV was giving record sales and finally started supplying the channel with clips. Most of the record companies were starting to view video as an increasingly important part of promotion, though they weren't yet making a video for every release by every artist. Indeed, although the sales slump that had started in 1979 was now worse than ever, and labels were laying off scores of workers (CBS Records dumped three hundred people that September), the industry was making twice as many clips as it had the previous year. Equally important, labels and artists were increasingly willing to invest substantial cash in each clip. The video for Billy Joel's latest single, "Pressure," reportedly had cost $80,000—almost three times as much as the average clip.

With MTV providing exposure and the record industry providing the capital, the music video scene was hotter than ever. TV shows like *Night Flight* and *Video Jukebox* were still on the air, now with more clips to choose from, and more clubs were beginning to show music videos. Perhaps most significantly, the video music industry itself—the number of people who actually shot the videos—was growing. In London, where much of the industry was based, a number of firms were churning out several videos per week for American and European record labels. More young directors were being drawn to the medium as well. It was a perfect place for a filmmaker to start out; budgets were relatively small, and they could be creative.

Of all the directors making clips at that time, Russell Mulcahy probably had the best reputation. Some saw him as video's first auteur. A twenty-seven-year-old Australian, Mulcahy had started making clips as a teenager before moving to London in the mid-1970s and continuing his career there. Since then, he'd worked with

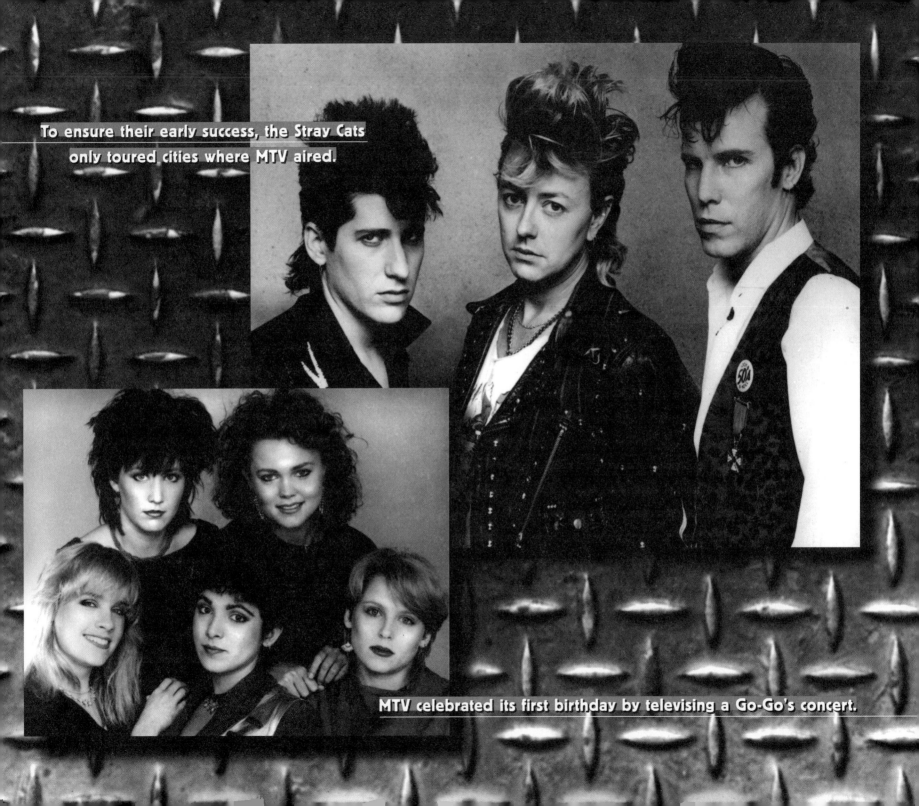

To ensure their early success, the Stray Cats only toured cities where MTV aired.

MTV celebrated its first birthday by televising a Go-Go's concert.

a number of acts, including Buggles (he directed their "Video Killed the Radio Star"), Ultravox, Rod Stewart, Kim Carnes, and Bonnie Tyler. His videos tended to be more stylish and visually adventurous than anyone else's. They frequently featured slow-motion shots of water splashing or objects breaking or curtains blowing, as well as other evocative images. His clip for Billy Joel's "Pressure" was filled with nightmarish scenes that were supposed to represent Joel's subconscious.

But he wasn't the only one doing interesting work. With bigger budgets, almost all the directors had gotten more creative. Straight performance videos, where the band just stood around and played the song, were becoming more and more rare; many clips either featured surreal images or even a rough storyline. It made sense. Not only did the music tend to inspire more imaginative ideas, but almost all the directors making the clips were young people—some of them just in their twenties—who'd grown up with TV and movies. They were TV babies. It was only natural for them to push the envelope.

Many of the directors were also starting to push the envelope in another way. There had been racy videos in the past, but suggestive images in videos were becoming more prevalent. One young director, Brian Grant, had made a clip for Olivia Newton-John's song "Physical" in which the comely singer pranced around in a skintight leotard. Others put scantily clad women in clips whenever they possibly could. Not that this should have been too surprising. After all, what was rock and roll without sex? Then again, what was advertising without sex? Hell, what was cable without sex?

It was particularly fitting that now, in the early fall of 1982, videos were getting sexier than ever, because MTV was about to debut on

the cable system that all those years ago had given cable viewers such programming as *Transsexuals* and *The Bath*.

After a year, the virus was about to hit New York.

* * * * * *

Two companies provided cable TV in the borough of Manhattan. Westinghouse-owned Group W Cable covered the upper portion of the island, while Manhattan Cable, owned by Time Inc. subsidiary American Television & Communication (ATC), covered the lower portion. Of the two, Manhattan Cable was generally considered by program suppliers to be the more critical one to be carried on. Not only did it have a larger number of subscribers, but it was also the cable company that served many of the ad agencies on Madison Avenue.

Negotiations between WASEC and Manhattan Cable with regard to MTV had started the previous year, even before the channel went on the air. The biggest hurdle was channel capacity. While Manhattan Cable's system had room for twenty-six channels, the large number of New York broadcast stations, the public access channels the system was required by law to carry, and the ever-increasing variety of satellite cable networks all made getting onto one of those channels difficult. In fact, many services shared channels with other networks, at least when they first started on the system. One service would be on from, say, 6:00 A.M. to 6:00 P.M., the other for the rest of the time. That was the deal WASEC worked out for Nickelodeon; the kids' channel aired every morning from 6:00 A.M. to 10:00 A.M.

But no one at WASEC would agree to such an arrangement for MTV. The main reason was the impact on advertising; not only would MTV salespeople constantly be explaining why they weren't on all day and all night in New York, they'd also have to start selling time slots instead of twenty-four-hour rotation, as they had been doing since the channel launched. And so negotiations continued all through the fall and into spring. By summer, the two sides were close to a deal, but there were still a few items to be worked out.

It was at that point that WASEC bought time on several broadcast stations in New York and debuted the "I Want My MTV!" spots. The response was phenomenal. Within a couple of days after the commercials started running, the phones at Manhattan Cable's offices were ringing uncontrollably. The kids had done exactly what Mick, Pete, Adam, Pat, and Stevie had told them to do: They'd called their cable operator and demanded their MTV.

Now they were going to get it. A couple of weeks after the spots started running, WASEC and Manhattan Cable cut a deal to put MTV on the system. The ads obviously weren't the main reason for the deal, but they surely helped.

MTV debuted in Manhattan at the end of September. To celebrate, MTV threw a party at the Ritz. What a feeling! Everyone would finally get to see the channel live, the way the rest of America was seeing it. What's more, so would the execs at the New York-based record companies and the decision-makers at the Madison Avenue ad agencies and the influential Manhattan-based news media.

Of all those groups, the media were arguably the most important. Despite the spread of MTV in the towns and suburbs of America over the past year, and despite the rise of video music in general, the national press hadn't paid a great deal of attention. Yes, *Fortune* called MTV one of 1981's products of the year and the *New York Times* ran a couple of brief pieces on the channel and *Rolling Stone* did a story about both MTV and USA's *Night Flight*. However, for the most part,

the mainstream press (the three broadcast networks, news magazines like *Time* and *Newsweek*, the big circulation papers like the New York *Daily News* and the *Wall Street Journal*) had reacted the way the rest of America's business establishment had: with a huge, rude yawn.

Within six weeks of MTV's debut on Manhattan Cable, all of that changed. The channel got so much press attention so quickly, in fact, that it was as if someone had suddenly pointed a huge spotlight on this venture that had been operating in near darkness for over a year. The first rays shone from *New York* magazine, which ran a feature at the end of October called "Can't Stop the Music Channel." Over the next few weeks practically every major news organization in New York followed suit—the *Times*, the *Journal*, *Time*, the *CBS Evening News*, NBC's *Today*, Channel 2's *Talk of the Town*, and others.

The national media, most of which were based in New York, could now finally see the channel for themselves, and that made a significant difference. It was one thing to have some correspondent out in Des Moines yapping over the phone about some cable network that played these things called music videos; it was something else to sit in your own living room and see the MTV flag planted in the moon and some half-man–half-bird singing a tune called "I Ran." Beyond that, MTV was just a great story. It was new, it broke all the rules, and it was socially significant, merging the two great cultural forces of post-war America, television, and rock and roll.

All of which made the channel a perfect candidate for the "rising star" story, about up-and-coming people or events. Nearly all of the stories covering MTV that fall presented it as a rising star. Each explained what MTV was, and then most of them practically gushed about the success the channel's programming was having, all but ignoring the company's financial troubles. *Time*, for example, raved that "the best videos enhance the mood of a song and expand TV's generally unadventurous visual vocabulary," while Channel 2 in New York called MTV "the cable channel that seems to be sweeping the nation." On the *CBS Evening News*, reporter Charles Osgood interviewed the Rosenfeld family from New Jersey. After showing the Rosenfeld parents—"Mr. and Mrs. Average America," as Osgood introduced them—the camera turned to the Rosenfeld children, who talked about the impassioned feelings America's youth had for MTV.

"I do everything while I'm watching it," said the average American teenage girl.

Her average American brother backed her up. "Some kids do their homework while they watch," he said. "Some kids even have TVs in their bathroom. I mean, they watch *all* the time."

The Rosenfeld parents expressed concern about some of the racey images on the channel, but from MTV's standpoint, that was the point: This was not supposed to be television for them, it was television for their kids.

Although all the MTV executives, from Schneider on down to John Sykes, gave interviews during this first great wave of press attention, the one who clearly stood out was Bob Pittman. Not only did he look like a young corporate hotshot in his gray suits, power ties, and horn-rimmed glasses, but he did his best to emphasize the revolutionary nature and deeper meaning of all this.

"We had a choice," he told one TV reporter, his Mississippi drawl still audible. "We could either take music and try to make it fit the form of TV, the format of TV, or we could reinvent the form of TV to make it match the music—which is what we did."

Within a month after the media blitz began, the virus had taken hold of Manhattan. As in practically every other market where MTV was available, when the young people in New York saw these rock stars and heard these songs right in their living rooms, they could hardly believe it. Awareness of the channel was becoming so great that even *Saturday Night Live* had started to satirize it, spoofing the "I Want My MTV!" spots with a fake commercial for DTV: the All Dead Channel. "All dead, all day," the announcer said. "If you're not getting the All Dead Channel in your area, call your cable operator and demand it now." The piece ended with a shot of a very dead Soviet leader Leonid Brezhnev exclaiming, through the magic of cheap special effects, "I want my DTV."

Just like that, everything changed for all the MTV employees in New York. While two months earlier people had responded with blank expressions when the pioneers said they worked for MTV, now people were incredibly impressed. MTV was now considered cool. The five veejays felt it most of all. J. J. Jackson had been living in a second-floor apartment in Greenwich Village, where for more than a year he'd lived rather anonymously. Nobody in his neighborhood had paid the slightest attention to him. But within weeks after the channel went on in Manhattan, people started to recognize him. Even diners in the restaurant across the street had begun gazing up at the big window in his apartment and pointing. It got so weird that he finally moved to the Upper West Side.

All the attention was starting to help the struggling business side of the channel. With national television exposure, and with the "I Want My MTV!" campaign as successful in Los Angeles, San Diego, and Orlando as it had been in New York, distribution really took off.

They now had nine million subscribers, and they were adding more than a million more each month. Moreover, all the press had really given some real ammunition to the ad sales team. Once you'd been made fun of on *Saturday Night Live*, how could any advertiser or ad agency ignore you?

There was really a sense that the tide had turned. Morale was better; the future looked brighter.

Unfortunately for John Lack, it all came a little too late.

* * * * * *

He wasn't the first to go. Back in October, ad sales chief Gary Koester and WASEC marketing chief Richard Gilmenot had been given their walking papers, and Bob McGroarty had been moved from senior vice president of sales and marketing to senior vice president of ad sales. While technically McGroarty's move wasn't a demotion, it sure didn't look to the rest of the company like a reward for a job well done.

The changes went beyond that. In November, Warner AMEX Cable president Gus Hauser, the man who'd turned faltering Warner Cable into a powerhouse, the man who'd brought John Lack out to Columbus to help invent the future of television, resigned. Though Hauser looked at the tens of millions of dollars Warner AMEX was now losing as an investment in the future—once built, the company's new cable systems would generate tremendous revenues for years—American Express and Warner were having trouble seeing it that way. Ultimately, the relationship fell apart.

Warner AMEX wasn't the only company going through this sort of shakeup. In September, just eleven months after venturing out onto the cable frontier, CBS announced it was reversing course and shut-ting down CBS Cable. Although the network was a favorite of critics, advertisers had stayed away, and the Tiffany Network lost more than $30 million on the venture. Others were starting to lose their nerve as well. Westinghouse had recently pulled out of a deal with Disney to start a service called the Disney Channel. In the rocky cable marketplace, the two couldn't agree on the best format for attracting viewers. Things were changing so quickly that John Malone, the president of the country's biggest cable operator, Tele-Communications Inc. (TCI), predicted that in the coming year the cable industry would see doom and gloom, mostly because the big cable companies had promised too much to cities in order to win franchises.

An era seemed to be ending. The cable boom that began with HBO and Qube was clearly coming to a close, and the hard work of turning all this into a real business was at hand.

There was no single thing that cost John Lack his job. As the months went by, WASEC chief Jack Schneider had simply come to believe that the negatives had begun to outweigh the positives with Lack. Schneider viewed him as a lot of talk, but not much action. Lack's contract was up at the end of the year, and one day during the late fall, Schneider called him into his office and told him he wasn't going to renew it.

Lack wasn't totally surprised—WASEC was going to lose more than $20 million in 1982. Nor was he devastated. His dream of creating a magazine rack full of channels, the vision with which he'd inspired all the early pioneers, seemed like it wasn't going to happen anyway. He and Schneider worked out a severance package—Lack figured it to be worth half a million bucks—and at the end of the year he left the offices at 1211 for good.

SEVEN

THE REVOLUTION

WINTER 1983 — WINTER 1984

It was a chaotic time—the virus hit Manhattan, and the press went berserk, and Gus Hauser and John Lack left Warner AMEX. And as the weeks went by, the momentum didn't let up; the virus just kept on spreading. On New Year's Eve, as MTV hosted its second New Year's Eve Rock and Roll Ball (this time featuring A Flock of Seagulls, the Producers, Jack Mack and the Heart Attack, and Duran Duran), the Group W System serving upper Manhattan began carrying the channel. A few weeks later the Group W system in the Los Angeles area also added MTV, giving the channel 175,000 new viewers there. By the end of January, the music video pipeline was available in more than eleven million homes across America.

The momentum wasn't only noticeable in distribution. The channel was also beginning to cause tremors in the non-cable world. Scott Shannon, a deejay and program director from northern New Jersey, took his station to number one in the New York market with a simple formula: He used a Top 40 playlist during the day, the MTV playlist at night. What's more, Lee Abrams, the most powerful album rock consultant in America and the man perhaps most responsible for rock radio's reliance on oldies over the past several years, announced a cataclysmic change: The several hundred stations he programmed would switch from playing 75 percent rock classics to playing 75 percent new music. Although he didn't make any mention of MTV and the popularity of its new music playlist, the connection was clear.

Television was being rattled as well. Not only did the USA Network (which already featured *Night Flight* on weekends) add a daily music video show called *Radio 1990*, but all across the country local TV stations were starting their own video music programs. Not only that; those pole-climbing cable operators at Warner AMEX were finally going to get what they'd wished for two years earlier: Westinghouse announced it was launching The Nashville Network, a channel featuring nothing but country music videos.

Perhaps the most ground-shaking example of MTV's momentum was the impact it was having on the music business. Not only were videos breaking more and more new acts, but many of the acts that had already been broken were now making videos. In the late spring of 1981, just a couple of months before MTV's launch, only twenty-three of the songs on *Billboard*'s Hot 100 singles chart were supported by videos. Now, little more than a year and a half later, that number had grown to more than fifty. The acts that were making clips weren't exactly at the bottom of the pile, either. The Australian band Men at Work, for instance, whom MTV had started playing the previous summer, were now in their eighth week at the top of the album chart; the Stray Cats, the tattooed, pompadour-wearing rockabilly band from Long Island, were at No. 2; and several other acts MTV had helped break—including A Flock of Seagulls and rockers Billy Idol and Adam Ant—had albums in the top twenty.

Of all the bands MTV had aided and abetted, most interesting was the one nestled at No. 14 on the album chart that January, the British band Duran Duran. While video had clearly boosted bands like Men at Work and Stray Cats in their climbs to the top, no one thus far had been as shrewdly calculating about using music video as Duran Duran

was. The five young, poster-boy-pretty Brits, along with their management, had been image-conscious ever since they released their first record in England two years earlier. At that time, the "New Romantic" movement, in which a band's style was at least as important as its sound, was the rage in England, and Duran Duran had positioned themselves as part of it, teasing their hair, sporting frilly shirts, and wearing heavy eye makeup. The strategy worked, and their very first single, a New Wave-meets-disco track called "Planet Earth," went to No. 12 on the U.K. charts. When the New Romantic movement faded later that year, the Duranies, as their fans called them, transformed into more conventional teen idols, complete with bottle-blond hair, sharp suits, and Pepsodent smiles. That look, combined with their danceable pop tunes, made them even more popular, and over the next year they had several other hits in England, Australia, and Europe.

And their videos had much to do with their success. Not only were all the members of the band good-looking, they seemed to comprehend the innate power and potential of video—not so much for artistic purposes as for marketing purposes, as a way of projecting an image to the public. In their first video, "Planet Earth," director Russell Mulcahy showed the band in all their frilly, romantic splendor. By the time the group was set to make their second clip, this one for a song called "Girls on Film," the boys and their management understood that video could also be a way to attract attention and generate publicity. So they instructed directors Kevin Godley and Lol Creme (former members of the popular group 10CC) to create something controversial—something with plenty of sex in it—to be played in dance clubs. The duo didn't disappoint, creating a clip that featured two nude women wrestling in oil.

Boys on Film: Duran Duran understood as well as anyone what music video could be—not art, but marketing muscle.

By the summer of 1982, Duran Duran's catchy songs, pretty faces, and alluring videos had made them pop stars practically everywhere in the world—everywhere, that is, except the United States. Although the group had spent months traveling around to small clubs all over America, both of their albums, *Duran Duran*, released in the fall of 1981, and *Rio*, released in the spring of 1982, had flopped in America. The biggest reason was radio apathy. Since the Duranies' dance rock didn't fit the narrow format of either album or Top-40 radio, they had received little air play in the States (one of the few exceptions was a station called KROQ in Los Angeles). Both the band and their record label, EMI, hoped video might be the foot in the door they needed. In August, Duran Duran and director Russell Mulcahy flew off to Sri Lanka to shoot videos for songs from *Rio*. The strategy was to show the group as young, sexy, jet-setting playboys, the James Bonds of rock and roll. And Mulcahy delivered. All three clips he directed were filled with exotic South Seas locales, glimpses of the gorgeous boys in the band, and a boatload of beautiful babes.

In early September the band's American record label, Capitol, delivered one of the new videos, "Hungry Like the Wolf," to MTV. When Les Garland and the programming crew saw the clip in the weekly music meeting, they were knocked out. It was as good as anything any artist had done to date, and "Hungry Like the Wolf" went into rotation. When the clip became a hit with viewers as well, it stayed on the channel for the next couple of months. Slowly, both the single and the album, *Rio*, began to scale the charts, thanks almost exclusively to the exposure "Hungry Like the Wolf" was getting on MTV. In Dallas, *Rio* was actually a sellout in half of the city's record stores—those stores in the parts of town wired for cable. Finally, in December, radio stations all across America started adding the song to their playlists. By January, just after the Duranies played MTV's New Year's show, "Hungry Like the Wolf" was the third most popular song in America, and *Rio*, once considered a stiff, was in the Top 20.

Over the next six weeks, things only got better, with MTV giving air play not only to "Hungry Like the Wolf," but also to the song "Rio," "Save a Prayer," and a PG-rated version of "Girls on Film." By early March, when the group's newest clip, "Is There Something I Should Know?," was in heavy rotation on MTV, the press had started a round of rising star stories about the band. But you couldn't really blame the folks in the media. After all, when the group made an appearance at a store in New York's Times Square, several thousand young girls showed up to see them. The type of store said much about how the group had achieved their fame, too: It was a video store.

As *Rolling Stone* put it in its story about Duran Duran later that spring: "They may be the first rock band to ride in on a video wave."

By the time the Duranies hit the shores of rock and roll stardom, the temperature inside the Manhattan offices of Warner AMEX had cooled a bit. To begin with, American Express chief executive officer Jim Robinson and Warner chairman Steve Ross had hired executive Drew Lewis to replace Gus Hauser. Short in height but aggressive and intimidating, the forty-eight-year-old Lewis was an unexpected choice. Although he had a reputation as a corporate turnaround whiz, he'd actually spent the past two years serving as secretary of transportation in the Reagan administration (he was the man who'd canned America's air traffic controllers when they went on strike in 1981). By the end of 1982, Lewis was ready to return to corporate life, and when Robinson and Ross offered him the job as Gus

Hauser's replacement, he took it. The only difference was that while Hauser had overseen only the hardware side of Warner AMEX—WASEC's Jack Schneider reported directly to Ross, Robinson, and the Warner AMEX board—Lewis would run the whole operation. Even Schneider would report to him.

That was how far Jack Schneider, the onetime gatekeeper of the American Airwaves, had fallen in the eyes of WASEC's corporate parents. Schneider wasn't necessarily seeing eye to eye with his subordinates, either. One day, as Bob Pittman was talking to Schneider about giving bonuses to various staff members, they came to the name of Tom Freston, the pioneer who was overseeing MTV's marketing. Pittman thought Freston was doing a great job and wanted to give him a decent-sized bonus, but Schneider started shaking his head. "Those suits he wears," Schneider said, referring to Freston's rather colorful wardrobe. "And that hair." Another time, artist relations head Gale Sparrow came into her office at 1133 and noticed that her picture of punk singer Wendy O. Williams—who was noted for wearing nothing but electrical tape over her nipples—was gone. Apparently Schneider had torn it down. (Years later Schneider wouldn't recall either incident.)

If Jack Schneider's star was falling, Bob Pittman's kept right on rising. During the fall, the Keeper of the Vision had served more or less as chief executive officer of The Movie Channel, which even in the spring of 1983, was still in a state of flux. The original negotiations between WASEC and the movie studios had fallen through in September, but new talks had resumed in the late fall, this time with the industry's number two pay movie service, Showtime, also involved. Finally, near the end of the year, all sides had reached an agreement—only to hit a snag yet again. The Justice Department, smelling anti-trust problems as it had when the movie studios tried to launch their own cable network, put a hold on the merger until it could investigate.

Though The Movie Channel was in no man's land, Bob Pittman surely wasn't. The big bosses at Warner and American Express had pegged him as the person responsible for MTV's programming success—a young man who was going places. Pittman's relations with the Warner's brain trust (Steve Ross in particular) seemed to be growing closer every day. Early in the year, they made him an extraordinary offer: They would dump Jack Schneider and make Pittman chief executive officer of WASEC. At age twenty-nine, and with no formal business training (thanks to his meteoric radio career, he hadn't even bothered to finish college), Pittman himself was uneasy about the offer, particularly since it meant blowing Jack Schneider out of the water. Finally, that spring Pittman instead replaced John Lack as WASEC's executive vice president.

With both Pittman and Drew Lewis in their new jobs, and with things dark and dangerous out on the cable frontier, a new attitude emerged inside all of Warner AMEX that spring—one of austerity. Ross and Robinson had given Lewis a simple mandate—stop the corporate bleeding. The former Reaganite had wasted no time in getting to work, quickly laying off two hundred people on the hardware side of the company. Moreover, he gave Bob Pittman as blunt a charge as he himself had been given: Cut WASEC's losses in half—down to around $10 million—or the company would think about getting out of the cable programming busi-ness altogether.

As he took over his new position, it seemed to Bob Pittman that what was at stake was nothing less than the survival of the company.

And as it turned out, Pittman would have to improve the bottom line without the aid of two of WASEC's original pioneers, Seibert and McGroarty. Keeper of the Grooviness Fred Seibert, the man who'd played such a major role in giving MTV its look and feel, was miserable ever since he'd been put in charge of the creative services department a year earlier. While his personal clout remained high—Pittman continued to consult him about various MTV programming matters—the department he ran had no real impact on the channel; it was a support group merely there to serve other divisions of the company. Frustrated, Seibert and Alan Goodman decided to try things on their own, and they formed a production company called Fred/Alan.

McGroarty, maybe more than anyone else, had started to miss the vitality of the early days on the frontier, when all things seemed possible. Coming to work wasn't as much fun now. In addition, he was hardly thrilled at the idea of working for Bob Pittman. So that spring he quit WASEC and became a partner in a small media company. Still, McGroarty did go out on a high note: In the first quarter of 1983, with the MTV virus spreading through Manhattan, he and the ad sales crew had booked more ad dollars than in all of 1982.

Despite the upturn in ad sales and MTV's continued momentum, Pittman, Schneider, and the corporate powers at Warner AMEX knew that much work needed to be done to make the company profitable, they began making changes. Pittman became an absolute bear about expenses. They hadn't had much money to work with during the first couple of years—they were lean and entrepreneurial—but now things got even tighter. Underlings would bring Pittman the projected budget for covering some concert, and he'd go through it with a pen,

crossing out various items. Backup crew? Don't need it. Crane shot? Forget it. Caterer? Try brown-bagging it. He even formed a new unit of the company to oversee all revenues and expenditures.

The affiliate sales team—the men and women out there dealing with cable operators—was also revamped. From the very beginning, the regional salespeople said that dealing with local cable operators would be much easier if someone was also working things on a corporate level—schmoozing the major executives at TCI, ATC, or any of the other large multi-system operators. So they created something called the National Accounts Group to do just that.

Finally, Pittman and the other execs began a search for ways to increase the company's revenue, and by the time the late spring came around, they'd settled on two. First, WASEC was going to start accepting ads on previously commercial-free Nickelodeon. Second, they were going to start charging cable operators for MTV, which to this point had been free. Steve Ross was the one who pushed the latter idea. After all, CNN had charged cable operators fifteen cents per subscriber ever since it went on the air, and ESPN had recently instituted a charge, as well. While the strategy was both risky and difficult to pull off, it seemed to most of the decision makers at WASEC that the company had little choice. Without a second stream of revenue alongside ad sales, MTV would go the way of CBS Cable—scalped and left for dead on the cable frontier.

Equally significant in this decision was the belief that now, with the video virus spreading all over the country, cable operators would actually be willing to pay for the channel. How could the gatekeepers refuse? The kids continued to call their local cable companies and demand the channel, the press continued to write about it, and the cable industry itself continued to make buckets of money from it, as people signed up for cable just to get MTV.

Moreover, by the time the new charge was announced late that spring, someone else had ridden in on the video wave, someone who, as it turned out, would take MTV to a whole new level.

By the time he was twenty-three, Michael Jackson was already a legend in the music business. As part of the Jackson Five and as a solo artist, Jacskon had proved himself to be one of the most popular— not to mention most exciting—performers in pop music. In 1979, Jackson's first solo album, *Off the Wall*, had spawned four hit singles and sold more than eight million copies.

Could he top it? Jackson, his management, and the executives at CBS Records all hoped so. And by the time his next solo album, *Thriller*, was ready for release in the fall of 1982, it was clear that everyone involved was out to make the record a mega-success. They wanted to get as much radio air play on as many different radio formats as possible. In October, six weeks before the album itself came out, Epic released a single from *Thriller* called "The Girl Is Mine," a duet with Paul McCartney. Just as they'd hoped, Top-40 radio ate it up, and by December the song had risen to No. 2 on *Billboard's* Hot 100. Then in January, with "The Girl Is Mine" sliding back down the charts and *Thriller* having just hit the stores, Epic released two singles simultaneously, hoping to get both in the top ten at the same time. One was "Billie Jean," a dance track aimed at urban and Top-40 radio; the other was "Beat It," a rock-flavored song featuring heavy-metal guitarist Eddie Van Halen that was targeted at album rock radio.

Radio was only one part of the strategy that Epic and the Jackson camp had plotted out for turning *Thriller* into a mega-hit. The other

was music video. In many ways video was a natural for Jackson. While offstage Michael might have been painfully shy, the instant he stepped in front of an audience or a camera his every move demanded that you watch him, as he danced and spun and slid and darted and dipped to the music. He was a truly visual performer, the kind you needed to see in order to fully appreciate, and the kind for whom music video was ideally suited.

Nevertheless, all involved with *Thriller* knew that getting MTV to play Michael Jackson videos was anything but a sure thing. The reason was simple: In the channel's first eighteen months, as it had become a cult hit among white suburban teenagers all over America, it had played only a handful of clips by black artists. From Bob Pittman's and everyone else at MTV's point of view, it was simply a matter of format. Ever since the MTV flag was planted in the moon during the summer of 1981, the channel had positioned itself as a rock and roll station. And because only a few black acts—Tina Turner, Prince, Joan Armatrading, the Bus Boys—played what most people called rock and roll anymore, only a few had their clips played on the network. For Pittman, programminghead Les Garland, and the rest of them, the situation was no different from radio, where few album rock stations played many black artists.

But that argument didn't fly with everyone. MTV's original head of talent and artist relations, Carolyn Baker, who was black, had questioned why the definition of music had to be so narrow, as had a few others. What's more, as MTV received more and more press attention, a growing number of journalists and music critics and black artists really began to slam the network for its segregated view of music. True, the critics said, album rock stations didn't play many black acts, either. But other radio formats did, and black music was still widely available on the radio. MTV, on the other hand, was still the only music video channel on television, and therefore, according to the critics, it had an obligation to expose blacks acts and to educate its viewers as to what else was out there.

Probably the most vocal critic of MTV was black musician Rick James. Despite the fact that his most recent album, *Street Songs*, had sold more than three million copies in 1982, MTV had passed on clips for his songs "Super Freak" and "Give It to Me Baby." The funk star clearly wasn't pleased by what he considered a snub, so in early 1983 he took every opportunity to publicly call MTV a racist network.

Despite the inability of Rick James and other black artists to get their clips on the air, and despite the fact that the music on *Thriller* was no more "rock and roll" than anything on *Street Songs*, in January Michael Jackson and Epic went ahead and made videos for the two singles they had just released. Steve Barron, a twenty-seven-year-old British director who'd done clips for the likes of Human League, Rod Stewart, and Adam and the Ants, shot the video for "Billie Jean." Bob Giraldi, a forty-four-year-old American commercial director best known for his Miller Lite "Tastes Great, Less Filling" ads, shot "Beat It."

"Billie Jean" was finished first, and in the middle of February Epic delivered the clip to MTV—at which point Bob Pittman and Les Garland and everyone else involved with programming MTV found themselves facing a dilemma. On the one hand, "Billie Jean," with its thumping beat and bass line and heavy use of synthesizers, was clearly not a rock and roll song—at least not the way MTV was defining it. But by the time the video itself was delivered to them, there were some equally compelling reasons why the channel should play it.

"Billie Jean" was as hot a song as the music industry had seen in years. After only a handful of weeks on the charts, it was already in the Top 10, and it looked as if it was headed for No. 1. Moreover, CBS and Epic had a great deal invested financially, strategically, and emotionally in Michael Jackson, and they desperately wanted the clip played.

Finally, and maybe most compelling of all, the video itself was irresistible, the best a number at MTV had ever seen. Though the concept itself was enticing enough—in it Michael played a sort of mystical healer, one whose powers allowed him to appear and disappear at will—what really made the clip work was Michael's performance. Dressed in a glittering black jacket and wearing one white glove, he jumped and spun and slid all over the clip's surrealistic city street set. You couldn't take your eyes off of him.

It was a tough call to make, and years later there would be some disagreement about what exactly happened. The way Les Garland would remember it, the day he first saw "Billie Jean," he called Bob Pittman, who was in Los Angeles on business, and said that despite "Billie Jean" not being a perfect fit musically, he and the others in programming really thought they had to play it. Pittman agreed to look at it, so Garland sent it to him in California via overnight mail. The next day, Pittman, looked at it, called Garland back, and, after the two of them discussed it for a few minutes, told him to go ahead and put it on the air.

Others would claim the decision wasn't that simple. That spring, a story began circulating that CBS Records boss Walter Yetnikoff and some others at the company had threatened to pull all of the label's videos off the air if MTV didn't play "Billie Jean." Years later Pittman and Garland would deny that any such threat was made, pointing out that such a stunt would have been ridiculous. How would Yetnikoff ever explain to Billy Joel or Journey or any other CBS act that their clips were going to be sacrificed for the good of Michael Jackson's career?

Either way, on March 2, one week after the song hit No. 1 on *Billboard*'s Hot 100, the "Billie Jean" video debuted on MTV.

"Beat It" arrived a couple of weeks later, and if they were all impressed by "Billie Jean," they were absolutely floored by "Beat It." This second clip was even better than the first. Costing more than $150,000 and directed by Broadway choreographer Michael Peters, the video looked like an updated, inner-city version of *West Side Story*. They even got members of real Los Angeles street gangs to appear in it. But what made it great was the dancing. Michael, dressed in a red leather jacket, snapped and stepped and shrieked to the music, this time with more than a hundred talented extras moving along with him.

Never before had there been a video like this one. Almost single-handedly, this shy former child star had taken the entire field of music video and lifted it up a notch artistically. The reaction to both clips once they'd been aired—and to the songs, and to the album, and to Michael himself—made that clear. All across the country, in bars and basements and breakfast nooks and anywhere else that the MTV pipeline reached, people were watching the two clips and nodding that, yes, these were the best they'd ever seen, these were what video had the potential to become. Certainly record sales reflected people's excitement. *Thriller* had already sold more than two million copies by the time MTV first played "Billie Jean," but after the video went on the air, the album began to sell at a remarkable eight hundred thousand copies per week.

And as that spring went by, Michael seemed only to get hotter. In early May, forty-five million people tuned in to watch him perform a version of "Billie Jean" on an NBC-TV special called *Motown 25*. By June, "Billie Jean" had racked up an incredible thirteen weeks at No. 1, "Beat It" had spent several weeks in the Top 10, and *Thriller* had sold more than seven million copies.

Michael Jackson was the hottest pop star on the planet in nearly twenty years—and you could see him almost hourly on your favorite music video channel. While Michael and MTV were both absolutely on fire, the two weren't competing with each other; they were helping each other. Some would turn on their televisions merely to catch "Billie Jean" and "Beat It," and then find themselves mesmerized by the rest of what they were seeing on MTV. Others would tune in merely to watch MTV, and then find their jaws dropping at Michael's videos. The synergy was phenomenal. It was as if a couple of super-charged rockets had somehow hooked up in midair, and now the two of them were hurtling toward the heavens, linked together and moving faster than anyone could ever have imagined.

After "Billie Jean" and "Beat It," everything changed. Everything. With MTV spreading like never before and Michael demonstrating how mesmerizing these promo clips could be, music video was suddenly everywhere. It was as though, after eighteen months of methodically infecting a select audience in American cities, the video virus just said, the hell with it, and began infecting everyone. The entire culture had been exposed.

Music video was everywhere that summer. Only four years earlier, Michael Nesmith had been forced to create *Popclips* just so he'd have a venue for showing his own videos—now there were pop clips all

Gender-bending Boy George. By playing new acts such as Culture Club, MTV helped the record industry out of its slump.

Though conservative groups complained about some clips, MTV lifted rockers like Billy Idol to the top of the charts.

over the tube. All across the country, in big cities and small towns, at large network-owned-and-operated stations and tiny UHF outfits, local TV outlets were producing their own video clip programs or signing up for one of the dozen or so syndicated video shows that were coming down the pike. The record labels gave out the clips for free, and the ratings were usually terrific, so they couldn't help but make money. A few bigger players had started getting in on things, too. Cable's Playboy Channel announced it was launching a show (developed by none other than Fred Seibert and his partner Alan Goodman) that would feature R-rated videos like Duran Duran's "Girls on Film." Ted Turner's superstation, WTBS, debuted its own weekend-night clip show called *Night Tracks*. Even the broadcast networks, which years ago had decided there was little money in rock and roll, got involved. In July, NBC premiered a weekly ninety-minute program called *Friday Night Videos*.

But video's ubiquitous presence wasn't limited to television. Someone had developed—or rather redeveloped—a video jukebox (long live the Scopitone!) and was installing it in restaurants and bars all over America, while every dance club worth its plastic and chrome had now put in a video screen. RockAmerica, a company that supplied clips to clubs, reported that it was serving three hundred clients that summer, a substantial increase from the year before.

No one had a bigger case of video fever than the record companies themselves. While just twenty-four months earlier, Bob Pittman and Carolyn Baker had practically had to beg the industry to let MTV use their clips, now, having finally seen the channel for themselves and witnessed just what video had done for acts like Michael Jackson and Duran Duran, executives in both New York and Los Angeles

were taking to the form like kids to a new toy. They couldn't get enough. At almost every record company, video departments were expanding, and video itself was suddenly being viewed as a serious promotional tool. Executives had finally caught on to the tremendous potential video had when it came to marketing artists. Consequently, the number of clips being made skyrocketed, as did the money labels were willing to put into each one. Probably the best place to see the change was in MTV's weekly music meeting. While a year earlier programming head Les Garland and his team had been looking at four or five new videos each week, these days they found themselves screening up to thirty-five new clips per meeting.

That spring the music industry finally broke out of its three-and-a-half-year slump—sales in the first half of 1983 were up 10 percent. And most people weren't shy about giving music video the credit for the turnaround—rightfully so. Michael Jackson and Duran Duran were the best examples of the effect the channel could have, but they certainly weren't the only ones. A slew of new acts on the charts had broken through commercially because of video, and they were a pretty diverse bunch. Some, like the British band Culture Club, who hit it big with "Do You Really Want to Hurt Me," were brand-new acts. Others, like heavy-metal act Def Leppard, whose *Pyromania* album was now flying out of record stores, had been around the block a time or two without much luck. Still others, like Texas blues band ZZ Top, whose videos for "Gimme All Your Lovin'" and "Legs" were among the most popular on MTV, had scored hits before, but now found themselves catapulted to an entirely new level by music video. Another success story wasn't even a band; it was a movie. Back in the spring, MTV had started playing a video pulled from the film

Flashdance. The result was that the movie, which owed much of its own visual style to music video, was tops at the box office for weeks, and just a month after its release the *Flashdance* soundtrack had sold 1.5 million copies.

Most infected by the video fever were the people in the creative communities in New York and Los Angeles. Following the lead of commercial director Bob Giraldi, who'd made such a splash with Michael Jackson's "Beat It," directors from other media were suddenly on the phone with their agents trying to line up video work. Filmmaker Tobe Hooper, who'd directed the movie *Poltergeist,* shot Billy Idol's clip "Dancing with Myself," while commercial director Tim Newman did ZZ Top's videos, and another commercial director named Jay Dubin was doing Billy Joel's newest clips. They all loved doing them, because video gave them a chance to be experimental and creative.

The artists themselves were also beginning to take video seriously. In the wake of Michael Jackson's amazing clips, the feeling that had been bubbling below the surface for several years suddenly came rushing up: namely, music video could be art. Most of the clips hadn't yet achieved that status. As performance artist Laurie Anderson put it that summer, "Much of it is just boys playing guitar on the roof, boys playing guitar in the shower." But things were changing. Singer Kim Carnes, who'd had a hit a couple of years earlier with the song "Bette Davis Eyes," announced that video was transforming the way she made albums: As she was recording, she was already thinking of what was going on visually. Singer/songwriter Rickie Lee Jones did her one better: She said she was actually writing the videos as she was writing the songs.

Not surprisingly, the obsession with music video did wonders for MTV. In recent months, the press—through shows like *Nightline* and *20/20* and publications like the *New York Times Magazine*—had all but officially upgraded the channel's societal status. MTV was no longer just a rising star; the channel that had started in a basement in Fort Lee, New Jersey, was now a full-fledged cultural phenomenon.

On screen, the channel looked slicker than ever. With more money being spent and better directors becoming involved, the videos themselves had a new sheen. At the same time, Pittman, Garland, Sykes, and the rest of them at MTV were doing things to keep the channel fresh. Over the past few months, they'd added a number of new shows and features to the mix. There was a monthly *Guest Veejay* segment, in which a celebrity came on and played his or her favorite videos (Dan Aykroyd was the first); *The Cutting Edge,* a show featuring underground videos; *The Basement Tapes,* a program showing the best clips by unsigned bands; and *Friday Night Video Fights,* a weekly feature in which viewers could call in and vote for one of two new clips.

With video-mania raging all across the country, inside the walls and halls of MTV's offices the feeling was electric. Everyone at MTV had to continue with his or her job—churning out veejay spots, creating more irreverent channel IDs, or schmoozing the record companies—but there was just no denying the fact that everything had changed.

In the first three quarters of 1983, advertising sales jumped an amazing 300 percent from the previous year. They were hardly at broadcast network levels when it came to revenues, but things were looking up. And there were other signs of sales progress—like the fact that advertisers were now actually making commercials just for

MTV. Kraft had been the first to do it, creating a spot featuring fast-paced, sexually suggestive shots of some of its products—everything from Velveeta to Miracle Whip—all while the Devo song "Whip It" played in the background. Since then, a number of other advertisers, including Warner's own Atari, had done similarly MTV-esque ads, each clearly influenced by the frenetic videos that were constantly flowing down the MTV pipeline. The most obvious homage was in a Miller Beer ad. Their spot looked exactly like a music video; the band Southside Johnny and the Asbury Jukes stood on a stage and performed a Miller Beer jingle. At the end they even went so far as to put a small ID label in the bottom left-hand corner of the screen that read,

"'Miller Time'

Southside Johnny and the Asbury Jukes

Miller Beer."

Why had things changed so much? First, distribution continued to grow—by September they were reaching fifteen million subscribers—and as a result, more national advertisers were willing to consider the channel. Moreover, for the first time MTV's audience was measured by A. C. Nielsen, the company that had always taken the ratings for the broadcast networks. MTV and the cable industry in general had been leery about the whole issue of ratings. In a narrowcasting environment ratings were really beside the point; how many people watched was nowhere near as important as who watched. Still, the ad community had insisted on some sort of measurement, and so one by one, as they reached Nielsen's minimum distribution level (15 percent penetration of American television homes), each cable network started to be rated. MTV hit the 15 percent plateau in the spring, and it couldn't have asked for better

numbers. It got a 1.2 rating for the second quarter of 1983, the highest ever for a basic-cable channel.

As important as both distribution and ratings were, the biggest factor in the sales turnaround was the spread of the video virus itself. With the channel now a full-fledged cultural phenomenon, and with Michael Jackson-mania sweeping the nation, whatever hesitation the advertising world felt in MTV's first couple of years was beginning to pass. For the ad sales crew, the days of "M-what?" were certainly over.

Viewer response was more hysterical than ever, as well. For example, though most of the promotions that John Sykes and his crew put together in the channel's first couple of years drew about one hundred thousand entries each, one that summer called "A Party Plane with the Police," which gave the winners a chance to hang out with the platinum-selling band, pulled in an incredible four hundred thousand entries. Of course, when it came to viewer response, no one felt it more than the five veejays. Each of them was getting hundreds of letters per week, and none of them could go anywhere—a restaurant, a club, a concert—without being recognized. One day, Nina Blackwood was standing on a street corner in the middle of Manhattan trying to hail a cab, when all of a sudden a police car pulled up right next to her. One of the cops rolled down his window and said, "Hey, what are you doing?"

Nina was startled. Had she done something wrong? Quickly, she told them she was just trying to get a taxi.

The cops looked at her for a moment. "We watch you all the time," one said finally. "Hop in. We'll give you a ride."

At which point Nina Blackwood was taken, by patrol car, to her dentist appointment.

The five veejays weren't the only ones receiving such perks. MTV was now so hot that practically everyone who worked there garnered VIP treatment when people found out what he or she did for a living. They all felt like celebrities during that glorious summer and fall of 1983. And some of them really milked it. For example, if someone needed to get on an overbooked plane, they'd simply mention to the attendant at the check-in desk that they were from MTV and had to get to a big meeting. The vague promise of an MTV T-shirt or an MTV lapel pin was usually enough to do the trick. Getting friends into sold-out concerts was another sure bet. In fact, this kind of schmoozing became so commonplace that at one point a joke started going around the office:

How many MTV people does it take to screw in a light bulb?

Five. One to screw it in, plus four on the guest list.

Not all of the perks were so wholesome. After all, this was New York in the early eighties, and this was the rock and roll business. Access to illegal substances was plentiful, and at least a few of the staffers weren't shy about indulging.

The whole experience of working at MTV was incredible. To stand inside 1133, or Telectronics, or any of WASEC's offices during those summer days of 1983, was to feel as though you were standing at the center of the universe. They had the sense that everybody was watching what they did, that people everywhere were talking about them. And it wasn't just the culture watchers in the media, or the slick suits on Madison Avenue, or the pole climbers in the cable industry, or the hepcats in the music business. Regular folks who lived average lives were watching, too. They weren't all saying wonderful things about the channel, of course. The racism issue was still hot, as was the debate about music videos themselves. But people were talking. How else could you explain the fact that someone as mainstream as Johnny Carson was now making references to MTV in his *Tonight Show* monologue?

"In Southern California, they've updated the math books," Johnny told his audience one night. "For example, one problem says, 'If Sally's mother gets $500 a week in alimony, but spends $200 on an analyst, will there be enough for Sally to buy MTV?'"

While all at WASEC received their share of the glory, three in particular stood out from the rest. The first was the network's programming chief, glib, outrageous Les Garland. Garland remained Garland; he was as out of control as ever, which was one of the reasons why, earlier in the year, Bob Pittman had brought in a former radio executive named Dom Fioravanti to become general manager of MTV. Under Garland, things in programming had become a little loose from a management standpoint, and Pittman hoped that the low key, forty-something Fioravanti, with whom Pittman had worked at WNBC, might settle things down a bit. But there was no denying Garland's value to the network. Not only did he keep the rock and roll spirit burning, but his relationships in the entertainment business— with record executives, with managers, with artists themselves—were unbeatable. He was the one person at MTV who seemed to best understand the industry's agenda, what they wanted from MTV.

Young John Sykes was becoming a star, as well. Though at twenty-six he was still a baby, Sykes, who'd given up his job with CBS Records and moved to New York three years earlier just because he loved the idea of MTV so much, was doing very well. He'd recently been promoted to vice president of promotion and production, and while some at the network thought he was a little too ambitious for his own good, Bob Pittman believed in him.

A bit of a rivalry had actually developed between Garland and Sykes. From the way it looked to others at the company, both were constantly vying for Bob Pittman's attention. At one point, a rather dark joke started circulating about the two of them. Apparently, not long after he'd arrived at the channel, Garland had developed an eye disease and had to have his left eye removed (an odd coincidence, given Pittman's own visual handicap). The joke said that when John Sykes learned about this, he was so jealous, he immediately went out and had both of his eyes removed.

Though both Les Garland and John Sykes were flying high thanks to MTV's success—and were even starting to look like Pittman in their expensive Italian suits—they were still in a different class than the Keeper of the Vision. He had the highest profile in the press. In almost all the press coverage, it was Pittman who was MTV's top spokesperson. He really had the spiel down, throwing out phrases like "TV babies" and "mood and emotion." Sykes and a couple of other guys at the network had even started to tease Pittman about it. "Tay-vay babies," they'd say in an exaggerated Mississippi drawl. "Thaie think in non-lanear patterns."

But reporters devoured such stuff, and Pittman seemed to know it. What was most interesting about Pittman's relationship with the press was how they'd managed to anoint him as the guy who'd invented MTV. Less than a year after John Lack left the company, his name had all but disappeared when it came to the roots of the channel. Story after story was written, and story after story left Lack's name out. All the reporters, in fact, basically put things the same way:

"MTV's game plan was formulated by Bob Pittman," or "MTV is overseen by Bob Pittman," or "If MTV has a driving force, it's Bob Pittman." It's not that such statements weren't true—it was just that friends of Lack really thought the man at least deserved a mention, and they often blamed Pittman for taking too much of the credit.

And yet, nine months after Lack had left, there was no denying that WASEC really was Bob Pittman's company. Not only were people like Steve Ross, Jim Robinson, and Drew Lewis frequently bypassing Jack Schneider to deal directly with Pittman, but among the troops Pittman was known as the man in charge. He hadn't grown any less demanding, either. One day, Marci Brafman, the head of the on-air promo group, came down with the flu and missed an important meeting. Pittman called her at home. "I hate to bother you when you're sick," he said, "but you wanted to be a success, didn't you?"

Though he was a tough boss, many of his employees grew to respect him. He was just twenty-nine, but somehow he had an aura about him that made people, for one reason or another, really care about pleasing him.

As the months passed, Pittman continued his fight to improve the company's bottom line, and by the fall things were looking better. The Movie Channel deal was finally completed—in the end the movie studios dropped out and the channel merged with Showtime. This allowed Pittman and Schneider to slash dozens of people from WASEC's payroll. Revenues were also improving. Not only was the company pulling in more money from advertising, but some cable operators had finally begun paying for MTV.

And MTV's rocket was still ascending.

* * * * * *

In the middle of October, *People* magazine upped the ante in the media's coverage of MTV, doing a six-page cover story on the channel. You couldn't blame them. There were now more than two hundred video clip shows on the air in the United States. Moreover, places like bowling alleys and hair salons had started installing video screens. You couldn't dodge these things—even if you wanted to.

The record industry's enthusiasm hadn't let up, either. Having been revived by video, the labels were now keeping video directors in New York and Los Angeles busier than ever; 17 of the Top-20 albums on the latest *Billboard* charts were being supported by videos. Some companies were even trying to sell the clips in stores. Sony had recently introduced what it called the Video 45—a twelve- to twenty-minute tape featuring a couple of clips by an artist. And it now seemed as if every performer in music wanted to make a video, including such an unlikely artist as Bob Dylan. The man who'd made the words worth listening to in rock and roll filmed a couple of clips for his latest

popular album in the history of CBS Records and had sold more than ten million copies in America alone. Three more singles from the record had gone into the Top 10, for a total of six. And though Michael hadn't made videos for any other songs from his own album, he did have a new clip coming out. His latest, "Say Say Say," was another duet with Paul McCartney, this one from McCartney's new album, *Pipes of Peace.* McCartney and his record label spent $250,000 on the video and hired Bob Giraldi, of "Beat It" fame, to direct. MTV world-premiered the clip at the end of October.

By the time "Say Say Say" came out, Michael had already decided to increase the stakes in the music video game and make a clip that would top them all. The song he wanted to do it with was "Thriller," the title track from his album. An upbeat tune featuring a "rap" by horror movie star Vincent Price, the number was a natural for a horror-movie video treatment—and that's exactly the approach Michael wanted to take. To direct the clip he hired filmmaker John Landis, who'd direct-

Michael Jackson and friends in the ground-breaking, $1.1 million "Thriller" video. Together, Michael and MTV were responsible for what *Time* called "a musical revolution."

album, *Infidels.* But as surprising as it was to see Dylan's face in a clip, he didn't win the Most Unexpected Video Performer award: Hoping to revive his career, crooner Dean Martin had made a music video as well.

Though MTV was hotter than ever, so too was its partner in fame, Michael Jackson. Ten months after its release, *Thriller* was the most

ed the movie *An American Werewolf in London*, and the two of them came up with a concept and a script.

But there was one problem. Shooting the video the way they really wanted to shoot it was going to cost a lot more than either CBS Records or Jackson himself was willing to put up. So they decided to

The channel's execs initially balked at playing his clips. But Michael Jackson and MTV hoisted each other to new heights; after "Billie Jean" and "Beat It," videomania took hold like never before.

approach MTV and ask if the channel would be interested in paying for the clip.

The request put Bob Pittman in a bind. On the one hand, a new Michael Jackson video—particularly one as grandiose as this promised to be—would be an incredible boost for MTV. On the other hand, the channel had never paid for a clip before, and Pittman didn't want to set a precedent. Finally, both sides found a solution. Instead of actually buying the rights to "Thriller," Pittman agreed to pay $250,000 for the rights to a documentary that was being shot, *Making Michael Jackson's "Thriller."*

Filming began in Los Angeles at the end of October and lasted for a couple of weeks. One day during shooting, Les Garland got a phone call from someone in Michael Jackson's camp, saying that Michael wanted to meet him. Garland hopped on a plane to Los Angeles the next day and then drove over to the set, where he met John Landis and was eventually taken back to Michael's trailer. When he got there, Michael was just coming off the set. Les said hello, but Michael just smiled. Michael's assistant said that the singer had to go take care of a few things, and asked Garland to come back a few minutes later, which he did. As he sat inside the trailer talking with Michael's assistant and some other people, a sock came flying out of the trailer's bedroom and hit him in the shoulder. Garland looked up, startled.

"That's Michael," the assistant said. "He wants you to come back."

Garland picked up the sock and walked back to the bedroom. It was pitch-black inside. He couldn't see a thing.

"Michael?" he said into the darkness.

"Les?" a soft, high-pitched voice said back.

Garland still couldn't see anything. "Where are you, man?"

"I'm over here," Michael said.

Garland turned, and finally saw Michael lying on the bed, taking a break. He walked over and sat in the chair next to him.

"How ya doin', man?" Les said.

Michael looked up at him. "Listen, I just wanted to tell you thanks."

"What?" Garland said.

"I just wanted to tell you thanks," Michael repeated.

"For what?"

"For everything you guys have done for me."

"Oh no, man, you've got this backwards," Garland told him. "Let me tell you thanks. If it wasn't for guys like you and the videos you make, there would be no MTV. Let me thank you, okay?"

Even Garland was amazed at the scene: sitting there in a dark trailer in the middle of a Hollywood movie lot, talking with the biggest star in the world.

As the production of "Thriller" continued, rumors began spreading around the entertainment business about how huge the clip was going to be. It wasn't just a video; the word on the street was that it was a mini-movie. *Billboard* reported that "Thriller" was going to cost $500,000—ten times as much as the average video. As the weeks went by, the anticipation just kept building.

The video was finally finished in mid-November, and a few days after it was done an executive named Harvey Leeds, who earlier in the year had been named head of video promotion at Epic (Michael's label), brought two copies of it over to MTV. One was on a 3/4-inch cassette; the other, the master copy, was on a one-inch reel. With practically everybody in the company packed into Les Garland's office, Leeds put the cassette in the VCR and pressed play. It was even more terrific than the rumors had predicted. Fourteen minutes long (and costing $1.1 million, not $500,000), it actually had dialogue and a whole story line, not to mention fantastic choreography, and the usual incredible dancing by Michael and the rest of the cast. Best of all were the makeup and special effects—at one point Michael transformed into a werewolf; at another, he danced with a couple of dozen "corpses" in a graveyard.

When it was over, everybody in the room went crazy. It was the best video most of them had ever seen.

The video "Thriller" had its world premiere in the third week of November at the Metro Theatre in Westwood, California. Michael and John Landis and the producers chose to debut it theatrically so that it would be eligible for an Academy Award as best short-subject film. Two weeks after its theatrical premiere, on December 2, the world's most anticipated video debuted on the world's first twenty-four-hour video music channel.

The reaction was amazing, even in this year when everything had been amazing. With MTV hyping the clip like crazy (they actually announced the times it would be shown), "Thriller" pulled in phenomenal ratings. For the whole fourth quarter, MTV's Nielsen rating jumped to a cable record smashing 1.5.

Obviously, Michael was benefiting from all this. One full year after its release, when even most hit albums have been long forgotten, *Thriller* was selling at the astonishing rate of six hundred thousand copies per week. What's more, in the middle of the month, *Making Michael Jackson's "Thriller"* was released on videocassette, and it was flying out of record and video stores. It really seemed as if everything that Michael Nesmith had envisioned years earlier was coming true: People were buying these pop clips and taking them home to watch.

The incredible attention and excitement generated by "Thriller" didn't elude the media. At the end of December *Time* magazine did a cover story on music video, and in so doing raised both video's and MTV's status even higher. According to *Time*, what was happening was a full-fledged "musical revolution."

"Increasingly, and perhaps irreversibly, audiences for American mainstream music will depend, even insist, on each song's being a full audiovisual confrontation," the magazine predicted. "Posterity can rest easy . . . but for rockers, popsters, and soul brethren, video will be the way to keep time with the future."

It had been quite a year—one filled with unbelievable good fortune and amazing events and intense emotion. It had been such an incredible twelve months, in fact, that few of those inside the offices on Sixth Avenue in New York even noticed what may have been the most astonishing feat of all that year.

Up there in a place now occupied by MTV and Michael Jackson, somebody finally found long-lost Satcom III.

	Dollar	Pound	SFranc	Guilder	Peso	Yen	Lira	D-Mark	FFranc	CdnDlr
Canada	.7376	2.1152	1.1903	.26894	...	.02573	.00203	.56195	.27890	...
Portugal	4.8559	7.5770	4.2036	.99797	.61364	.04760	.00305	3.4492	...	3.5
PratHt	1.PHC	2.1967	1.0075	19.2873	21779	.03816	-.06316	...	.28992	1.0395
PrePdLegal	159	2483.1	1388.9	1009.3	201.17	15.682	...	1130.4	327.72	1175.0
	101.40	158.33	89.196	64.354	12.827	...	.06376	72.075	20.894	74
Netherlands A	PRSA	2.4603	1.3830	1230	...	.01554	.00099	1.1200	.32470	1.1642
Switzerland	1.7575	1.7751	...	.24149	.14381	.01121	.00071	.80806	.23427	.83998
PriceCom	.6416	...	.56336	...	...	.00834	.00093	.45523	.13198	.47321

Source: Dow

-V-W-X-Y-Z-

4922.75   +50.94

ecProfDntl	PRO	...	cc	15	1⅜	1¼	1⅜	...		
PropCapTr	PCT	.48	5.8	15	98	8⅜	8½	8⅜	...	
ProvenaFood	PZA	.15	4.0	64	3⅛	4⅛	4⅜	4⅜	...	
ProviEngy	PVY	1.08	6.5	13	24	16½	16¼	16½	...	
Psychemed	PMD	...	52	247	5⅜	5	5¼	...		
PubStor9	PSK	1.29a	7.1	11	25	17	16¼	16½	...	
PubStor10	PSE	1.40	8.6	10	11	17½	17¼	17½	...	
PubStor11	PSM	1.36	7.9	12	...	...	...	...	...	
PubStor12	PSN	1.32a	7.0	11	6	18⅜	18⅛	18⅜	-⅛	
PubStor14	PSP	1.36	7.8	11	12	17⅜	17⅜	17⅜	...	
PubStor15	PSQ	1.20a	6.9	12	24	17½	17½	17½	...	
PubStor16	PSU	1.08	7.1	12	22	15¼	15¼	15¼	...	
PubStor17	PSV	1.40e	8.5	13	17	16⅝	16⅜	16½	...	
PubStor18	PSW	1.42e	8.4	13	20	17¼	17	17	-¼	
PubStor20	PSZ	1.41e	8.6	13	4	16⅜	16⅜	16⅜	...	
PutnmCalInv	PGA	.93a	6.7	...	20	13⅞	13¾	13⅞	...	
PutnamInvGr	PML	.80	6.8	...	11	11⅞	11¾	11¾	...	

6¾	2⅜	Viacom wt97		...	...	...	1092
8¹³⁄₁₆	4¼	Viacom wt99		...	...	...	120
3⁷⁄₁₆	1	Vitronic	VTG	...	...	12	1081
▲ 9⁷⁄₁₆	2½	ecVoiceCntrl	VPS	...	...	dd	345
12⅝	10	VoyagrAriz	VAZ	.73	6.0	...	186
13⅛	10⅛	VoyagrColo	VCF	.70	5.7	...	86
12½	10	VoyageurFla	VFL	.72	6.0	...	54
12⅞	10¼	VoyageurMinn II	VMM	.80	6.7	...	230
12	9¼	VoyageMinn III	VYM	.72	6.5	...	9
14¾	12¼	VoyagrMinn	VMN	.93	6.8	...	107
17½	13⅞ ▲	WashRlTr	WRE	1.00	6.6	18	263

EIGHT

THE GOLD RUSH

WINTER 1984 — FALL 1984

Even with the hoopla surrounding MTV, the furor over "Thriller," and *Time*'s proclamation that the music video revolution was, in fact, being televised, not all were true believers. And not everyone was infected with the MTV bug. A backlash had started to develop along both sides of the political and social spectrum. From day one, there had always been a few souls—parents mostly—who looked upon this newfangled form of TV as a threat to social decency, the same kind of feeling people had when Elvis first swiveled his way into the American consciousness a quarter-century earlier. But now, with all the publicity the channel had received, there was a growing contingent of folks who wondered whether these clips and this channel were good for young people. Some argued that the videos, usually three and a half minutes long and filled with lightning-fast edits, were shortening the already short attention spans of America's youth. Others were uneasy about the frequently racy content of the clips—the surrealistic images, the scantily clad women, the occasional violence. The video that British punker Billy Idol had made for the song "White Wedding" even included Nazi-style salutes.

There was such concern about all of this that a few prominent citizens mounted their soapboxes to warn about the dangers of music videos and MTV itself. One was C. Everett Koop, the Reagan administration's surgeon general, who theorized that the combination of pornographic and violent images in some of the clips could be dangerous to healthy emotional relationships between young men and women. However, the surgeon general was hardly MTV's loudest critic—that title belonged, ironically enough, to Ted Turner. The ad sales deal that Turner and Lack had struck in Boston not long after MTV's launch had fallen through the previous summer. Ever since then, Turner rarely passed up an opportunity to bash MTV. At one point he even proclaimed that the channel was producing a nation of "Hitler Youth."

On one hand, MTV welcomed such histrionics. Hadn't that been the point all along—to be outlaws? To tap into the rebellious spirit of youth? Wasn't that the very thing the people who worked there loved about the channel—that it challenged the establishment? You could hardly ask for better publicity than to have some fuddy-duddy like Koop or some loudmouth like Ted Turner denouncing the channel. On the other hand, practically everyone at the company was sharp enough to understand that, for business reasons, MTV couldn't appear to be any real menace to society, so Bob Pittman and the others worked up a couple of arguments in their own defense. First, they said, MTV wasn't the artist; it was merely the art gallery. It was the record companies and the artists who made these clips, the argument went, so if people had problems with the images they were seeing, they ought to be directing their fury at the labels and the musicians and the directors, not at MTV. Pittman and his crew were also quick to note that the network had the same rules that the broadcast networks did about nudity, violence, and salty language. Although there was no formal standards department (one would be formed that summer), in the previous two and a half years the programming crew had been sensitive to anything that might cross the

boundaries of acceptability. It wasn't unusual for them to send clips back to the labels and ask for changes. What choice did they have? Advertisers and cable operators were still leery about the channel; nobody wanted to risk offending them further.

Ironically, conservatives were no longer the only ones outraged by the channel. While the initial reaction to MTV in the hard-core rock community had been positive, now, with the channel growing more and more popular and everyone from Dean Martin to Barbra Streisand making videos, some had already started longing for the network's good old days. Even a growing number of people in the rock and roll camp looked at MTV as a sham, a sell-out, the antithesis of all that rock was *really* about. Not only was the race issue still alive (although, following the success of Michael Jackson, the channel had started playing more black artists); many old-guard rock journalists began complaining about MTV's narrow format, its relentless self-promotion, and the commercialism of the whole enterprise. The most blistering assault to date came in December in *Rolling Stone*. In a cover story entitled "AD Nauseam: How MTV Sells Out Rock & Roll," writer Steven Levy portrayed both the channel and Bob Pittman as a seductive, evil monsters who were exploiting the magical, rebellious stuff of rock and roll to make a buck. "It's a sophisticated attempt to touch the post-Woodstock population's lurking G-spot, which is unattainable to those advertisers sponsoring *We Got It Maid*," Levy wrote, "After watching hours and days of MTV, it's tough to avoid the conclusion that rock and roll has been replaced by commercials."

Some musicians also counted themselves as part of the video resistance. One of the members of the band Devo, which had made some groundbreaking clips back in the late 1970s and received a lot of exposure during MTV's first year, said the channel had become "a parody of itself." British singer and songwriter Joe Jackson was equally distressed. Exposure of his videos on MTV helped Jackson's 1982 album, *Night and Day*, spend a couple of months near the top of the charts, but as he got ready to release his newest record, *Body and Soul*, Jackson decided his career as a clip maker was over. Not only did he think videos forced listeners to forever associate one set of images with a particular song (an argument made by many critics), but they also compelled musicians to become something that few of them were: actors. The fact was, many of the clips being made were pretty bad. "[Video] has become," Jackson wrote in a widely read *Billboard* article later in the year, "a shallow, tasteless, and formularized way of selling music."

Whatever you thought of his other arguments, it was hard to argue this last point. Despite the heights that Michael Jackson and a few others had reached when it came to marrying music and images, the majority of clips really were mediocre. Two years earlier, Russell Mulcahy's blowing curtains and spilling water had been fresh and evocative, but now such images were so omnipresent that they'd become video clichés. Not that this was surprising, given the way many record companies and artists approached making videos. From the industry's point of view the clips were merely promotional tools, and few record companies were willing to take any real artistic risks. Even *Time*, the leading evangelist in this video revolution, acknowledged that many of the videos being churned out by record companies were hardly high art. "The majority of clips now in circulation," the magazine reported, "are labored ephemera with heavy imitative association, fully worthy of one executive's dismissive characterization as 'this year's satin jackets.'"

Despite the grenades being launched by the video resistance, people everywhere tried to cash in on the clip craze. Music videos spawned a real gold-rush mentality in the television industry. Not only were there a couple of hundred clip shows on the air, but all across the country small, struggling UHF stations had suddenly started dumping their old-sitcom, old-movie formats and putting on nothing but music videos, just like MTV. When it came to programming, all these channels essentially made the same claim: We're better than MTV because we know what kind of music our local audience likes.

Within the creative communities of New York and Los Angeles, the music video style—loud rock and roll soundtrack, machine-gun-style editing—was in vogue. Everywhere you looked, you could see the mark being made by music video—in the advertising industry, the fashion industry, and the movie business. The "MTV look" had such cachet that some folks had started coming to the network's creative people asking how to make their work look just as cool.

There was little reason to think that people's passion for either video or for MTV was going to let up. MTV took steps to keep its programming fresh. In the spring a weekly show, the *Top-20 Video Countdown*, premiered. The channel continued to break exciting new acts, the latest being a one-time female pro wrestler, Cyndi Lauper. A thirty-ish Brooklynite with a squeaky, Betty Boopish speaking voice, Lauper had been signed to CBS Records in 1983. The company was excited about her. Not only was she a wonderful singer, but she had a terrifically kooky look—multi-colored hair, outrageous clothes—that was perfect for video. MTV added her first clip, "Girls Just Want to Have Fun," in

With her colorful, outrageous look, Cyndi Lauper was part of a generation of stars whose appeal was as much visual as it was musical.

the fall of 1983. By the time she played the channel's third New Year's Eve rock and roll ball that winter, both the song and Lauper's debut album, *She's So Unusual*, were near the top of the charts.

MTV was also still riding the Michael Jackson rocket. Michael and his brothers, with whom he was now getting ready to release a new album, had recently signed a multi-million-dollar sponsorship deal with Pepsi, calling for the group to appear in several commercials, directed by Bob Giraldi. At the end of January, during the filming of the spots, everyone received a scare. As Michael descended a set of stairs on the set, he got too close to some pyrotechnical special effects, and his hair caught on fire. Fortunately, he suffered relatively minor injuries. Strangely, the whole incident put even more of a spotlight on the spots, which were due to debut the night of the Grammy Awards in mid-February.

MTV music programming guru Les Garland was well aware of people's interest in the new commercials, so a week or so before the Grammys he called over to the ad sales department and asked if MTV was going to be showing them. They were—but not until after the Grammy telecast. Garland hung up and started making phone calls to people at Pepsi. Finally, he ended up speaking with the company's president, Roger Enrico.

"Roger," he said, "this may be the strangest conversation you've ever had."

"Why's that?"

"Well, you know how MTV world-premieres videos?"

"Yeah."

"I want to world-premiere your new commercials."

Enrico was certainly surprised, but because it wasn't going to cost Pepsi a dime—indeed, the publicity would be worth thousands—he agreed. On February 20, the night before the Grammys, MTV ran an interview with Bob Giraldi, followed by the new Pepsi spots.

Well, there you had it—rock and roll really *had* been replaced by commercials. But few people seemed to care. The kids tuned in just the same. Somehow, it symbolized the status that the channel had achieved. Like Elvis in the late 1950s and the Beatles during much of the 1960s, MTV was at the very center of the musical universe. While this was partly the network's own doing—after "Billie Jean," the channel had increasingly shifted from an album rock format to a "hits" format—mostly it was a reflection of just how popular this musical pipeline was. Simply put, the channel was so successful that it defined, merely by what it played, what was hot and what was not when it came to music. And if what was hot was a Michael Jackson commercial, then so be it.

* * * * * *

On the business side of the company, things were equally upbeat. There were some problems, of course; the relationship between Bob Pittman and WASEC head Jack Schneider had become strained since Pittman replaced John Lack as executive vice president. Warner chief Steve Ross and Warner AMEX boss Drew Lewis were now dealing directly with Pittman when it came to WASEC matters, and Pittman's friendship with Ross had grown closer. They were like father and son, and it seemed to Schneider that Pittman was schmoozing with Ross at meetings and doing his best to bump into the Warner chief executive officer outside the office. Schneider finally told Pittman not even to talk to Ross and Lewis anymore. The Keeper of the Vision couldn't believe it.

Despite their growing rift, there was a definite sense of momentum among MTV's business types. The channel now had twenty million subscribers, nearly ten times what it had two years earlier. More important, advertising sales were stronger than ever. The channel's strong ratings were part of the reason for this. After all, it was much easier to say to a potential client that you represented the highest-rated cable channel in America than to say that you represented an outlaw rock and roll channel, as the guys had to do that first summer. Even better, the ad community was slowly beginning to lose its resistance to cable in general. Despite the weeding-out process that was going on in the cable business, the ad community was getting more and more comfortable with the pipeline idea of advertising—if only because a growing number of people were signing up for cable. In 1983, clients spent nearly $400 million advertising on cable—seven times what they'd spent in 1980. That was still nowhere near what they were spending with the broadcast networks, of course, but progress was definitely being made.

When it came to ad sales, the biggest impact was being made by the department's new boss, Bob Roganti, a slender, graying forty-one-year-old. The former head of MTV's New York sales office, Roganti was about as different from ex-sales chief Bob McGroarty or any of the other CBS-reared pioneers as you could imagine. A native New Yorker, he began his professional life as an academic, teaching political science at St. John's University in Queens. He then moved over to the world of UHF television, eventually becoming president of an advertising rep firm called Field Communications.

Roganti came across as a tough-as-nails city guy who swore like a son of a bitch and would do anything to make a sale. His image was amplified by the fact that, thanks to an eye condition, he always wore dark glasses, even indoors. Roganti was the quintessential UHF ad salesman. If the guys who worked at CBS in those days were seen as the classiest in broadcasting, the guys who worked for UHF stations were considered broadcasting's used-car salesmen. This wasn't surprising; their stations, frequently reliant on schedules of old sitcoms and old movies, generally had the worst ratings in the market. Consequently, they had to scratch and scrape and go after every table scrap they could.

Roganti brought that underdog attitude with him when he started at WASEC in late 1981. While Jack Schneider, John Lack, and Bob McGroarty saw MTV as a sophisticated sell—a state-of-the-art narrowcasting vehicle that delivered the difficult-to-reach youth market to advertisers—Roganti saw things differently. To him, MTV was nothing more than a UHF station made big, a struggling, little piece-of-shit channel that was charging too much for ad spots and that had better wake up and smell the damn coffee before it was too late. Consequently, Roganti approached ad sales in much the same way the people in programming approached their jobs: Just get it done. Don't worry so much about the rate you're charging and don't worry about long-term relationships with the clients, just sell the spots and deal with that other crap later. And his approach worked. Though rough and unpolished, Roganti was also the most effective guy in the department, and several months after Bob McGroarty left, Jack Schneider and Bob Pittman put him in charge of ad sales.

Roganti's management style was as unusual as everything else about him. A night owl, he would sometimes call staffers at home after midnight and keep them on the phone for endless hours, talking about work. And according to many who worked for him, his favorite motivational tactic was fear. "This video thing is probably just a flash in the pan," he told them. "You better sell this shit while you can."

But there was no arguing with the results Roganti got. All together, MTV pulled in $25 million in ad sales in 1983, up from $7 million in 1982. Furthermore, this new year looked even better: In just the first quarter, the network had garnered nearly $11 million in ad revenue.

That was enough to put WASEC, which had lost more than $82 million since forming in 1979, over the hump. In the first quarter of 1984—four and a half years after Jack Schneider, John Lack, and all the other pioneers had first arrived at 1211, two and a half years after MTV itself had gone on the air, and one year after Bob Pittman ascended to the position of chief operating officer—WASEC finally earned a profit.

Needless to say, the Keeper of the Vision was ecstatic. For one of the few times in his whole life, he really let himself enjoy the moment. In fact, as soon as he found out they were actually going to make money, he hustled over to Steve Ross's office and told him the news. Ross's reaction wasn't quite what he expected.

"That's great," the Warner boss said. "But here's what we should do now."

Steve Ross had never been one to rest on his laurels. When it came to business, be believed that you had to seize the day, take advantage of the position you're in, and build on your success. And so, as profitability approached, that became the attitude inside MTV.

Despite the jolt that MTV had given the industry over the past two years—breaking new artists, making old ones bigger than ever—

executives at most labels had never abandoned the idea of MTV paying for the clips they played. NBC's *Friday Night Videos* had been paying for clips since it went on the air the previous summer, and most in the record industry really felt they deserved some sort of compensation. Not only were they supplying most of MTV's programming, but their own video budgets had just exploded in the past year. They were making more videos than ever, and each one was costing more than the one before.

With the improvement in MTV's financial position, Bob Pittman and the others at the network realized that they were going to have to pay something. But nobody at the channel was about to give away the farm—especially since its relationship with the record industry had already started to change. Early on, Pittman, music programming chief Les Garland, and Gale Sparrow from artist relations had done their best to suck up to the industry—putting ID labels on the clips, plugging various acts on the air, and playing new artists. But ever since the channel had hit New York and Los Angeles, the balance of power had begun to shift. With the video virus having spread throughout the country, and the MTV pipeline hooked up to an ever-growing number of family rooms, it was now possible to argue that the music industry needed MTV as much as MTV needed the music industry. In many ways, MTV had become the equivalent of a huge national radio station.

People at the labels certainly recognized this shift. Several labels put some of their top radio promotion people on the music video beat to deal with MTV the way they'd dealt with the nation's hottest radio stations all these years. The folks at MTV recognized the change as well. And while Les Garland and his staff were still doing their best to appease the labels by promoting their pet acts (no easy task, either, given the ever-increasing number of videos that were being submitted each week), the channel's execs were starting to throw a little of their own power around. In February, after CBS Records allowed *Friday Night Videos* to premiere the newest clip by the Rolling Stones, "She Was Hot," the video oddly never made it past light rotation on MTV. A few months later the same thing would happen to Billy Joel, when he chose to debut his latest clip, "The Longest Time," on NBC's *Today* show. While all the executives at MTV knew they would eventually have to start paying the labels for the videos, they also knew that they could demand something in return—the exclusive right to show the clips.

The reason was simple enough: It was a way of protecting MTV against its competition, specifically the hundreds of video clip programs and all-video UHF stations that had sprung up in the past year. While publicly the channel's executives welcomed the other video outlets, saying such exposure was good for video music, they also knew that too much music on the rest of television could only harm MTV. Which was why, in late 1983, when they first started discussions with record executives in New York and Los Angeles about payment for the clips, they put the issue of exclusivity on the table. For the record industry it was a touchy issue. On the one hand, they wanted money from MTV, and they understood that if they were going to get it the channel needed something in return. On the other hand, these clips were promotional tools, and the labels obviously didn't want to be limited in where they could promote their artists. As a result, the negotiations dragged on. Still, though the talks were tough, by the late spring of 1984, deals were close to being signed.

And when it came to seizing the day, Ross, Pittman, and the rest of them weren't going to limit themselves to the record industry.

Meanwhile, the financial situation at Warner had grown dire. Thanks to Atari's continued decline, the company lost more than $400 million during 1983. As if that weren't bad enough, late in that year, Australian media mogul Rupert Murdoch started buying up shares of Warner stock, clearly gearing up to take over the company. To hold off Murdoch, Steve Ross had finally turned to Herb Siegel, the chairman of a manufacturing company called Chris-Craft. Siegel had become Warner's white knight, buying up a significant amount of the company's stock and frustrating Murdoch's effort to take control.

Even when the Murdoch threat disappeared, many changes needed to be made and much belt-tightening needed to be done if Warner was to survive. So in addition to looking around for a buyer for Atari, the company considered going public with a portion of Warner AMEX Cable stock. There was bound to be some interest in it on Wall Street, and certainly AMEX, given its view of cable, was not likely to object to cashing in part of its investment. But when the company's financial staff really started taking a look at things, it came to the conclusion that an even more attractive vehicle to take public was none other than the red-hot MTV. Why not get some money out of this thing while it's on fire? So in the middle of February, they quietly formed a new entity called MTV Networks, and in mid-June announced they were going to offer one-third of the company's stock to the public.

Inside MTV there was plenty of excitement about this, because most of them would receive shares of stock. But no one was more excited, or took more pride in this offering, than WASEC chief Jack

Schneider. In many ways, the past few years had been odd ones for him. On the one hand, deep down, he remained very much a network guy, a stranger out on the cable frontier. Who could blame him? He'd practically ruled at CBS during a time when network television was at its most powerful and most exciting, and clearly no network had been more powerful or more exciting than CBS. Consequently, there was just no way any new cable programming company, no matter how successful it became, would ever be able to top CBS in Schneider's heart. Besides, things at WASEC had not always been pleasant. Not only had Schneider clashed over the years with everyone from cable operators to the Warner guys to some of the young MTV pioneers, but he had always seemed slightly embarrassed about presiding over this rock and roll channel; it just didn't seem very dignified.

Despite all the unpleasantness, Jack Schneider really did have a chunk of his soul invested in WASEC. It was only natural. He'd been the one who came over from the world of network broadcasting and led the WASEC wagon train in its early days, who'd given the company its direction and style, and who'd taken all these young pioneers from their ordinary little offices in midtown Manhattan all the way to the *Tonight* show and the cover of *Time* and now to profitability and the gilded corridors of Wall Street itself. As much as anyone, he had the right to say that this was *his* company.

With MTV Networks ready to go public, Schneider couldn't have been more in his element. A major part of taking a company public was doing what was called the Road Show—going around the country and making presentations to investors, trying to persuade them that your company was worth sinking a few dollars into. And who was better at leading potential investors through perfectly prepared

charts and graphs and financial statements than Jack Schneider? It was exactly the kind of situation in which all his CBS class and polish could really shine through. It was perfect.

*   *   *   *   *   *

On July 17, the day before the MTV Road Show was set to begin and nearly five years after Jack Schneider had first arrived at WASEC, Warner AMEX chief executive officer Drew Lewis called Schneider into his office at 75 Rockefeller Plaza and asked for his resignation. They were going to replace him, Lewis said, with David Horowitz, the Warner executive who had been the liaison to WASEC the previous five years.

As some would later recall it, the timing of the decision had much to do with what was happening at Warner. As time went by and Chris-Craft's Herb Siegel had continued his push to cut costs, there was increasing pressure on Warner boss Steve Ross to jettison some of the company's top-heavy corporate management, including David Horowitz, the company's co-chief operating officer and one of the members of the office of the president. But what to do with him? Finally, the suggestion was made to have Horowitz replace Schneider as the head of MTV Networks. Ross and the rest of the Warner crew were no fans of Schneider, nor was Drew Lewis. Such a switch was not without risks—changing chief executive officers right before going public was bound to raise questions—but it did seem to solve two problems at once, and so the switch was made.

As he sat there in Drew Lewis's office, receiving the news of his dismissal, Jack Schneider couldn't believe what he was hearing. The more this all rattled around in his head, the more furious he got. Hadn't he gotten himself in a jam with Warner at least partly because he was trying to look out for American Express's interest in this operation? Where the hell was Jim Robinson now that he needed him? It was one thing to be asked by Bill Paley to leave the glorious confines of CBS; it was something very different to be shot dead on the cable frontier by Steve Ross and Drew Lewis.

* * * * * *

In many ways, David Horowitz was an even less likely leader for MTV than Jack Schneider. A lawyer by training, Horowitz, fifty-five, had joined Warner in 1973 after several years with a New York law firm and several more with both Screen Gems and Columbia Pictures. He'd done well under Steve Ross, becoming part of the company's unique four-man office of the president in 1976, with responsibility for both the cable television and records divisions. Five years later he added the title of co-chief operating officer of Warner.

always tried to guide and encourage him. Pittman, in turn, saw Horowitz as the rabbi among Warner's top management, the one who would listen to your problems and concerns and offer his advice. He liked and respected Horowitz so much that he was the one person other than himself he would have accepted as chief executive officer.

In the summer of 1984, Horowitz and Pittman hit the road together to sell MTV Networks to the investment world. It was a whirlwind trip—two cities a day for two weeks straight, all over America and Europe. The new chief executive officer and the Keeper of the Vision had a wonderful time together peddling their hot commodity. Not only was the company now profitable, but in June, MTV finally signed contracts with several of the major record labels, giving the network exclusive use of certain videos in exchange for payment.

Thoughtful and soft-spoken, MTV Networks chief executive officer David Horowitz's manner was different from that of his predecessor, Jack Schneider.

In terms of style and personality, Horowitz couldn't have been more different from Jack Schneider. Where Schneider was aggressive and occasionally abrasive, Horowitz, a small, balding man with wire-rimmed glasses and a big, bristly mustache, was quiet and soft-spoken, a genial and gentle sort who loved literature and music. What's more, unlike Schneider, Horowitz got along wonderfully with Bob Pittman. From the Keeper of the Vision's earliest days in the company, Horowitz had been impressed with his drive and intelligence—he really thought he was a quick study—and he had

Meanwhile, across America, the video revolution was picking up even greater momentum, with more people loading up their mules and searching for video gold. In Hollywood, music video had become the rage. Filmmaker Brian DePalma and actor Timothy Hutton were directing videos (DePalma did Bruce Springsteen's "Dancing in the Dark," Hutton the Cars's "Drive"). Others, like comic Rodney Dangerfield, were appearing in them. It was the thing to do. The Hollywood/music video connection worked the other direction as well, as hot movies like *Stayin' Alive* and *Footloose* freely borrowed the fast-paced, often chaotic look of video clips. Herbert Ross, the director of *Footloose*, was said to have prepared for the film by studying hours and hours of MTV. Other movie producers took a more sure-fire way of achieving the video aesthetic: They actually hired music video directors (like "Hungry Like the Wolf" auteur Russell Mulcahy and "Billie Jean" director Steve Barron) to make features for them. Even the biggest stars in Hollywood were riding on the video bandwagon. One day, Clint Eastwood showed up at the MTV offices to play them some tunes from his new Dirty Harry flick, *Sudden Impact*. Any chance the network would play them? After being given the okay, Eastwood went ahead and put together a video.

The music video style was everywhere that summer. The "beast" had even entered the world of politics. Convinced by a staff member that it would be the best way to connect with young voters, the sixty-nine-year-old governor of Indiana, Robert Orr, made a music video-style campaign ad. His opponent in the race responded by sending the governor a Boy George costume, along with the suggestion that he wear it in his next clip. But Orr got the last laugh: He won reelection with 53 percent of the vote.

As a result of the strong numbers, the deals with the record companies, and the relentless spread of the video virus, most financial analysts expected big things for MTV Networks. Indeed, in early August, as David Horowitz and Bob Pittman brought the Road Show to a close in San Francisco, it looked like the company's stock offering would be a sellout at around $18 per share.

Then, as if the summer hadn't been trying enough, Ted Turner got involved.

*   *   *   *   *   *

On August 7, two days before MTV Networks's stock was to go on sale, Ted Turner sent a letter to eight thousand cable operators around the country announcing that he was considering starting up his own music video network. It would be family oriented, Turner said—no Hitler Youth here—and cable operators who signed up for the new service within two weeks would get it free for five years. According to Turner, if he got commitments for ten million subscribers within that period, the network would be a go.

Turner's motivation for his all-out assault on MTV appeared to be a moral one; he told cable operators at the CTAM convention that same month that they could get "clean" videos from his channel, or "dirty" ones from "that sleazy company," MTV. But most people believed that there was a whole lot more to it, such as money. MTV was now obviously a successful business, and Turner undoubtedly thought he could share in the wealth. Some of the WASEC sales people remembered how amazed Turner had always been by MTV. One day a couple of years earlier, David Houle, a young ad sales rep in MTV's Chicago office, was on a sales call with Turner when Ted turned to him and said, "Hey, how's that MTV thing doing anyway? How much are you getting for a spot?"

When Houle told him, Turner's eyes popped. It was more than Turner was getting for CNN.

Others believed that some of the country's larger cable operators had put Turner up to the fight. After all, the WASEC affiliate sales people had spent much of the last year trying to get the cable companies to pay for MTV. If there were a second video service out there—one that was free—then MTV would almost certainly have to lower the price it was charging, or maybe even get rid of the fees altogether.

Whatever Turner's motivation, his announcement certainly put a hell of a scare into those at MTV. This was the most serious threat that MTV had ever faced. Turner was one of the savviest guys in the cable business, and his company was probably the only one that could successfully take on MTV. Not only would Turner be able to take advantage of economies of scale and be able to promote his new network on his other two channels; not only did he already have relationships with the advertising community; but, most important, he had strong relations with the cable community. In style and attitude Turner was one of them, a tough-talking, risk-loving renegade who'd ventured out in the frontier years before it was fashionable and set up camp. As Turner himself was fond of saying, "I was cable before cable was cool."

It was that Operation Defeat Ted went into effect. When David Horowitz and Bob Pittman heard about Turner's plans, they were still in San Francisco, finishing up presentations on the Road Show. Not wanting to waste a single second in fighting back Turner's charge, Pittman and Horowitz summoned all of MTV's top executives out to the West Coast. Then Horowitz and Pittman put everybody, including themselves, on a plane together and headed back to New York. On board the flying "conference room," the group began to plot their strategy.

The biggest danger, they decided, was channel capacity. According to the affiliate sales group, there were around fifteen million homes whose cable systems had enough room to handle a second music channel. Therefore, even if not one single cable operator dropped MTV in favor of Turner's channel (admittedly a fair-weather scenario, given that Ted's service would be free), Turner would still be able to get enough subscribers to cause severe damage to MTV's advertising revenue. Because the ad pie, despite its recent growth, was still not large enough to split in two, it was possible that the two channels would end up putting each other out of business. Consequently, the executive team ultimately decided that their best strategy would be to do to Turner what Turner had done to Westinghouse when it tried to compete with CNN in 1981: start a new channel of their own, a fighting brand. If America's cable companies had room on their systems for a second music video channel, then it would be MTV that gave it to them, not Ted Turner.

But exactly what type of service should it be? As far back as the John Lack era, people inside the company had identified at least two other possible niches: an urban music channel and an adult contemporary channel. Because an adult channel that was aimed at twenty-five- to fifty-four-year-olds was likely to be a better weapon in fighting Turner, that was the one they decided on.

On August 10, MTV Networks's stock went on sale. Unfortunately for the company, however, the Turner announcement had made investors leery, so instead of selling out at $18 per share the stock went for $15 per share, costing the corporate parents millions. As tough as that was to swallow, all were aware that the real threat Turner posed was long-term, so with their battle plan in place, they set out to make it work.

From the outset, it was clear that the most important job was to win the support of the cable companies. They focused on the industry's two largest operators: TCI, which boasted 2.5 million subscribers, and ATC, the Time Inc.-owned company that had 2.1 million subscribers. Together, the two outfits had so many customers that if MTV lost them, the network truly put at risk its status as a national advertising vehicle. Unfortunately, relations with the companies had never been great, particularly with ATC.

Shortly after Turner's announcement, David Horowitz called Nick Nicholas, the executive who oversaw cable at Time Inc., and asked what the situation was. Nicholas put it to him straight: "You might be too late, David. Our guys are so ticked off with MTV that I think they're going to go with Turner." Though it looked bleak, Nicholas told Horowitz that most of ATC's big guns were meeting at the cable company's headquarters in Denver the next day. He offered to have the Time corporate jet fly Horowitz there.

The next day Horowitz, Bob Pittman, and David Hilton, who'd taken over the previous fall for pioneer Andy Orgel as the head of affiliate sales and marketing, all jetted out to Denver to meet with the top brass at ATC. They made their pitch, telling them about the new adult contemporary channel they were going to launch and also making a few financial concessions with regard to MTV. While they didn't seem to make a lot of progress, the door was left open. The ATC guys were going to meet once more, on August 20, to make a final decision.

When he returned to New York, David Horowitz called the top guns at TCI, also based in Denver, and arranged for a meeting with them on the very same day, August 20. On the nineteenth, Horowitz, David Hilton, and Drew Lewis flew out to Denver, and the next morning they met with TCI chief John Malone and his lieutenants. They were able to reach an agreement—MTV made some concessions on the price per subscriber, and TCI agreed not to add Turner's service. TCI wanted the contract signed that day, however, so David

Hilton began working out the details. Horowitz, meanwhile, got on the phone and called the folks across town at ATC. He just happened to be in the neighborhood, he told them, and thought maybe he had an approach that might help bridge the gap between them. They told him to come over; everyone was there.

Horowitz took a cab over to ATC, and by the time the afternoon was over and the evening rolled around the two sides had worked out a deal. They signed the contract right there. David Hilton, meanwhile, had worked out the final details with TCI, and signed a deal with them as well.

That night, Horowitz and Hilton were ecstatic. They had two signed deals with the country's two largest cable operators, and they felt at that moment as if the company's future was secure. When they got back to the hotel they called Bob Pittman, who was in Atlanta working on a deal with Cox Cable. They told him the news.

"Shit," the Keeper of the Vision said, "I wanted to be there."

*   *   *   *   *   *

Despite MTV's deal with TCI and ATC, and despite not getting the ten million subscribers he'd hoped for, in early September Ted Turner announced he was still going ahead with his music video channel. The plan was to launch at the end of October, by which time Turner figured they would have five million subs lined up.

As summer came to a close the mood inside MTV was frantic, as they all threw themselves into this latest battle. In programming, Les Garland and John Sykes were busy dealing with the record companies, trying to ensure that none of them gave Turner any help, while ad sales vice president Bob Roganti and his crew stormed Madison Avenue, solidifying the network's position there. And, of course, there was the whole matter of starting this new channel, which they'd decided to call (in a name reminiscent of Pittman favorite TV-1) Video Hits-1, or VH-1.

To oversee the programming of the new service, Bob Pittman turned to another former WNBC colleague, Kevin Metheney, who'd joined MTV back in the spring. Metheney had a bear of a job to do. They only had a few million bucks to get this channel operational, so everything had to be done on a shoestring. What's more, since Pittman had given strict orders that VH-1's playlist should be separate from MTV's, Metheney had to find some way of making a coherent format out of the wide variety of music that supposedly appealed to adults—everything from ballads by Barry Manilow to country tunes by Willie Nelson to R & B songs by the Commodores.

The affiliate sales group and their boss, David Hilton, had also thrown themselves into the battle. A small but aggressive and hard-driven young man, Hilton had joined WASEC in 1980 as head of film acquisitions for The Movie Channel, and had stayed with the movie service through the merger with Showtime in 1983. That fall, Bob Pittman, who was always a big supporter of Hilton, brought him back to WASEC, this time as head of affiliate sales and marketing. There in the fight against Turner, Hilton was driving everyone hard. He was turning out to be as much of a battlefield commander as Bob Pittman himself. As the weeks went by, the sales crew spent every possible moment on the road, negotiating with cable operators. It was so intense that many of them began to feel the same way the programming crew had felt launching MTV three years earlier: as though they'd gone to war. It was hard work, but they felt invigorated.

* * * * * *

Although most of the company had gone to war with Ted Turner, the channel itself had hardly shut down. Ads kept selling, veejay spots kept being churned out, new clips kept being added, and out in America young people kept tuning in.

But not everything went so smoothly. That summer, the channel had conducted its latest giveaway, the Paint the Mother Pink contest. Ever since the first One-Night Stand contests back in 1981, MTV had tried to make each contest bigger and better and more outrageous than the one before it. One night, the staffers were out at the Russian Tea Room, sucking down the vodka, when somebody said, "Hey, we should do a real rock and roll contest. We could give away a house or something." Everyone loved the idea. They cooked up a scheme involving John Cougar Mellencamp, as a way of promoting his latest album, which contained the hit song "Little Pink Houses." MTV would buy a house in the singer's hometown in Indiana, paint it pink, and give it away to a viewer, along with a pink Jeep and other prizes. The whole thing would be topped off by the singer and his band giving a concert in the living room of the new pink house.

The network got a pretty good deal on a house and set about painting it pink. But one day while the MTV crew was there, John Mellencamp rushed over to producer Marci Brafman.

"Are you in charge of this production?" he asked.

"Yeah," she said.

"Well, I want to talk with you. I'm really upset about something." At which point he took her inside the house.

"Do you realize," he continued, "that you have purchased a house to give away with *my name* connected to it . . . that's sitting on a toxic waste dump?"

It was true. It seems that these MTV sharpies from New York had been suckered by a local realtor. The network ended up buying another house to give away.

Even with such setbacks, the channel's momentum didn't let up; they were still at the very center of the musical universe. That September, they even put together their largest event yet: The very first MTV Video Music Awards. While an awards show honoring the top videos of the year was hardly a revolutionary concept—several other outfits had already done video award shows—such a project was a natural for MTV. In addition to giving them a signature event, it was bound to pull in plenty of cash through advertising and syndication rights for broadcast television.

The show was terrific. Produced by Ohlmeyer Communications and shown live from Radio City Music Hall, the two-hour program pulled in a phenomenal (for cable, anyway) 8.6 rating in the Nielsens. Not only did viewers get to see the year's top videos honored (the Cars's "You Might Think" was named video of the year, and Herbie Hancock's "Rockit" won three other awards), but they also got to see some of the biggest names in show business. Comedian Dan Aykroyd and singer Bette Midler hosted the show, everyone from Eddie Murphy to Roger Daltrey to Hall & Oates gave out awards, and Cyndi Lauper and Tina Turner were among those who performed live.

Perhaps the biggest hit of the evening was the latest MTV-created star, a young singer named Madonna. A Michigan native, Madonna had come to New York when she was nineteen, tried to make it as a dancer, failed, then knocked around with a couple of bands on the downtown club scene before getting a record deal of her own, and finally, in the summer of 1983, releasing her first album, *Madonna*. While the album didn't get much initial interest, in the spring of 1984 MTV added to its playlist a video for the song "Borderline," and slowly the record began to climb the charts. By summer, Madonna's debut album and another single that MTV was playing, "Lucky Star," were near the top of the charts.

Like Michael Jackson before her, Madonna was ideally suited to video—hearing her was only half the experience. While dancing made Michael's videos so wonderful, in Madonna's case it was something else. The woman just oozed sex. The video for "Borderline" was hardly sophisticated; it was really just Madonna, wearing a black cut-off shirt and black skirt, dancing and rolling around against a white background. But it was incredibly alluring. Viewers couldn't take their eyes off it.

MTV wild man Les Garland couldn't take his eyes off it, either. Garland got to know Madonna as they worked together on the MTV Awards show. During the program, Madonna was slated to perform the title song from her latest album, *Like A Virgin*, complete with giant wedding cake. One day during rehearsal, Garland happened to be holding the ladder as Madonna climbed to the top of the cake. He looked up and noticed two things: first, that the back of Madonna's dress was open; second, that she wasn't wearing any underwear. Always a gentleman, Garland politely informed her of this.

"Oh, really?" she said. "How does my butt look?"

A couple of days after the show, Garland called Madonna to congratulate her on her performance, which many said was the most memorable of the evening. Then he moved on to more important matters.

Madonna: from Boy Toy to Material Girl to platinum-blonde starlet, the singer was constantly reinventing herself—and using music video to show off each new look.

"Madonna, I don't really know how to go about doing this," Garland said. "You see, I'm really kind of a shy guy. But, uh, do I have a chance with you?"

"That's funny," she said. "I was wondering when you were going to get around to asking."

"Well, I'm asking."

"I did some checking on you," she said, "And I found out you talk too much."

Garland laughed. "You can bet on that."

"Well, that's not the only problem," Madonna continued. "You see, I just met somebody else. Sorry."

As Garland later found out, the guy she'd met was actor Sean Penn, who she later married.

* * * * * *

At noon on October 26, Ted Turner's Cable Music Channel (CMC) went on the air. It was hardly the event that Turner had hoped for. Thanks to MTV's exclusivity

announced he was shutting the channel down and that MTV had agreed to buy CMC's assets for $1.5 million. As Turner executive Bob Wussler put it, explaining the decision, "We felt the outlook for adding additional subscribers was weak."

Inside MTV, there was euphoria. This was particularly true among the affiliate sales people, whose hard work among the cable operators had really driven Turner under. Somebody even made up buttons with the numbers "851:59" printed on them—the exact number of hours and minutes that CMC had been on the air.

Not long after that, new MTV Networks chief executive officer David Horowitz flew out to Los Angeles to go to the annual Award for Cable Excellence (ACE)—the Emmys of the cable business. As he stood talking to some people at a reception before the event, Horowitz heard a voice screaming out to him:

"Dave! Dave!"

He turned and noticed somebody at the other end of

Madonna, in a publicity still for her first album. Oozing sexuality, she was a natural for music video.

agreements with the record industry, CMC couldn't play many popular videos. The channel had only fifteen advertisers and distribution problems. Although CMC claimed that it had 2.3 million subscribers at launch, a week later revised that number, in large part because of a challenge from MTV, whose executives were certain Turner was inflating his numbers. Due to "internal errors," Turner's company said, they'd miscalculated. In reality they had only 350,000 subscribers.

Several weeks after CMC's launch, at the end of November, Turner

the room waving at him. It was Ted Turner.

"Are there any photographers here?" Turner said. "Please, everybody, gather 'round."

When a sufficient crowd had formed, Ted reached over and pulled the handkerchief out of some bystander's pocket. Then he dropped to his knees and started waving it.

"Dave," Turner confessed to Horowitz. "We surrender. You guys kicked our ass."

MONEY FOR NOTHING

W I N T E R 1 9 8 5 — S U M M E R 1 9 8 5

Despite CMC's demise, MTV went ahead with plans for VH-1, and the new channel set sail at noon on New Year's Day, playing as its first clip a version of the "Star Spangled Banner," performed by Marvin Gaye. Naturally, the company held a party to celebrate the launch, though it turned out to be a fairly subdued affair; most people were still hung over from the tequila and other substances they'd partaken of the night before at MTV's fourth annual New Year's Eve show. But maybe the lack of energy and excitement was fitting for VH-1. Despite the affiliate sales crew doing a good job signing up three million subscribers by launch day, it remained an austere operation. Consider its veejay spots, for example. While MTV's veejay segments were now being shot in a custom-configured space at Unitel Studios in midtown Manhattan, the VH-1 veejays—New York radio veterans Don Imus (whom Bob Pittman had fired and then rehired when he was at WNBC), Scott Shannon, and Frankie Crocker, along with former Sha Na Na member Jon "Bowzer" Bauman—shot their spots in a remodeled broom closet in the Brill Building. You couldn't have asked for better symbolism.

Despite the ugly-stepchild status afforded VH-1, in the afterglow of the Turner victory there was now an undeniable sense of confidence in the company, one that stretched from David Horowitz and Bob Pittman all the way down the corporate ladder. From a business perspective, everyone felt invincible.

After years of being seen by cable operators as arrogant, quasi–broadcast network know-it-alls, they had finally smoothed over and solidified their relationship with the cable community. Distribution now topped twenty-five million; more important, they had long-term contracts with almost all the country's largest cable companies. True, getting those contracts had meant sacrificing a few cents per subscriber in revenue, but it was a small price to pay for security.

Things were equally bright when it came to ad sales. During the past year the channel and Madison Avenue had gone positively goo-goo-eyed over one another, as advertisers began to get more and more heated up about the idea of sending their messages down the MTV pipeline and into the homes, hearts, and minds of America's youth. Things were so good in 1984, the company showed a profit of $11.9 million, its first year ever in the black.

Three and a half years after MTV's launch, two and a half years after hitting Manhattan, and one year after *Time* had proclaimed that a video revolution was underway in America, the music video virus showed little sign of letting up. As more creative types had started to use elements of music videos in their work, many observers proclaimed that MTV was changing not only the music industry, but television in general—they saw MTV as the force that was changing the way the rest of TV looked and sounded.

The hottest new TV show of the season, for example, was NBC's *Miami Vice*. While in many ways it was a typical good-guys-chasing-bad-guys cop show, the same kind the broadcast networks had been showing for thirty years, *Vice* distinguished itself by using a real rock and roll soundtrack and by using all the visual tricks—moody lighting, quick edits, slow motion—that music video had brought into vogue. The show's style had hardly come about by accident; the previous year, Brandon Tartikoff, NBC's whiz-kid programming chief, had become infatuated with MTV, spending an entire weekend staring bug-eyed at the channel, like some seventeen-year-old. The following week he came into his office, worked up a concept he called "MTV Cops," and gave it to a couple of producers named Michael Mann and Anthony Yerkovich. *Miami Vice* was born.

Not surprisingly, all of this change—the rout of Ted Turner, MTV's evolution into a solid business, the unchecked march of the virus—continued to have its effect on people inside the company. Those who worked at MTV were already being treated like celebrities. But as MTV started to shape the culture and mature into a solid corporation, those same people were now being treated with a certain respect.

For example, at the end of the year, Bob Pittman was named Man of the Year by the Creative Fashion Designers Association (CFDA), one of the most prestigious groups in the industry. Though the award seemed like a stretch at first, when you thought about it, the honor made sense. Not only had fashion designers begun to use video to show off their latest designs, but all over America young people were copying the styles of artists such as Cyndi Lauper and Madonna and Boy George and the others they'd seen on MTV. Pittman and his wife, Sandy, invited Marci Brafman and Judy McGrath from the on-air promo department to go with them to a CFDA dinner, and at one point during the evening Brafman found herself talking to designer Perry Ellis. She was thrilled to meet him. The thing was, Ellis seemed equally thrilled to meet her. "You guys are making a wonderful contribution," he told her. "You're changing American style."

This new-found status came to other individuals in the company as well. A few months earlier, senior programming vice president Les Garland had been invited to the White House to watch Michael Jackson receive an award from President Reagan, and had gotten to meet the Gipper. And Garland added some of his own kind of spice to the event. At one point he started hanging out with some of the Secret Service guys, who, as it turned out, were big MTV fans. Garland got one of the agent's names, and when he got back to New York he mailed him a bunch of MTV T-shirts. A few days later Garland received a package—several Secret Service golf shirts. It turned out the U.S. government had promotional items, too.

John Sykes was also enjoying the perks of working for MTV; he'd been seen around town with singer Carly Simon. And Bob Pittman was flying even higher than the others. With Jack Schneider left for dead on the cable frontier and Ted Turner still trying to see straight over the pummeling MTV had given him, Pittman's reputation inside the company was larger than ever—particularly among the younger members of the staff, who hadn't been around five years earlier when Pittman was just "that young radio guy who ran programming at The Movie Channel." To many of them, the Keeper of the Vision was god-like—a perception that he seemed a little amused by. One night, Pittman and a bunch of MTV staff members were out to dinner in New York. During the evening, the Keeper of the Vision leaned over to J. J. Jackson and whispered, "I heard this really terrible joke today. But you just watch how everybody falls out of their chairs when I tell it." He told the joke, which was, in fact, terrible. But as soon as the punch line rolled out of his mouth the whole table erupted in dutiful, subservient laughter. Pittman just looked over at Jackson and smiled.

Earning $200,000 a year and $1.5 million in stock options, Pittman had begun to live the life of a powerful corporate honcho. And the outside world continued to acknowledge him. In addition to the CFDA award, Pittman was also given a testimonial dinner by the American Cancer Society in 1984. Perhaps most impressive of all, at the end of the year *Time* named Pittman runner-up for its prestigious Man of the Year award, presented to the person who had the greatest impact on world and national events during the past twelve months (Los Angeles Olympic Committee chairman Peter Ueberroth won the honor). The magazine gushed about the Keeper of the Vision, though it exaggerated slightly when it came to his role in getting MTV off the ground. "Pittman's idea for MTV was simplicity itself," *Time* said. "Get the record manufacturers to produce video commercials for their records and then use those elaborate and often fanciful commercials for most of MTV's broadcasting."

When John Lack's friends read it, all they could do was groan.

*   *   *   *   *   *

Nevertheless, there were some problems bubbling underneath the channel's surface. To start with, there was the whole MTV Is the Devil movement, which only seemed to be getting stronger as MTV grew. Recently, a group called the National Coalition on Television Violence condemned many of the clips the channel was playing as excessively violent. Following a year-long study in which it examined nearly nine hundred different music videos, the organization found that on average, MTV broadcast 17.9 violent acts per hour. All together, about 22 percent of the videos contained violence between men and women, it said, and 13 percent of violent videos contained sadistic violence, where the attacker took pleasure in committing the violence. While MTV didn't address the study specifically, not much later Bob Pittman did announce they were cutting back on clips by heavy-metal bands—generally the biggest offenders in the sex and violence category.

The music industry began griping about the channel as well—not over content, but over exposure for their clips. Because the labels were making more videos than ever, it was now simply impossible for MTV to play all of them, a fact that frustrated record company executives in New York and Los Angeles. Les Garland, John Sykes, Gale Sparrow, and the rest did their best to appease each of the labels—expanding the playlist, adding three more categories to the original light-medium-heavy rotation format—but they were tough to satisfy. On the flip side, there were now some managers and label executives who thought their artists were getting too much exposure on the channel. Some people in the record industry believed that the burnout rate—that point at which the public goes from loving a video to hating it—was much shorter with video than it was with radio, and they had actually started requesting that MTV take their artists' clips off the air.

These developments, along with the ever-increasing size of the MTV programming staff, made the weekly music meetings a real drag. One person would push for so and so's clip because the channel owed Capitol Records. Someone else would advocate for a different clip because Epic Records was really behind it—or that the channel should play only the most artistic clips or the biggest hits. Les Garland started to think that what they really needed was a benevolent dictator.

Perhaps the biggest area of concern was the atmosphere inside the company itself. On one hand, the place—particularly programming—

was still as wild and rock and roll as ever, and so were many of the people in it. Somehow, something was changing. First, money began to get in the way. When MTV Networks had gone public the previous summer, each person who'd been at the company for more than a year received some stock. The problem was that senior management had also been given stock options to buy large numbers of shares at reduced prices—a fact that rankled many of the people below, particularly those who'd been there from the earliest days. By this point, it was clear that they were no longer just a tight-knit, hard-working, happy little band of pioneers out on the cable frontier. As MTV grew more successful, the size of the staff had naturally grown, and while they were far from big, the company now employed more than five hundred people. But many of these new folks were, by definition, a different breed. While four and five years earlier, the original group had hopped on the WASEC wagon train without much of a clue as to where it was heading, this new crew knew exactly what they were in for—they were going to work for the hottest entity in television. In fact, some of the youngest staff members were the very kids who'd drooled over the channel when it first went on the air in 1981. For them, working at MTV was no leap of faith; it was a dream fulfilled.

Undeniably, the stakes had gotten higher. The press attention was relentless; big-name advertisers were spending big money on the channel; record companies had entire careers riding on whether MTV did or didn't play a clip; and stockholders had to be answered to. For at least a few at MTV, such pressures had started to spoil the fun. The real turning point came the previous summer, when the company held a corporate retreat at a place called Arrowood in upstate New York. The idea of MTV even having a corporate retreat struck a lot of them, especially those in programming, as completely out of whack. Why couldn't they just go to some bar and drink a few? What made it even worse was how the retreat went. While the other companies that were meeting at Arrowood spent a lot of time hunkered down by the pool or at the bar, the MTV group spent endless hours in meetings, talking about things like goals and business philosophies and management styles. The whole thing was so corporate it made some of them long for a hotel room that smelled like corned beef.

But maybe all of this was nothing but nitpicking. After all, things were still going well. Being attacked by the conservatives was a good thing, right? And the record companies were making more videos than ever, weren't they? And the fact that the corporate culture was changing was merely a sign of success, wasn't it? When you thought about it, they'd been amazingly lucky. In the summer of 1981 they'd created something, and in the three and a half years since then they'd seen it grow from a tiny baby of a company that inspired "Huhs" and "M-whats" and unreturned phone calls into a handsome, strapping young lad, one capable of taking on any problem or slaying any giant.

And the ride wasn't nearly over.

* * * * * *

By early 1985, American Express had lost patience with the cable business. Not only had AMEX itself shifted directions since 1979—it was now essentially a financial services outfit—but, more significantly, cable television hadn't quite lived up to all the hype of those early days. People were becoming part of the Wired Nation (more than 43 percent of America's television households now had cable),

but it didn't seem to be quite as revolutionary as everyone had expected. It was now clear that the interactive Qube technology that Warner had launched out in Columbus was, at best, ahead of its time. In fact, early in 1984, in one of his many attempts to improve Warner AMEX's bottom line, Drew Lewis all but shut down the Qube Network that had started the previous year. What's more, it was clear to the executives at AMEX that the cable business was not going to be a major part of financial services, at least not in the foreseeable future. Finally, Jim Robinson and the rest of his team decided it was time to get out of cable altogether. By the spring of 1985, they had initiated discussions with several corporate suitors—including Viacom, Time Inc., and TCI—about buying out their interest in Warner AMEX and MTV Networks.

When word filtered down to David Horowitz and Bob Pittman that American Express wanted out, there naturally was some concern. A large block of MTV Networks stock could suddenly end up in new hands. Just how large a block depended on how things played out; if Warner decided to sell its interest as well, two-thirds of the company would be owned by someone new. Horowitz and Pittman were pondering the consequences of all this, when slowly it began to dawn on them: What if they bought MTV Networks themselves?

At first it truly seemed like an outrageous idea—buying a company worth hundreds of millions of dollars, according to its stock price. Yet by 1985, changes in the business world—particularly the advent of leveraged buyouts (LBOs)—made the idea plausible. In an LBO, a group of investors—usually a combination of a company's management and outsiders—together borrow the money needed to buy a company, using the business's assets as collateral for the loans and its cash flow to pay off the loans. (It's a bit like going to a bank and, despite not having any cash or collateral of your own, borrowing money to buy a car based on the idea that with the money you make using the car, you'll pay the bank back.) Such deals were usually extremely inviting, since those involved frequently put up little of their own money, but were still able to make huge profits. Of course, to the older players in American business at that time—a generation with vivid memories of the Depression and the war—the idea of a business taking on the huge debt an LBO required was abhorrent, the antithesis of all they believed about how money should be managed and a company run. But by the early 1980s, a new generation with a new attitude was beginning to establish itself on Wall Street— a generation with little use for the way its elders said things should be done. It was as if the rock and roll spirit itself had entered the world of American business. Be free! Unshackle yourself! That was the mood that took hold, and that's precisely what many did.

With LBO-mania sweeping through American business and a spirit of invincibility surging within the walls inside MTV, the possibilities seemed limitless. Buying the company would only be the beginning, Horowitz and Pittman thought. Once they had control, they could build on the three networks they already had—MTV, VH-1, and Nickelodeon—and turn this company into a mini-conglomerate. Or maybe even the dominant media company of the next generation. So in the spring, Horowitz and Pittman approached Steve Ross and Drew Lewis and told them they wanted to try a leveraged buyout of MTV Networks. Both executives gave the effort their blessing. They could hardly say no, given that each of them was considering putting together his own LBO—Lewis trying for Warner AMEX, Ross trying for Warner.

Horowitz and Pittman began looking for backers. A number of venture capital firms had recently sprung up, specializing in such deals. They would supply the cash, the targeted company's management would supply the expertise, and together they'd be able to get the financing from various banks and insurance companies and other investors. Unfortunately, given the unusual and unpredictable nature of MTV's business (most LBOs to this point had been done with manufacturing companies), many were leery of becoming involved. Finally, David Horowitz hooked up with a group called Boston Ventures. A venture capital group comprised of five partners, the firm was a natural for the deal. The previous year they'd backed the management of Metromedia in its buyout of that company. Both sides now worked out an agreement: Boston Ventures would put up several million dollars in equity and receive a majority share of MTV stock in return, while Horowitz, Pittman, and the rest of the senior management team at MTV would receive the remainder of the stock.

In the middle of May, the group went to the MTV Networks board of directors and made an offer for all of the company's stock. Unfortunately, the board declined to consider the offer. Although the group had a letter from the investment banking firm of Salomon Brothers saying they were highly confident they'd be able to supply the remainder of the financing for the deal, the money wasn't totally locked up. Consequently, the MTV Networks board said they couldn't consider the offer.

But Horowitz and Pittman weren't ready to give up.

* * * * * *

As spring turned to summer, the hectic pace inside the company continued. Bob Pittman went off to Harvard Business School for a management seminar that Drew Lewis had urged him to attend as a way of sharpening his business skills (he'd done the first half the summer before). Meanwhile, in New York events happened fast and furious. In June the company moved to new offices at 1775 Broadway. Not only had they outgrown the other space, but Bob Pittman felt it important that the entire company should be in the same building. On top of that, changes were taking place at Nickelodeon. The network had been a favorite of critics and parents since it first went on the air, but children themselves never quite took to it. In 1984, Pittman put Gerry Laybourne in charge of the channel, and brought in the Keeper of the Grooviness himself, Fred Seibert, along with Seibert's partner, Alan Goodman, to work with her. Together they completely revamped Nickelodeon, transforming it into a fun channel that kids actually liked. That spring, they'd taken the next step, putting on an evening schedule for the channel called Nick at Nite, featuring nothing but old sitcoms like *Donna Reed* and *My Three Sons* that TV babies loved.

Meanwhile, the music video virus was as strong as ever in America. Three years earlier, only 30 percent of the songs on *Billboard*'s Hot 100 chart were backed up by videos. That number had now risen to more than 75 percent. Moreover, one of the hottest videos of the summer was one that actually immortalized MTV itself, Dire Straits's "Money for Nothing." A satiric diatribe against the rock and roll life told from the point of view of the average working stiff, the song included a guest vocal by Police leader Sting. As synthesizers hummed eerily in the background, the blond singer sang longingly, "I . . . want . . . my . . . MTV. . . ."

Despite all the activity and the channel's continued success, it was the LBO that dominated people's lives that summer, and by July, Horowitz and Pittman had lined up new backers, the New York-based investment firm of Forstmann Little & Co. Formed in 1978, the firm, owned by two brothers, Ted and Nick Forstmann, and another man named Bill Little, was one of the oldest and most successful LBO firms going. Their biggest deal had come a year earlier, when they bought the then-struggling Dr Pepper company for $512 million. What made them really attractive as partners in this venture was the fact that they had a billion-dollar capital fund to draw on, solving the subordinated debt problem the MTV crew had faced with Boston Ventures.

But by the time David Horowitz and Bob Pittman had hooked up with the Forstmanns, the situation had changed with AMEX. In mid-June, after several months of negotiations with several companies, AMEX announced that it had accepted a $900 million offer from Time Inc. and TCI to buy all of Warner AMEX. This, in turn, had put into effect a buy-sell clause in the Warner AMEX partnership agreement. Under the terms of the agreement, Warner now had two options: It could accept the offer and split the $900 million with American Express, or it could buy out American Express's interest itself for $450 million. Warner had until August 14 to decide.

Steve Ross desperately wanted to retain Warner's cable holdings, particularly the cable systems. Unfortunately, finding the cash to do that was not going to be easy, given the considerable financial strain the company had been under for the past several years. As the months went by, relations between Ross and one-time Warner's savior Herb Siegel had reportedly grown more and more strained. With Siegel providing financial pressure, it was clear that there were only two ways Ross could hold on to Warner's cable operations: Find someone to replace AMEX as Warner's partner, or sell off some other part of the company.

As the summer wore on, Ross had talks with various people and considered various deals. The one group he wouldn't talk to was Forstmann Little. As Bob Pittman would later remember it, Ross was angry that Horowitz and Pittman had jumped ship from Boston Ventures, and he didn't want to negotiate with Teddy Forstmann, whom he didn't know.

One day that summer, Ross called Bob Pittman and told him they were ready to make a deal in which Viacom, with whom Warner already co-owned Showtime/The Movie Channel, would replace AMEX as Warner's cable partner, giving them a one-third interest in MTV Networks. Ross was well aware that Pittman himself longed to own a larger piece of MTV and wouldn't be thrilled with someone else buying the company. Nevertheless, he told the Keeper of the Vision he really needed him to stay at MTV after the deal went through. As the genius behind the channel, he was crucial to the deal.

"Listen, Steve, you've been really good to me," Pittman told him. "But I'll only agree to do it if you do one thing for me first—listen to Teddy Forstmann's offer. If you'll listen to Teddy Forstmann and consider his offer, and then you still want to do this deal with Viacom, then I'll go with you."

Ross agreed, and within the next several days he had a number of discussions with Forstmann about MTV. The talks turned out to be fruitful—the two sides actually reached a tentative agreement. On August 8, Forstmann Little, together with MTV's management, put $200 million in an escrow account and officially made an offer to buy

MTV Networks at $31 per share, or $470 million. The way the deal was structured, Warner would retain 20 percent of the company.

But the deal wasn't final. As the days went by, Ross had continued talking with Viacom, and the day after the Forstmann offer Warner made two announcements. The first was something that practically everyone had assumed anyway: namely, that Warner was exercising its right to buy out American Express's half of Warner AMEX for $450 million. The second was a backup agreement with Viacom: Within the next thirty days Warner could, if it wanted, require Viacom to either purchase MTV Networks for $470 million, or replace American Express as Warner's partner in the cable business for $450 million, whichever Viacom preferred. In any scenario now, Ross and Warner would be able to hold on to their cable systems.

Talks continued as the days went by. Because the AMEX/Warner deal had not officially gone through, any sale of MTV Networks also needed to be approved by AMEX. To ensure American Express's approval, on August 14, the Forstmann Little–MTV management offer was increased to $33 per share, or a total of $500 million. The only catch was that Warner, which would still own 20 percent of the company, would have no say in management. The offer was good until 5:00 P.M. on Thursday, August 22.

By the following Wednesday, August 21, things looked terrific. While nothing official occurred, Forstmann had reportedly received indications from both Ross and the folks at American Express that the offer was going to be accepted. It looked like such a sure thing, in fact, that Pittman and John Sykes took Teddy Forstmann to a Bruce Springsteen concert at Giants Stadium that night.

It was amazing how far they'd come in the four years since they'd launched this channel in a dingy bar on the outskirts of godforsaken Fort Lee, New Jersey. They'd given birth to a phenomenon, seen it spread all over the country, watched it start a revolution, and defended it against the most legendary guy in the cable business. Now, finally, they were going to get their piece of it.

As they sat there on a warm summer evening in the middle of New Jersey, listening to Bruce Springsteen sing about people's heartbreaking pursuit of the American Dream, it all must have seemed incredible to Bob Pittman. What had he been but a one-eyed fifteen-year-old who wanted to fly an airplane? Somehow, that desire had led him to a small radio station in Brookhaven, then on to Pittsburgh, Chicago, New York, and, finally, MTV.

The man was certainly flying now.

* * * * * *

The next day everything fell apart. At the very last minute, some issues developed between Steve Ross and Teddy Forstmann, and finally, Ross became so aggravated that he sent one of his lieutenants over to Viacom. If they would pay just fifty cents per share more, plus agree to buy Warner's stake in Showtime/The Movie Channel, they could have MTV Networks. Viacom took the deal.

On the night everything came crashing down, Teddy Forstmann, David Horowitz, and Bob Pittman were out to dinner at a small Italian cafe in Manhattan. Steve Ross called the restaurant to talk with Pittman. To have more privacy, Pittman excused himself from the others and went around the corner to Nick Forstmann's apartment, and he called Ross back. The Warner chairman told him they were going to do the deal with Viacom—the company would own MTV Networks outright. Still, he said, he didn't want Pittman to leave the company; he was crucial to the deal. The Keeper of the Vision told him he would have to think about it.

The next day he and Ross talked again. Ross told him once more how important he was to the deal, and also told him he would make sure Viacom took care of him financially. Pittman finally agreed to stay.

Still, the disappointment they all experienced was immense. David Horowitz felt as if he'd let all those young folks in the company down. But it was John Sykes who best seemed to understand what had happened.

"Wow," he thought to himself the night the deal fell apart, "we actually failed."

Three weeks later, "Money for Nothing" hit No. 1.

Press up sleeve hem.
Finish raw edge with seam binding or
or stretch lace.
Slip-stitch, easing in fulness.

NOTE: For view 1, the back neck interfacing may be omitted.

UNIT 1
front, back and
shoulder seams

Stitch front to back at
shoulder seams, easing
back to fit between
small dot and notch.

directions

t side of fabric
arenthesis.
ams, unless otherwise stated

RULES FOR KNIT FABRICS
and 10 to 12 stitches per

and a fine needle.
eams with a narrow zig-zag
t stretching, baste center o
seam line on front shoulder a
ms.
tching, 1/4" (6mm) from tr
es in place, trim outer c

THE NEHRU JACKET

FALL 1985 — SUMMER 1986

Given MTV's own CBS lineage, it was fitting that the channel's new owner, Viacom International, was also a descendant of the Tiffany Network. The company was created in 1971, not long after the FCC ruled that CBS had to divest itself of its program syndication division and the cable systems it owned. Over the next several years the company evolved into a small communications conglomerate, one that owned not only cable systems and a syndication arm, but also a number of local TV and radio stations around the country.

Why the interest now in MTV? Under Terry Elkes, the bespectacled fifty-four-year-old executive who'd become president of Viacom in 1978 and chief executive officer five years later, the company was striving to become a major provider of programming for both the broadcast networks and the cable industry. In 1978 Viacom had launched Showtime, the pay-movie service that later merged with WASEC's The Movie Channel, and in 1982 it launched the Cable Health Network, which two years later merged with the Daytime Network to become Lifetime. As a result, MTV Networks's four programming services—MTV, VH-1, Nickelodeon, and Nick at Nite—seemed a perfect fit, valuable additions that the Viacom executives believed would generate revenue and increase the company's clout with cable operators. True, some business analysts speculated that the growth potential of MTV itself was limited, but Elkes and his team disagreed. And they saw tremendous potential in Nickelodeon.

Unfortunately, within MTV headquarters at 1775 Broadway, the feelings toward Viacom weren't nearly so warm. Bob Pittman felt that Viacom had absolutely no business buying the company. Pittman and the rest of the pioneers had created MTV—it was their baby. There was also the issue of corporate culture. Warner, the dominant player in the Warner AMEX partnership, had always been a company that prized, encouraged, and rewarded the sort of creativity that made MTV strong, but Viacom's reputation was different. Indeed, from what Pittman and the rest at MTV had heard, the top executives at Viacom were little more than bean counters who didn't care a whit about creative people and who forced their own employees to work in offices with metal desks and linoleum floors.

The first meeting between the Viacom honchos and the MTV bigwigs didn't do much to resolve the situation. The folks from Viacom arrived a half-hour late, and when chief executive officer Terry Elkes finally walked into the room, he looked at everyone and said something like, "At ease, men." The guy was only joking, but it didn't do much to endear him to the troops.

Still, Bob Pittman resigned himself to remaining at the company, and in the late fall Pittman signed a new five-year contract with Viacom. It was quite a deal: In addition to a salary of more than half a million dollars a year and a $300,000 signing bonus, it also gave him Viacom stock options and other perks. It made him president and chief executive officer of MTV Networks.

David Horowitz just didn't figure into Viacom's plans. Because Pittman was clearly running things day to day at MTV Networks, and Viacom already had a full contingent of management, there was just no room for someone with Horowitz's background and skills. This

wasn't terribly crushing to Horowitz. He was disappointed at not getting MTV in the LBO, and it was rare that top management stuck around after losing an LBO bid anyway. And so, in December 1985, after eleven years with Warner and seventeen months as the head of MTV Networks, David Horowitz packed his things and left. Not long after he was gone, a few wags inside the company shared their assessment of the former chief executive officer. "David's a wonderful, bright guy. His only mistake was going to work as Bob Pittman's boss."

Pittman had finally reached the top. Almost six years to the day after he'd first gone to work as the head of programming for The Movie Channel, Bob Pittman was running the whole shebang, sitting in the very spot Jack Schneider had once occupied. Despite his powerful position and relative youth—he was only thirty-one—Pittman wasn't happy with the situation. Having come so close to pulling off the LBO, he found the idea of answering to Terry Elkes and the rest of the crew at Viacom irked him. It was, in his mind, quite a letdown from working under the likes of Steve Ross and David Horowitz.

Equally disturbing was what was now happening with MTV—four and a half years after launch, almost three years after they'd linked up with Michael Jackson, the high-flying MTV rocket finally looked like it was coming back to earth.

They were facing daunting internal problems. Over the summer, Pittman and Horowitz had made a few changes in the ranks at the company, moving Dom Fioravanti, who'd been general manager of MTV, VH-1, and Nickelodeon, to the newly created position of head of corporate development. Although Pittman thought Fioravanti had done good work, giving the channel some much-needed organization and professionalism, the Keeper of the Vision also believed that

Fioravanti was out of touch with the creative part of the company, and as a result, an us-versus-them mentality had begun to develop inside programming. To replace Fioravanti, Pittman turned to David Hilton, a young battlefield commander who'd done such an impressive job in affiliate sales during the war against Ted Turner. Like Fioravanti, Hilton didn't have a creative background, but he really wanted the position, and Pittman felt he deserved the opportunity.

The move soon turned out to be an absolute disaster. Though programming was no longer staffed by only pioneers and rock and rollers, and though the high stakes had taken some of the fun out of things, the department's culture remained loose and freewheeling. Consequently, when Hilton tried to impose the same sort of discipline on the programming staff that he had on the sales and marketing group, it just didn't work. For artist relations head Gale Sparrow, one of the people who'd been so disillusioned by the corporate retreat at Arrowood the summer before, it was the last straw. When Hilton told her she was going to have to start playing hardball with the record companies—demanding things from them, using the power that MTV had—Sparrow quit. Any success this channel ever had was because of the record companies, she told him. Find somebody else to play hardball with them. And Sparrow was hardly the only one to have a run-in with Hilton. By December, the situation had become so sticky that Pittman knew he needed to do something, so he told Hilton he had two options: He could go back to the creative people, proclaim *mea culpa*, and try to start over, or he could resign. Hilton chose the latter.

Unfortunately, things weren't going much better for the channel whose once-vital video virus was finally losing its virulence out in America. Ironically, the tide had begun to turn the previous summer, while all of the execitives were focused so strongly on the LBO. One of the first signs of trouble was Live Aid, the huge event that musician Bob Geldof had organized to fight famine in Africa. MTV agreed to air the concert, which was being held simultaneously in London and Philadelphia and featured practically all the biggest acts in pop music. Unfortunately, the channel kept cutting away from the performances to show its own veejays—a move for which it was crucified in the media afterward. The press also didn't seem to be impressed by the second MTV Video Music Awards, held in September. Though there was plenty of star power—comedian Eddie Murphy hosted, former Eagle Don Henley won best video award for his clip "The Boys of Summer," and acts such as Pat Benatar, John Cougar Mellencamp, and Sting performed—there were a lot of people who thought the program didn't have any of the adventure or spirit of the first MTV Awards. As *People* magazine put it, "The show made rock look as exciting and daring as the polka."

But as damaging as such press attention was, by the early part of 1986, the biggest problem the channel faced was its quickly sliding Nielsen ratings. In early January, Nielsen contacted MTV and informed them that the bottom seemed to have fallen out of its viewership. For the fourth quarter of 1985 the channel received a rating of .6, down substantially from the .9 it had earned in the third quarter and far away from the whopping 1.5 it had garnered during the height of "Thriller"-mania two years earlier. When Bob Pittman and the rest of the execs at the company got a look at the numbers, they broke out into a collective cold sweat. Not only would the drop-off in ratings add to their public image problem, but it could cost them plenty of cash. Like all networks, the channel guaranteed advertisers a certain minimum audience; if they didn't measure up to that, they had to provide free commercial time. What's more, a smaller audience would likely mean lower ad rates in the days ahead.

After receiving the news about the ratings, the company did two things quickly. First, it asked Nielsen not to make the numbers public. Second, it requested that the ratings service review its methodology to see if there was a reason for the downturn. As it turned out, there was. Nielsen had changed its audience sample in the fourth quarter, using fewer young people, a factor that obviously hurt MTV. Still, as Nielsen and others argued when the ratings were finally made public a couple of months later, even among the twelve-to-thirty-four-year-old demographic, viewership had dropped. There was no denying the trend of the past several ratings periods. Like a rocket rushing back to earth, the numbers were going down, down, down.

There were other signs that the video virus was dying. With the exception of the negative reviews and a handful of other pieces describing the vapidness of the channel, press attention of any kind had dropped off considerably. What more could be said about MTV that hadn't already been said? In addition, many of the video clip shows and music video networks that had sprung up in the previous couple of years were struggling as well. While this was partly due to MTV's exclusivity agreements with the record companies, you couldn't help but notice that the shows' and networks' ratings were dropping, too.

But why? After years of spreading throughout America, what was causing video-mania to lose its momentum? The most obvious explanation was that the whole ride hadn't ever been meant to last any

longer than this. All along, naysayers insisted that music video and its main purveyor, MTV, weren't part of a revolution at all, but were merely another fad, something fashionable, no different from goldfish swallowing, phonebooth stuffing, the Hula Hoop, or the Nehru jacket. Ah, the Nehru jacket; a collar-less coat worn by Indian Prime Minister Nehru and then promoted as the look of 1967 by fashion designers, and now a laugh-inducing reminder of an earlier, weirder time.

Though few people inside the company wanted to say it out loud, the notion that the channel was a fad had begun to creep into the MTV staff's collective consciousness. This was not the kind of thing the mind accepted easily. Was that really all the past few years had been, just fashion? Worse, could that really be what was in store for them in the future—being stuffed into the back of the cultural closet and trotted out only for some wretched retrospective on how wacky life was in the 1980s? It was too much to believe—that despite all the hype and hoopla, they'd really been nothing more than an eighties version of the goddamned Nehru jacket.

There were other potential explanations for the downturn besides the overly mystical "Our time is done." Namely, that the channel simply had more competition for viewers than ever before. While the explosion of new cable channels had essentially stopped back in 1982, the construction and expansion of cable systems hadn't. The number of 36-channel (as opposed to 12-channel) cable systems had increased dramatically. As a result, when kids flipped the dial, the chances that they'd land on MTV were forever decreasing.

On top of that, the music industry itself had hit a down period. While acts like Michael Jackson and Duran Duran had revved up the business in 1983, and Cyndi Lauper, Bruce Springsteen, Madonna, and

Prince had done the same thing in 1984, no act in the past year had yet caught the country's fancy. Perhaps more significantly, the videos themselves weren't particularly exciting. With few exceptions, they seemed to have deteriorated into nothing but babes and leather and blowing curtains and splashing water.

Plenty of people were upset about video's deterioration. Video director Kevin Godley, half of the team that had made Duran Duran's racy "Girls on Film" and Herbie Hancock's award-winning "Rockit," even commented about it at the recent MTV Awards. "Where once there was imagination and excitement and invention and soul," he said upon receiving an achievement award, "now there is stagnation and overkill." Partly this was because the record companies still considered the clips promotion, not product. Though *Making Michael Jackson's "Thriller"* had sold more than a million home video copies, other attempts to get consumers to buy these clips—to turn them into the pop records of the future, as Michael Nesmith once dreamed—had come up short. Music fans just didn't seem willing to shell out $19.95, or whatever it was the companies were charging. Ironically, one of the reasons for the lack of creativity these days was MTV's own success. As it had grown harder to get a video on the network, record companies had instructed directors to make clips that looked like those that were already on MTV. You didn't want to take a chance on being so out there that you didn't get played.

The final reason for the ratings downturn had to do with the rest of television. MTV had first gone on the air with a look and sound and feel that seemed miles ahead of network television; now TV itself was catching up. The music video style was all over the tube, in commercials, in network graphics, in programs, in coverage of sporting events. And rock and roll, which four years earlier was still something of a corporate taboo, was suddenly becoming more acceptable. Once-staid establishment advertisers like Ford, Del Monte, and Procter & Gamble were now using Beatles tunes and other classic rock and roll songs to sell products. When consumers—baby boomers especially—heard the tunes, their minds jumped back to the glory days of their youth. Advertisers hoped that consumers would associate some of that good feeling with their product.

Not all of the changes directly resulted from MTV. After all, a whole new generation was now making TV. So it wasn't surprising that by the early part of 1986, MTV looked and sounded less distinctive and less interesting. After almost five years of rebelling against traditional television, of sticking a finger in the eye of CBS and the other broadcast networks, of fiercely fighting conformity, no one ever really stopped to ask what may have been the most important question of all in this battle:

What do we do if we win?

* * * * * *

Interestingly, despite the fear of Viacom, the weakening of the virus, and the Nehru jacket complex that had crept into the company, MTV's financial health had never been better. Ad revenues jumped 30 percent in 1985 to $90 million. But with ratings declining, Bob Pittman knew they needed to shake things up on the creative side of the company. The Keeper of the Vision had always been a believer in change for change's sake. It was like putting a new cover on a magazine, he said. You had to do it to keep the channel looking fresh. That was one of the reasons the channel had added shows like *Basement Tapes*, *The Cutting Edge*, and *Top 20 Video Countdown* over the years.

Most recently, they'd made their first foray into episodic TV by airing a British sitcom called *The Young Ones*. A bizarre show about the antics of four housemates in London, the program, shown late Sunday nights, became a real cult hit when it first aired in the fall of 1985.

But with ratings sagging, Pittman believed the channel needed a major facelift, and the man he wanted to perform the surgery was MTV's new general manager, Tom Freston, who years earlier had first discovered the MTV virus in Tulsa. A laid-back, craggy-faced, shaggy-haired forty-year-old, Freston had had an interesting career at the company, as well as an interesting life. He'd grown up in suburban Connecticut, gone off to school at tiny St. Michael's College in Vermont, and earned an MBA at New York University, finishing first in his class. He wasn't really the buttoned-down corporate type, however. He lasted only a year in his first job, as an account executive for the ad agency Benton &

Freston started at WASEC in January of 1980, one month after Bob Pittman. He'd sold his business, he thought cable had tremendous potential, and he loved rock and roll, so when he saw a *Billboard* article in which John Lack talked about the possibility of creating a music video channel, he was extremely interested. He got himself in to see McGroarty and Lack, and they ultimately hired him as the head of marketing for WASEC's eastern region. When MTV was being put together a year later, Freston became head of marketing.

Since then, he'd handled a number of different jobs at the company. In 1982, not long after he'd overseen the early stages of the "I Want My MTV!" campaign, Freston had been shipped over to The Movie Channel to oversee marketing there. He didn't want to leave MTV, but for the good of his career he took the assignment. A year later, when The Movie Channel was merged with Showtime, Pittman and Dom Fioravanti

MTV pioneer Tom Freston. With his down-to-earth irreverence, the one-time import/export company owner was one of the most popular people in the company.

Bowles. The job seemed ridiculous to Freston. He spent most of his time that year working on the Hasbro account, trying to find a way to sell G.I. Joe dolls at a time when much of the country was clamoring for an end to the Vietnam War. When that campaign ended and his bosses asked him to work on the Charmin toilet paper account, Freston decided he'd had enough and spent the next year traveling around the world, supporting himself as a bartender in places like Aspen and Bermuda. Finally, he and a partner formed an import/export clothing company.

brought Freston back to MTV to become marketing vice president. During the summer of 1985, Freston had replaced David Hilton as the top man in the company's sales and marketing division. Pittman's reason for now wanting him as general manager of the flagship channel made complete sense. In addition to having the business and management skills necessary for the job, Freston, un-like either Fioravanti or Hilton before him, was a real rock and roll guy. Not only did he love the music—as a kid he'd listened to everything from Elvis to Dylan to the Beatles to the blues—but he also wasn't afraid to down the tequila with the rest of them now and again. He could frequently be seen out in the clubs of New York, grooving to the latest tunes. Above all, he was a funny, friendly, down-to-earth guy and one of the most popular people at the company. During the early days of WASEC, he was the one person who had actually been able to straddle the wide gulf between Bob McGroarty's business types and Bob Pittman's programmers, and he hadn't lost any of his charm.

Assessing the situation, Freston thought MTV's current problems were fairly simple: It had lost its edge. It had become what you can never afford to be when you're trying to lure a young demographic: stale and predictable. In addition to low ratings, there was some anecdotal evidence to back up this observation. One day around that time, Viacom chief Terry Elkes was at home riding his exercise bike and watching the channel. A few hours later the fifty-one-year-old Elkes went to a meeting and made a major announcement.

"Fellas," Elkes began, "we've got huge problems with MTV. I'm actually starting to like it."

Throughout those first few months of 1986, Bob Pittman, Tom Freston, and the rest of them oversaw what amounted to the reinvention of the channel. They added several new shows and features. Some, like the phone-in request program *Dial MTV*, were designed to get the audience more involved. Others, like the weekly *New Music Hour* and the new alternative show, *120 Minutes*, were signals to both the audience and the record industry that the channel was still committed to breaking new acts and exposing new videos. Finally, still other programs—most especially the old 1960s sitcom *The Monkees*, featuring none other than Michael Nesmith—they threw on just for the hell of it. The rights for that series had recently become

available, and because the price was cheap and they were in the mood to experiment, MTV picked it up. They made quite a fuss over the show, too. For only the second time in their history (the previous summer's Live Aid had been the first), they scrapped the one-video-after-another format for an entire day and presented nothing but Monkees episodes. The result was the highest ratings in a couple of years. Afterward they started showing the program a couple of times per day.

That winter and spring, the channel's programming powers worked to get the veejays out of the studio more. In March, the network broadcast from Florida during spring break; a couple of months later they broadcast from the Montreaux Rock Festival in France, where a number of the rock world's biggest bands were performing. The idea behind all the travel was simple: to take MTV to where the music and the young people were.

Finally, and most significantly, the decision was made that it was time to put some new faces on the air, and in the spring both Nina Blackwood and J. J. Jackson were informed that when their contracts expired in June, they wouldn't be renewed. Neither of the video jocks was totally surprised, as it turned out. As the months had gone by, the role of the veejay seemed to be less and less important. In fact, they weren't even responsible for interviewing artists anymore. When the day finally came for both to sign off, the production crew threw a party for them at a club in New York. Mark Goodman hired a white female stripper for J. J. and a black male stripper for Nina, and they all stayed late and loud and said goodbye. It wasn't easy, though. As Goodman thought to himself that night, it truly felt as if an era was coming to an end.

Morale was lousy. Despite the work everyone there was doing to breathe new life into the channel, a sullenness had descended on the company itself. True, like any other business, MTV had long had its share of bickering and infighting and politicking, but as the rocket was rising an overriding sense of camaraderie had pushed most of the usual troubles to the background and made them seem unimportant. Now, with both their Nehru jacket complex and the frightening prospect of metal desks and linoleum floors bouncing around in their heads, it was the bickering and infighting and politicking that seemed to make up the day. There were all kinds of grievances—some were angry about not being promoted, others about how much stock certain people had received, still others about the channel's direction. About the only thing that seemed to bond them together now was how tired they all were. From the moment the work had begun in pea-soup-colored hotel rooms five years earlier, the pace had never really let up. It was so grueling that some of them had started comparing MTV years to dog years—you had to multiply everything by seven to get an accurate read on what it took out of you.

Marci Brafman, who in that early morning cab ride five years earlier had made the decision to see where this adventure might lead her, was one who really felt ground down. It just wasn't fun to come to work anymore. Things got so bad that one day she actually went to Bob Pittman and told him she was thinking about quitting. "Please don't leave yet," the Keeper of the Vision told her. "This isn't a good time to go. I'll tell you when you can leave."

As the summer came, changes at the network continued. In addition to sending veejays out of the studio more—covering things like the star-studded Amnesty International show and Liberty Weekend

in New York Harbor—the first new veejay, Downtown Julie Brown, made her debut on the channel. A flamboyant, twenty-something Brit, she'd been a dancer on the BBC's *Top of the Pops* and a veejay on a British music video network called Music Box, which was where the MTV crew had spotted her. Along with handling the 8:00 A.M. to 1:00 P.M. shift, she was now also the host of another of the channel's new shows, *The MTV International Video Hour*.

To keep viewers interested, Tom Freston and the folks in the promotion department also tried to make the contests bigger and more outrageous than ever. In the spring, for example, the channel that had started by giving away One-Night Stand trips to concerts, moved on to home entertainment equipment, and trips, and even a house, decided to give away an entire town—MTV Town, they called it. The winner, to be announced at the end of the year, would actually receive a few hundred acres the network had bought near Shamrock, Texas (as it turned out, the winner opted for the cash equivalent—$300,000). That summer, the network also did a promotion with musician Prince. To create publicity for his new movie, *Under the Cherry Moon*, the rock star/actor/director agreed to premiere the film and also play a concert in the hometown of some lucky MTV viewer. And where did the winner turn out to be from? New York? Chicago? Los Angeles? Try Sheridan, Wyoming. In the middle of July the cast and crew of the movie, the executives from the movie studio, several dozen MTV staffers, and Prince's sizable band and entourage descended on Sheridan, population forty thousand. It was lunacy. As if the culture shock weren't bad enough, it turned out there wasn't really any place to have a concert. Ultimately, they ended up putting it on in the ballroom of the local Holiday Inn, where

As part of a typically outrageous MTV contest, the artist then known as Prince performed in Sheridan, Wyoming for the opening of his film "Under the Cherry Moon."

the ceiling seemed to be about six feet high. At one point Prince said he wasn't going to do the show, although he finally changed his mind and performed. The young winner was so excited that all she could say was, "It was better-er than I thought it would be."

Were any of these high jinks and programming changes making a difference? A small one, yes. During the second quarter of the year, MTV's Nielsens edged up from .6 to .7. And just as it had throughout 1983 and 1984, the network proved it could still break artists—sort of. The biggest MTV success story that year was . . . *The Monkees*. Thanks to the channel's rebroadcast of the show, records by the group, which had disbanded in the late 1960s, were flying out of the record stores. There was so much interest in them, in fact, that three of the four original members regrouped for a successful concert tour that summer. Ironically, the only one missing was Michael Nesmith, who was already committed to producing a movie.

fits. Maybe worse than that, two of the biggest acts in music, Van Halen and Journey, released albums that spring but decided not to make videos. While the strategy didn't work out for Journey—when their album stiffed they actually did shoot a clip—the lack of exposure on MTV certainly didn't hurt Van Halen. Their album, *5150*, spent several weeks at the top of the charts.

The press, too, had taken a new view of the channel over the previous months. Thanks to MTV's low ratings and programming changes, a round of what could only be called "falling star" stories began to appear—ironically in some of the same publications that had helped the MTV rocket get off the launching pad years earlier. *Forbes* and *Business Week* both ran pieces talking about the troubles the channel was facing, while the *New York Times* slammed the network as being "the ultimate in pseudo-hip." Although Bob Pittman and Tom Freston did what they could to mitigate the damage,

Years after providing the idea for MTV, music video pioneer Michael Nesmith (far right) played another key role. Rebroadcasts of *The Monkees* gave some life to MTV's sagging ratings.

Despite the small successes, the downward spin they were in had a momentum all its own. The attitude toward MTV among people in the record industry had also started to change in the last several months. Back in the spring Al Teller, the president of CBS Records, announced that his label was cutting back on the number of clips they were making. The cost had simply begun to outweigh the bene-

they weren't optimistic. As *Business Week* asked ominously: "How many teenagers still want their MTV?"

The lack of any new musical breakthroughs, the record industry's changing attitude, and the hostile tone of the press made morale even worse as the summer of 1986 wore on. It got so bad that in July, John Sykes, who in six years had risen from an enthusiastic puppy dog of a staffer to senior vice president of programming, announced he was leaving the company to join superagent Michael Ovitz's Creative Artists Agency.

That same summer, Marci Brafman went in to see Bob Pittman for a second time. She'd tried, she told him, but she was still terribly unhappy.

"Okay," the Keeper of the Vision said, as if everything had changed, "you can leave now."

*   *   *   *   *   *

As the months went by, Bob Pittman seemed to have settled into the job of MTV Networks's chief executive officer. In addition to trying to revive and reinvent MTV, he was also doing what he could to help the company grow. Much of his time was being spent on expanding MTV around the world. The channel had already done one international deal: In 1984 the Japanese broadcasting company Asahi began showing four hours per week of MTV. But the biggest market for MTV outside the United States was obviously Europe, and over the past couple of years Pittman and others in the company had tried to get the channel going over there. At one point, they were close to doing a deal with Richard Branson, the Englishman who owned Virgin Airlines and Virgin Records, to become a partner in his London-based video network, Music Box. But talks fell through, and so more recently, some people at Viacom had started discussions with British publishing giant Robert Maxwell, and it now looked like they were close to completing a deal.

Despite losing the LBO bid, Bob Pittman's reputation hadn't suffered at all. He received the White House Conference on Small Business Award for Entrepreneurial Excellence, and that summer he

was invited to Washington and honored by President Reagan at a small White House reception. And it wasn't only presidents who were high on Pittman. While the press may have soured on MTV, it remained in Pittman's camp. *Esquire* included Pittman in a special issue it called "America's New Leadership: Men and Women Under Forty Who Are Changing the Nation." Calling the decision to put MTV on the air "brilliant," the story noted that the company was now worth more than $600 million. "And remember," the magazine added, without a word about John Lack or anyone else, "Bob Pittman thought it all up."

Despite the invigorating challenge of growing the business and the continued praise he was receiving, Pittman (who'd made $2.3 million from his MTV stock options when the company was sold) seemed to be suffering from the same malaise as many of his colleagues. His heart just didn't seem to be in it anymore. Partly it was because of losing the LBO—after all, if he and Horowitz and the Forstmann group had pulled it off they would have been extraordinarily wealthy men. The plan all along was to buy the company, batten down the hatches for a few years to reduce the debt, and then take the company public again, at which point they would all have been worth tens if not hundreds of millions of dollars. But it wasn't only the lost money that seemed to weigh on the Keeper of the Vision now; he just didn't feel stimulated by the network anymore. One night, when he was out to dinner with Irving Azoff of MCA Records, Pittman started telling Azoff that he really wasn't sure what he wanted to do. Azoff mentioned that Sid Sheinberg, the president of MCA Inc., would love to have Pittman working for him, and he suggested that the two meet.

So Pittman and Sheinberg did just that. And it turned into a real let-your-hair-down kind of lunch for Pittman. He told Sheinberg that this LBO experience had really opened his eyes to a whole other side of business, the deal-making side, the buying and selling of companies. He said that what he really wanted to do was go out and buy a company, because having gone through the experience once, he realized what you could do to make a lot of sure money—you could buy a company that was already doing well and then just wait for it to grow some more. Sheinberg listened to him that day, and a week or so later he and Lew Wasserman, the chairman of MCA, came to Pittman's apartment in Manhattan. They had a deal for him, they said. They wanted to finance a company that would do whatever it was Pittman wanted to do. MCA would own one half, Pittman the other. He could take out a salary commensurate with what he was making now.

Pittman knew it was a hell of an offer—the freedom to pursue whatever it was he wanted to pursue. Finally, after mulling over the opportunity Sheinberg and Wasserman had just presented him with and the frustration he felt at MTV, he told them he'd do it—assuming he could get out of his contract with Viacom.

By the time Pittman sat down to hash things out with Viacom's Terry Elkes, Elkes had already heard about the Keeper of the Vision's negotiations with MCA, and he wasn't happy about it. Given the deal Pittman had signed just eight months earlier with Viacom, Elkes wanted to know what Pittman wanted. More money? Pittman told him he didn't want anything. Elkes responded by telling him that Viacom wasn't going to let him out of his contract.

As talks between the men continued, the Keeper of the Vision told Elkes flat out that he was leaving—whether Elkes let him go to MCA

or not. He assured Elkes that he wasn't going to start another MTV, and even offered to be a free consultant for him forever.

Elkes understood there really wasn't much he could do about it. While he might be able to stop Pittman from going to work for some other company, he couldn't force him to work for Viacom—contract or no contract. In the end, all sides managed to work out a deal. Pittman had to return the signing bonus that Viacom had given him back in December, cut Viacom in for a small piece of the action on this new company, and sign a commitment not to raid any of MTV's employees for six years. On August 7, six days after MTV's fifth birthday, the official announcement came: Bob Pittman was leaving the company.

Inside 1775 Broadway the reaction was mixed. Some believed the company was now doomed. Pittman had been the man, after all, the Keeper of the Vision. But others saw this as an opportunity to advance in the company themselves. In any event, hardly anybody was totally shocked. Ever since the LBO had failed, Pittman just hadn't seemed very interested.

The Keeper of the Vision stayed on through a brief transition period, and finally left the company during the fall. Shortly before he did, MTV threw a huge going-away party for him at a restaurant in Manhattan, where they all got loud and drank plenty of tequila and smashed plenty of glasses. It seemed like the rock and roll thing to do.

That same fall, Pittman spent a day talking with Larry Tisch, the financier who earlier in the year had bought CBS. The Tiffany Network, like ABC and NBC, was struggling a bit these days, since the combination of cable and the VCR had cut into its audience. Tisch was looking for some new ideas on programming, so his son Tommy, a friend of Pittman's, had suggested that the two of them get together. When the two men met one weekend at Tisch's home in Rye, New York, Pittman told the new head of CBS all about the theory of mood and emotion and the TV babies and how this new generation was different from the one that had come before it. Tisch was impressed by what he heard. He liked Pittman's ideas and fresh approach, so he offered him a job at CBS.

Here he was, being offered a job in broadcast television—the very thing he and the rest of the pioneers had been rebelling against all these years. Hell, as far as Pittman could tell, Tisch might actually have been offering him Jack Schneider's old job, head of the CBS broadcast group. He politely declined. He told Tisch he wanted to remain an entrepreneur.

Of course, had Larry Tisch known Bob Pittman better, he probably wouldn't have even bothered offering. After all, once you'd loaded up the wagon and traveled out to the frontier and built something like Bob Pittman had, going back to civilization just wasn't in your bones anymore.

ELEVEN
THE TWO KINGS OF SPARTA

FALL 1986 — SUMMER 1987

The changes in MTV's programming continued through the late summer and early fall of 1986. To coincide with their its birthday that August, the channel did a series of pieces called "Amuck in America." The concept was to send veejay Alan Hunter, executive producer Julian Goldberg, and a small crew on a trip across the country to see how many weird, wild things they could come across. They came across plenty of them, as it turned out—twelve stories a day, featuring everything from a house made out of beer cans to a mountain of snow in Las Vegas to a dinner at Aretha Franklin's house in Detroit, where the Queen of Soul made chicken Italiano for the gang and then sat at her piano and played a few songs.

As the programming crew searched for ways to breathe some fire into the MTV pipeline and to recapture some of the energy—and ratings—of the early days, the business side of the company was cruising along without a hitch. Ad sales had never been better. Given the sorry state of the Nielsen numbers, how could this be? Partly it was due to MTV's size. Even if the ratings were below what they'd once been, the channel's distribution continued to grow—they were now in thirty million homes—the total number of people seeing the channel hadn't dropped. Inertia, too, was a big factor. Just as the advertising community had been slow to attach itself to the MTV rocket when it was ascending to the heavens, now, as the channel poised for atmospheric reentry, the decision makers on Madison Avenue were slow to leap off.

And as things worked out, MTV's continued success on the ad front played a big part in picking a successor to Bob Pittman as the head of MTV Networks. Pittman's own choice was Tom Freston, whom he'd always liked and who had continued to impress him during his tenure as general manager of the channel. Freston was smart, popular, understood business, and, perhaps most important, he understood the irreverent spirit of MTV itself. The problem was that if they picked Freston over Bob Roganti, the head of ad sales, Roganti would be pissed off, and no one at Viacom felt they could afford to do that. Not only was sales the one part of the company that was doing well, but, because of the way Roganti operated, no one else in the company really understood how things worked there. Roganti hadn't even anointed a clear number two man who could take over if he did leave. Finally, the Viacom guys suggested that Freston and Roganti be made co-presidents. Having already clashed with Elkes on being let out of his Viacom contract, and wanting to get out of the company as quickly as possible, Pittman endorsed the idea. In mid-September it was announced that MTV Networks was being split into two divisions, with a different president for each: Tom Freston would run MTV Entertainment and oversee programming, marketing, and distribution; Bob Roganti would run MTV Operations and supervise advertising sales and research. Neither would have the title chief executive officer.

The two men couldn't have been more different. Freston was warm and outgoing, a stylishly dressed, hip guy who never looked like he was hustling—even when he was. Roganti was a sunglass-wearing, street-

wise tough guy few people in the company really knew and even fewer understood. The Prince of Darkness, some called him, and to most he was an enigma. This was even true among the people who worked directly under him. While they all respected his intelligence, many also thought he tried to intimidate and manipulate those around him.

The two men's attitudes toward the company weren't alike, either. While Freston thought MTV Networks, despite whatever troubles it was experiencing, had tremendous potential for growth, Roganti appeared to see MTV as a successful scam that wasn't likely to last much longer. In fact, Tom Freston would later remember, shortly after being named co-president, that Roganti suggested shutting down VH-1, which wasn't doing very well with either viewers or advertisers. "It'll make our lives easier," Roganti said. They didn't.

Finally, there were differences in the two men's approaches to the whole idea of a co-presidency. If only because he understood little about ad sales, Freston really believed such an arrangement could succeed, assuming the two of them worked together. But Roganti? The former political science instructor and student of power was far more skeptical about the future of this partnership. He remembered the ancient story of the two brothers who became co-kings of Sparta. The result?

One killed the other.

*   *   *   *   *   *

As it soon became clear, there was an important reason that Viacom's Terry Elkes had fought so hard to keep Bob Pittman around, a reason that, when it was revealed, even the Keeper of the Vision could understand and appreciate: Elkes and the other top management of Viacom were planning an LBO of their own.

Viacom had long been an inviting takeover target. The previous December, several investors had bought up large amounts of stock, and, though it never came about, for a brief period there was speculation that one of them was going to take a run at the company. Something similar happened several months later with well-known Wall Street corporate raider Carl Icahn. Icahn began purchasing shares of Viacom in the spring, eventually acquiring nearly 17 percent of the company. After considering an offer to merge with Icahn's group, the Viacom board ultimately decided to buy Icahn out.

Afterward, Elkes and the other executives at the company—Terry and the Pirates, some at MTV had started to call them now—began looking seriously at the possibility of buying the communications conglomerate themselves. LBO fever was as hot as ever, and they certainly believed in Viacom's growth potential. In mid-September, just a month after Bob Pittman announced he was

one whose most visible holding was a rock and roll cable network aimed at young people. But the man had certainly lived an interesting life. A native of Boston, he had graduated from Harvard in two and a half years and was then chosen for an elite intelligence team that broke Japanese codes during World War II. After the war he moved on to Harvard Law School and then to the Justice Department, before returning to Massachusetts to run his family's chain of drive-in movie theaters. Under his stewardship, National Amusements grew into one of the most successful movie theater outfits in the world, in large part because of its leadership in building multiplexes all over the country.

A tall man with a quick smile and a thick Boston accent, Redstone was in many respects a quintessential New Englander—an unassuming, frugal sort who, despite a personal net worth in the millions, still lived in a three-bedroom house outside Boston.

pg 157

Bob Roganti, sans his customary dark glasses. The former political science professor, dubbed "The Prince of Darkness" inside MTV, led the company's sales group to new heights.

leaving MTV, the group and its financial backers made an offer of $2.7 billion for Viacom. Finally, on October 17, the board accepted in principle Terry and the Pirates' offer to buy the company.

Except that it wasn't that easy. Not all of Viacom's stockholders were pleased with the deal, and perhaps the loudest of the holdouts was a sixty-three-year-old New Englander named Sumner Redstone. The chairman of National Amusements, a Massachusetts-based movie theater company, the white-haired Redstone was hardly the most likely suitor for a growing entertainment conglomerate, especially

Redstone and National Amusements had first bought stock in Viacom more than a year earlier, in the summer of 1985. At that point, Redstone was solely making an investment, much as he'd done in previous years with various Hollywood movie studios (at one point his outfit owned nearly 10 percent of Columbia Pictures). As he began doing more investigating and talking to people about where the media in general were headed, Redstone began to believe that cable television—in particular the kind of holdings that Viacom had—was really the flip side of the already mature theater business. As a result, Viacom management's offer for the company seemed far too low to him, and he blocked it.

By early December, Redstone and National Amusements had increased their interest in Viacom to nearly 19 percent. Still, Redstone was unsure about whether he wanted to make a run at the company himself, at least partly because Elkes and the rest of Viacom's management were denying him access to much of the corporation's financial information. Redstone's broker, Danny Tisch, suggested that he talk to none other than Bob Pittman about the company. Although Pittman had spent less than a year working for Viacom, he would undoubtedly be able to offer information about MTV Networks. By this point, Pittman was well on his way to launching his new company, which he was calling Quantum Media. With MCA's backing, his hope was to make Quantum into a powerhouse entertainment conglomerate geared toward the under-forty audience. When Redstone called, Pittman said he would be more than happy to get together with him. Pittman saw it as a way of getting revenge against Terry Elkes for making it so difficult for him to get out of his Viacom contract the summer before. Sometime that winter, he and Redstone met at Redstone's suite in the Hotel Carlyle in New York, with Redstone complaining how little information Viacom was giving him and Pittman offering his insights into the company. A week or so later they met again. This time Redstone said that Elkes and his team had threatened to resign if he tried to buy the company. Since Redstone himself wasn't knowledgeable enough about Viacom's businesses to run the operation on his own, he was obviously concerned.

Pittman suggested that Redstone talk privately with MTV Entertainment head Tom Freston and Nickelodeon chief Gerry Laybourne.

They and MTV Networks were the future of the company, Pittman told him. If Redstone had them on his side, the rest of the guys could walk. Pittman even said he'd set up the meeting for him, an offer that Redstone accepted. Pittman went downstairs to a pay phone in the lobby of the Carlyle, called Freston, and told him he really ought to have dinner with Redstone.

"I can't do that," Freston told him. "If the Viacom guys found out, they'd fire me."

"Listen, if Redstone comes in and you're the one who pledged his loyalty early, MTV is going to have a special place in his heart," Pittman said. "Elkes and those fellows aren't bad guys, but they're never going to let you on the inside, they're never going to be good for MTV because they don't understand the creative process." He paused.

"Tom," Pittman said finally, "those guys don't love MTV like we do."

* * * * * *

As the months went by, the feelings inside MTV toward Terry and the Pirates hadn't gotten any warmer. Elkes and his crew hadn't necessarily done very much to bring about such ill will. They were so preoccupied with the LBO that they'd all but ignored MTV. Still, the harsh feelings remained and actually increased as the MTV staff speculated how tight things would be financially if the management group actually succeeded in the LBO.

As a result, when Tom Freston and Gerry Laybourne went over to the Carlyle to meet with Redstone, they were quick not only to lay out their vision of the company but also to offer their support and encouragement. Redstone, in turn, inspired the two of them with his vision of how the company might be able to grow. The meeting went so well that Freston told Redstone he should come over to MTV's offices some day to get a feel for the place.

He showed up the next day. It was quite a sight—the sixty-three-year-old New Englander walking around the MTV offices, which, despite the blue mood in the company, had as much college dorm lunacy as ever. The youthful, rock and roll energy of the place knocked him out. If he hadn't made up his mind by that point, within a couple of days he was sure he wanted to buy the company.

On February 2, Redstone and his backers officially made an offer for Viacom. Unfortunately, the Viacom board decided the offer was no better than that presented by Elkes and the management team. Over the next several weeks Redstone and his group modified their proposal several times, with the management team making counter-offers each time. Finally, on March 3, the board met to evaluate the two most recent—and, as it turned out, final—offers from both sides. At daybreak the following morning, after sixteen hours of debate and negotiation, the board took a show of hands. Redstone's offer of nearly $3.4 billion was accepted.

What did he have planned for the company? "The next step is sleep," Redstone told reporters as he walked wearily out of the meeting that morning. "The next step after that is to play tennis. Then I'll go to work."

* * * * * *

By the time Sumner Redstone bought the company, it was clear that the relationship between the two kings of Sparta, Tom Freston and Bob Roganti, wasn't going very well. More accurately, it wasn't going at all. Though their offices were near each other, Freston and Roganti hardly spoke. Roganti, who'd never kept normal office hours,

now sometimes didn't come in at all. What's more, in the months that they'd been running the company together, the two men had no more than a few meetings.

Below them, life inside the company was just as unsettled. With Bob Pittman gone and the channel fading and much of the fun having disappeared, many of the original pioneers had left. Executive producer Julian Goldberg had resigned, for example, while "I Want My MTV!" campaign guru Dale Pon was no longer doing the channel's ads (he was replaced, ironically, by Fred/Alan, Fred Seibert and Alan Goodman's company). Finally, the legendary Les Garland had left the company, as well. Garland's contract had expired at the end of 1986, and despite Tom Freston offering him a great new deal, Garland, who'd been such a key part of MTV's relationship with the music industry, decided it was time to move on. Like the rest, he was just tired of the grind. Moreover, Pittman had made a place for Les in his new company. At the end of 1986 he left MTV and three months later officially joined Quantum Media as the head of the company's new record label, QMI Music.

This turnover wasn't all bad—at least not from the perspective of the pioneers' replacements, who saw all this change as a wonderful opportunity. The new general manager of the channel was Lee Masters, the same guy who, nine years earlier, had been Bob Pittman's co-host on *Album Tracks*, the late-night music video show Pittman had done at NBC. An easygoing, affable thirty-five-year-old with curly brown hair and a beard, Masters was another of those people who'd gotten hooked on radio as a teenager, starting his deejay career at a small station in his hometown of Doylestown, Pennsylvania, just outside of Philadelphia. From there he went on to be a deejay in various markets around the country—including a two-year stint with Pittman at WNBC in New York—before getting into station ownership and management. Pittman had brought him into the company in the spring of 1986 to be general manager of struggling VH-1.

Masters made a name for himself quickly. A few weeks after he started, the company had a retreat at a resort in the Caribbean. Unlike the gathering at Arrowood years earlier, this turned out to be a pretty crazy time. One night, a bunch of them were drinking flaming shots of tequila—blowing out the flame and then drinking the shot. Masters announced that he was going to show them how to really drink a flaming shooter. Unfortunately, he hadn't counted on a few things. First, it had been some time since he'd actually done a flaming shot. Second, the glasses they were drinking out of were wider than typical shot glasses. Third, he had a beard. He set his glass of tequila on fire,

"Are you kidding?" Pittman told him. "You're already a legend."

After Tom Freston ascended to the post of company co-president in September, Masters became general manager of both VH-1 and MTV, and he continued tinkering with the MTV's programming. While many of the adjustments he made were old radio tricks—simplifying the rotation schedule, instituting forced-viewing contests, toying with the station's clock (i.e., changing when they played commercials, station IDs, and so forth)—the biggest change he made was musical. He decided that the channel had strayed too far from its cutting edge, rock and roll roots—it was now much closer to a Top-40 format—so near the end of the year they tried switching back to more straight-ahead rock.

The effect of all these adjustments was practically nil. Out there in America, in the paneled family rooms, the video virus was now so weak that by the second quarter of 1987 the ratings had dropped back down to

Despite the difficulty he had downing flaming shots of tequila, Lee Masters (sans his post-nasal fire hazard), was crucial to the MTV's rebirth in the late 1980s.

picked it up, and threw it back into his mouth. Except that not all of it went into his mouth. He was standing there smugly, proud of showing these cowards how real men drink tequila, when all of a sudden he noticed that people were staring at him and pointing. His beard was on fire! He quickly smothered the flames, but he was really embarrassed. The next day, he was talking to Bob Pittman on the phone, and he started to apologize.

"I'm really sorry," he told Pittman. "You bring your old friend in here to work and I embarrass you by setting my face on fire."

.6. In addition, the record industry's love affair with video clearly looked like it was coming to an end. Despite the channel's strong effect on rock careers—rockers Bon Jovi and Poison were a couple of the latest success stories—the industry was cutting back on the number of clips it was making and the amount it was willing to sink into each one.

It was no longer just Tom Freston's side of the company that was struggling. By now, the late spring of 1987, the slump had finally begun to effect Bob Roganti's side of MTV as well. With the ratings off, the ad community had begun to back away from the channel; in the first half of the year, ad revenues actually dropped 10 percent from the previous year.

Not surprisingly, all of these troubles were more ammunition for the ever-increasing number of falling star stories that were now appearing in the press. Things had gotten so bad that at the end of June that even *Time*, the publication that just three and a half years earlier had proclaimed the arrival of the video age, wondered whether the dream was over. The magazine asked ominously, "Is MTV an idea whose time has already gone?"

* * * * * *

About the only bright spot that long, sad summer was the launch of the company's first full-fledged, twenty-four-hour-a-day foreign affiliate, MTV Europe. Back in the fall, Viacom had completed a deal with colorful British media mogul Robert Maxwell and another company called British Telecom. Under the agreement, Maxwell and British Telecom would put up all the cash in exchange for 75 percent of MTV Europe's stock, while Viacom would supply the MTV name and management expertise in exchange for the remaining 25 percent. The press conference announcing the deal, held in London, was a real hoot. Maxwell, a physically large man and a truly eccentric character, was there, as were Viacom's Terry Elkes and MTV's Mark Booth, a young one-time affiliate sales guy who was going to be the managing director of the new venture. First, throughout the press conference Maxwell kept referring to Elkes as *Elkeez*. Even better was the way the Englishman handled the questions the press fired at them. At one point, a reporter asked when the channel was likely to turn a profit. Mark Booth, doing the usual businessman's tap dance, told him that

it was hard to tell, given the nature of the business and the advertising climate, and all the unknowns in this sort of venture, not to mention. . . .

"Next year," Maxwell interrupted. "The channel will be profitable next year."

When the press conference was over, Terry Elkes looked at Booth and said, "Can you believe this guy? This is our *partner*."

For Mark Booth, one of the original pioneers, the chance to run this new venture really looked like a hell of an opportunity. A native of Lawrence, Kansas, the twenty-nine-year-old Booth had joined WASEC back in 1980 in affiliate sales, and over the years he had worked his way up the company ladder, eventually becoming the head of MTV's national sales division. When Bob Pittman and Tom Freston approached him the summer before about becoming involved in the European venture, he jumped at the chance. Not only was it an opportunity to move to London, where the new channel would be headquartered, but it was also a chance to be involved with a start-up all over again, this time at the top instead of the bottom. And so, near the end of 1986, Booth and a small team of MTV staff members flew over to London to set up shop in a small old house they were going to use as offices.

There were two options when it came to programming for MTV Europe. One was simply to take the American channel's signal and send it all over Europe—the approach that Ted Turner was taking internationally with CNN. The other option was to create an entirely new network, one that played music videos but was geared specifically for the European audience. For a variety of reasons, everyone involved decided the latter option was preferable. To begin with, musical tastes in Europe were different from those in America. While certain artists were big practically everywhere—Michael Jackson, Madonna, and Phil Collins, to name a few—there were many European favorites that Americans had never heard of and that American MTV never played. On top of that, the channel's personality had to be different. Because attitude had always been such an important part of the channel—from the promos to the veejays to the station IDs—it was clear that MTV Europe *had* to have a European flavor.

In launching the channel, Booth and the rest of them faced many of the same obstacles that Jack Schneider, John Lack, Bob McGroarty, and Bob Pittman had faced six years earlier. First, there was the difficulty of getting distribution. Like America in the early 1980s, Europe was just now beginning to be wired for cable TV. The only difference was that in Europe many of the cable systems were controlled by the government, which meant that instead of dealing with entrepreneurial pole climbers when trying to get distribution, Booth and his troops were often dealing with government bureaucrats. Then there was the difficulty of advertising sales. The biggest hurdle there was the fact that there had never really been a successful TV service that covered all of Europe before. Consequently, there wasn't a pan-European advertising market. Even big companies like Coca-Cola, Pepsi, and Levi's had separate budgets for each country in Europe, which meant that in order to put a spot on the new music service, a couple of dozen people had to sign off on it. Finally, there was the job of getting cooperation from the European record companies. Once again, just as had been the case in America six years before, the issue was payment. All the European labels were represented by an organization called the Video Performance League (VPL), which controlled

where the clips could be shown. The VPL was tough to deal with, too. At one point it looked like the channel wasn't even going to get off the ground; that's how bad relations were. After all, the record industry didn't think it needed MTV Europe; it already had ways of exposing artists. Ultimately, each side gave a little and an agreement was worked out.

On August 1, six years to the day after MTV had gone on the air in America, MTV Europe launched, with a total of 1.6 million subscribers in fourteen countries. The launch date and low subscriber count were about all the new channel's debut had in common with that of the original MTV, however. First of all, instead of getting a couple of buses and having the staff schlepped out to some lousy bar, as the American pioneers had done, the company chartered two 727s and flew a bunch of music industry types, advertisers, cable operators, press, and staffers to a huge, million-dollar bash at a club in Amsterdam. There were nude women with gold body paint walking around, and rocker Elton John threw the switch that actually launched the channel. The first clip was Dire Straits's "Money for Nothing," with its now-fulfilled pleas of "I want my MTV." More significant was what the service chose to play for its second clip—a video by an artist named Alexander O'Neill, who was black.

Nobody wanted to go through all that again.

* * * * * *

Though chief executive officer Terry Elkes and his management team had battled Sumner Redstone vigorously for control of Viacom, the new owner had initially remained open to the idea of Elkes and his team remaining at the company. But as the weeks went by that spring and summer, it became clear to both sides that it wasn't going

THE TWO KINGS OF SPARTA

to work out. Elkes and the rest were obviously disappointed that they hadn't gotten the company, and Redstone felt as though management still wasn't sharing information with him. Finally, in late July, Redstone hired an executive named Frank Biondi to become the new chief executive officer of Viacom. Biondi, forty-six, had most recently been head of Coca-Cola's entertainment division, and before that had been president of HBO.

Several days after the launch of MTV Europe, MTV Entertainment head Tom Freston was back in New York and received a call from Biondi. The new Viacom chief said he wanted to meet for breakfast the following morning at the Hotel Dorset. The next day, not really knowing what to expect, Freston walked in and sat down, and the two men started to talk.

"Having two guys running things at MTV just isn't working out," Biondi told him. "So we're going to make you CEO at MTV."

To Redstone and Biondi, it was clear that they needed one person to run the company, and given all the changes that had taken place at MTV already, they knew it would be better to stick with one of the two they already had. Freston seemed to be the better man.

"What about Roganti?" Freston asked.

"Do whatever you want," Biondi told him.

The meeting lasted about twenty minutes, and when it was over Freston walked back to the MTV offices a few blocks away and went directly to see Bob Roganti, not even bothering to stop in his own office. Sitting there behind his desk, a pair of dark glasses covering his eyes, the Prince of Darkness looked up at Freston.

"It's not working out," Freston said. Then he fired him.

The new, lone king of Sparta walked back into his office and sat down. He was the victor. Although just what he'd won was open to debate. After all, given MTV's sorry ratings and falling ad revenue, he had to wonder if he'd just been made president and chief executive officer of the world's biggest Nehru jacket manufacturer.

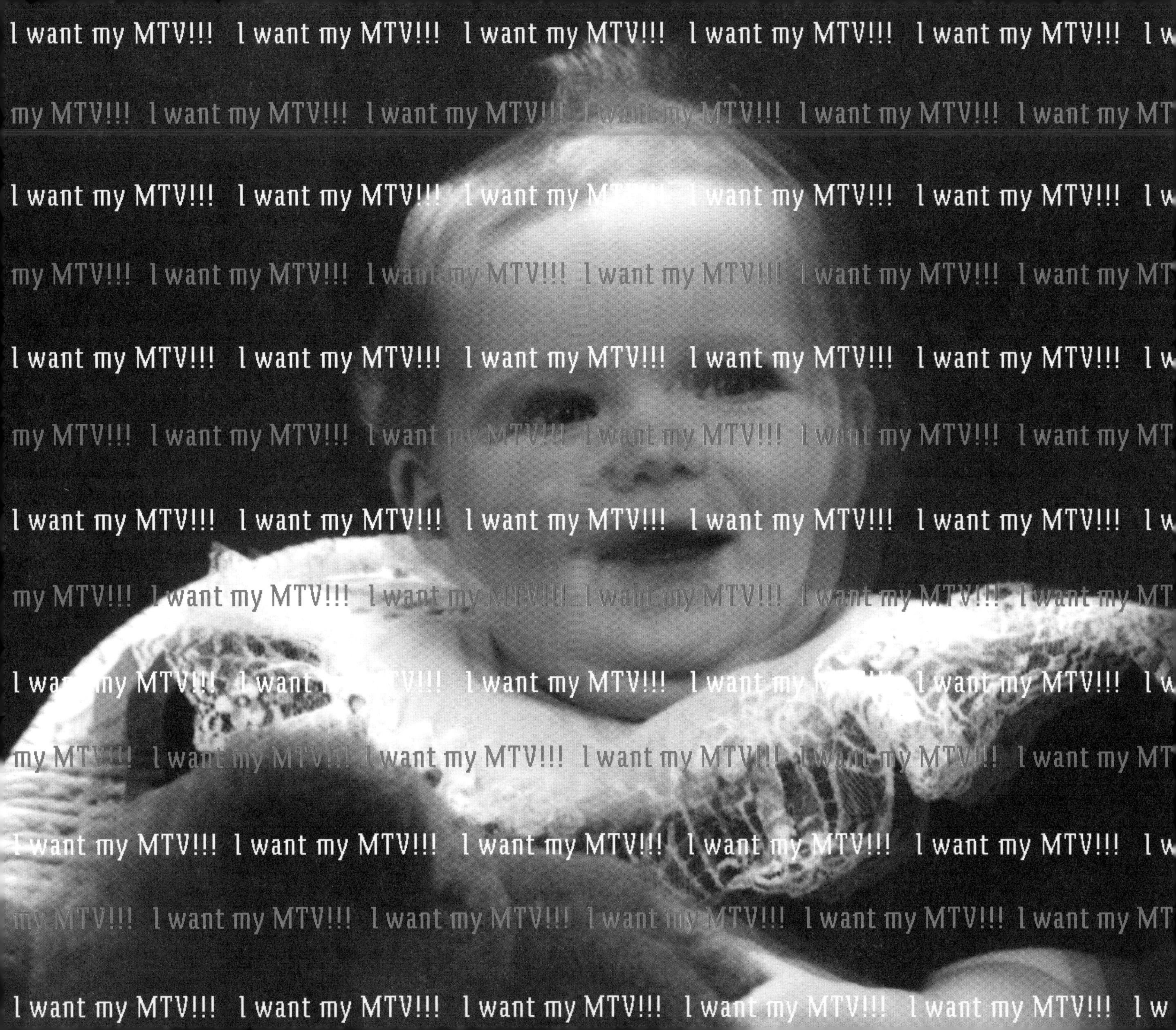
I want my MTV!!! I want my MTV!!! I want my MTV!!! I want my MTV!!! I want my MTV!!!
I want my MTV!!! I want my MTV!!! I want my MTV!!! I want my MTV!!!
I want my MTV!!! I want my MTV!!! I want my MTV!!! I want my MTV!!! I want my MTV!!!
I want my MTV!!! I want my MTV!!! I want my MTV!!! I want my MTV!!!
I want my MTV!!! I want my MTV!!! I want my MTV!!! I want my MTV!!! I want my MTV!!!
I want my MTV!!! I want my MTV!!! I want my MTV!!! I want my MTV!!!
I want my MTV!!! I want my MTV!!! I want my MTV!!! I want my MTV!!! I want my MTV!!!
I want my MTV!!! I want my MTV!!! I want my MTV!!! I want my MTV!!!
I want my MTV!!! I want my MTV!!! I want my MTV!!! I want my MTV!!! I want my MTV!!!
I want my MTV!!! I want my MTV!!! I want my MTV!!! I want my MTV!!!
I want my MTV!!! I want my MTV!!! I want my MTV!!! I want my MTV!!! I want my MTV!!!
I want my MTV!!! I want my MTV!!! I want my MTV!!! I want my MTV!!!
I want my MTV!!! I want my MTV!!! I want my MTV!!! I want my MTV!!! I want my MTV!!!

TWELVE

THE SECOND GENERATION

I f there was any irony in MTV's fall from grace, it lay in how much its one-time comrades-in-arms in the battle against the status quo were now thriving. Eight years earlier, when Jack Schneider and John Lack had first set out for the cable frontier, the industry was a raw and rugged place (at least in comparison to network TV), filled with more risk and adventure than most at CBS or ABC or NBC could have imagined. But the explosion of new networks had ended back in 1982, and whereas cable itself still stood in the shadow of the broadcast networks when it came to revenue, that shadow became smaller every day. Not only were services like HBO and CNN and ESPN now firmly entrenched in the communications landscape, but the wiring of America had continued without a hitch. Indeed, by now, the late summer of 1987, in what must have seemed incredible to early cable men like John Walson, cable's penetration rate exceeded 50 percent—more than half the television homes in America were wired for cable. All of this had transformed the nature and feeling of the business. Most of the pole climbers who'd started the industry were now either dead or spending their time on golf courses somewhere, contentedly counting the cash they'd made when behemoths like TCI and ATC bought them out during the early and mid-1980s. Replacing them were more and more business school types, guys who knew all there was to know about debt/equity ratios and earnings quotients and strategic planning, even if they couldn't have told you word one about how to string coaxial cable.

It wasn't only cable that was thriving. By now, rock and roll's place in the world had changed as well; corporate America had embraced it. Hardly any major act did a concert tour without a corporate sponsor, and the number of pop stars doing commercials had absolutely exploded ever since Michael Jackson and his brothers had filmed their first Pepsi spots back in 1984. Over the past few years, everyone from Eric Clapton to Lionel Richie to Whitney Houston had peddled one product or another. Although there had been outrage in the serious rock community about such commercial tie-ins, you couldn't really blame the companies for using these folks. More than ever before, rock and roll was the music of the culture—the music with which most consumers identified.

The final irony in MTV's downturn lay in what had happened to the company itself. It was unrecognizable from the earliest days of what was now WASEC; nearly 675 people were now employed at MTV Networks. And despite the falling star stories and the staff's Nehru jacket complex, there was still a certain power and cachet that came with working at the channel—a power and cachet that the early pioneers could only have dreamed about. While people like Nina Blackwood had practically needed to be wrestled into taking a job at MTV, these days working there had become a career goal for many people.

By the time Tom Freston took over as chief executive officer that August, a new era was clearly underway inside the company, and evidence of it started at the very top. Although he was Bob Pittman's hand-picked successor, in the past year Freston had proved he was no carbon copy of the Keeper of the Vision. Whereas Pittman had always exuded an aura of power and an air of mystery, Freston was far more down-to-earth and approachable, less the almighty emperor of MTV than the friendly fellow down the hall who just happened to be running this multi-million-dollar corporation. His own attitude toward managing the company was different from Pittman's, as well.

While Pittman had always been a deep-thinking theoretician concerned with social trends and cultural movements, Freston—though a bright, creative guy who was fascinated with pop culture—was a fly-by-the-seat-of-your-pants, go-with-your-gut type. If it smelled right, you did it. This was just television, for God's sake, not nuclear physics. Last, there was the difference in ego. Pittman went out of his way to keep his name in lights, but Freston was a much more modest man. Despite his humbleness, Freston could be extraordinarily demanding. He pushed himself hard, and he expected nothing less from those under him.

The names of the people beneath Freston were changing quickly. Many of the pioneers moved on to new endeavors, and by the end of July the three remaining original veejays—Mark Goodman, Alan Hunter, and Martha Quinn—had left as well, all moving West to try their luck in Hollywood. In addition to Downtown Julie Brown, they were replaced by a handsome Australian named Adam Curry and

MTV news anchor Kurt Loder. The former *Rolling Stone* writer gave much-needed credibility to the channel's news operation.

seventeen-year-old Dweezil Zappa, the son of rock star Frank Zappa. Some new faces had started to step forward in programming as well. In addition to Lee Masters, king of the flaming shooter, there was thirty-four-year-old former record exec Sam Kaiser. Kaiser had joined MTV in the fall of 1986, and now, with Les Garland and John Sykes both gone, he was the company's top liaison with the record industry. Doug Herzog was another new force. A curly-haired former producer at *Entertainment Tonight*, Herzog, twenty-nine, had joined the channel at the end of 1984 as the head of MTV's news department. He'd moved up quickly, and was now vice president in charge of long-form programming.

Masters, Kaiser, Herzog, and most of the rest of those who were now running the channel were a different breed. Whereas the original pioneers had all put their careers on the line to go to work for a start-up cable operation, this second generation had taken no such

the pioneers, then they'd let everybody down. And if they did measure up? Well, then, they'd merely done what was expected. What's the big deal? Pittman, Garland, and the rest did all the hard work.

Nevertheless, by the late summer of 1987, the second generation had begun to put their own stamp on the channel. As the ratings continued to be low, the real problem became increasingly clear: music videos themselves. Despite the drop-off in enthusiasm toward the clips the previous year, by now music video was an established part of the music business. Most label executives looked at the clips—and, by extension, MTV—as an almost irreplaceable way of marketing their artists. However, that was where the passion ended. The idea that had dominated three and four years earlier—that video was going to be the next great art form, or at least the next great product line—had faded. With the exception of the occasional piece that really did break

pg167

Adam Curry, one of the second generation of veejays. By the summer of 1987, all five of the original video jockeys had moved on to other endeavors.

risk. Though there was a temptation to dismiss this new group as a bunch of bandwagon jumpers who were merely trying to cash in on something somebody else had started, this wasn't exactly the easiest position to be in, either. While all of the new power people welcomed the opportunity to be working at MTV, in certain ways they were haunted by the pioneers' ghosts that seemed to walk the hallways of 1775 Broadway. This was particularly true of those near the very top. You really were damned if you did and damned if you didn't. If the newer generation failed to measure up to the standards set by

new ground, most clips were merely marketing tools, and hardly anyone would claim otherwise. In fact, the record companies had started to take a much more active role in creating the clips. Back in 1983 and 1984, they'd generally been content to hire hot directors like Russell Mulcahy, Steve Barron, and Bob Giraldi and let them work their magic. But today label executives were far more likely to tell the director precisely what it was they wanted to see. And why not? If you were dumping a hundred grand or more into something, you sure as hell had the right to get what you wanted, didn't you?

The problem was also with the audience, for whom video just wasn't that big a deal anymore. Not only was the clips' once-surprising visual style now all over the tube, but the whole concept of seeing a rock star jumping around in your paneled basement had become old. Moreover, just as there were now a bunch of younger siblings running MTV, there were a bunch of younger siblings watching the channel—thirteen- and fourteen-year-olds who couldn't remember a time when rock stars didn't make videos.

Which was why, after much thought, the second generation decided that the only solution might be to rebel against the very idea of MTV itself. Over the past couple of years, the only real boost to the ratings had come from the thirty-minute shows they had put on, like *The Young Ones* and *The Monkees*. And when you thought about it, that made sense. In addition to the novelty factor of such series, these and other traditional TV programs involved viewers for thirty minutes at a time. Videos, on the other hand, only lasted an average of three and a half minutes each, which meant that whenever a clip ended, it was really an open invitation for the viewer to switch to something else. Programming videos was like putting on a dozen shows an hour and hoping that viewers liked all of them.

Consequently, during the late spring of 1987, Tom Freston and the rest decided to cut back on the number of videos the channel showed and to produce some of their own programs. Such a switch in direction didn't come without a lot of debate. It went against Bob Pittman's original concept of non-narrative TV, of programming without beginning, middle, or end. On top of that, the whole MTV trademark had come to represent the idea of an endless stream of videos. In a lot of ways, some argued, this change was the equivalent

of Disney dumping family movies in favor of porn flicks. But as many arguments as there were for not trying shows, there was simply no denying the fact that everything else they'd tried—changing the clock or honing the playlist, for example—wasn't working. So what did they have to lose?

They started small. The first program was a natural for the channel, an after-school dance show called *Club MTV*. Hosted by Downtown Julie Brown and shown live from the Palladium in New York every afternoon, the show, which debuted at the end of August, was essentially an updated version of *American Bandstand* and the other teen dance shows that had been on the air practically since TV itself had first appeared. The channel played the music, Julie Brown bopped and said a few things in between clips, kids on the set danced, and, if all was working well, teenagers at home watched.

The second program, which premiered several months later, was called *The Week in Rock*. It, too, was a natural for the channel. From day one, MTV had done music news, and over the years the news department had grown larger and more independent. This was due in large part to current long-form programming vice president Doug Herzog and the head of the news department, Linda Corradina. An Emerson College graduate, the twenty-eight-year-old Corradina had spent three and a half years at ABC News before joining the MTV staff in 1985. Since then, she'd done much to bring some of the techniques of network news—basic things like getting videotape footage from network affiliates—to the channel. Herzog and MTV general manager Lee Masters placed her in charge of *The Week in Rock*—an hour-long weekly magazine show that covered what was happening in music. While Corradina was obviously excited about the challenge, to do the show properly she really felt she needed an anchorperson who had credibility in the music world. None of the veejays on MTV had that kind of stature. After interviewing and auditioning any number of TV types, radio people, and writers, Corradina settled on a boyish forty-two-year-old named Kurt Loder. A magazine writer who'd spent the past nine years at *Rolling Stone*, Loder had apparently gotten tired of the grind at the magazine and was looking for some new challenges. He took the job, and *The Week in Rock* went on the air.

The two programs didn't do badly when it came to ratings—both outperformed the music videos that had been playing in their time periods. Indeed, by the late fall *Club MTV* was doing well enough that Lee Masters and music vice president Sam Kaiser started adding dance cuts that premiered on the show to MTV's regular video rotation.

Despite the success of the two programs, it didn't do much to help the channel's overall ratings or the company's bottom line. In fact, when they tallied things up at the end of 1987, revenues and profits were down even more than the previous year.

* * * * * *

With Bob Roganti gone, a slew of new faces had started coming into power on the business side of the company, as well. On top was a young midwesterner named John Reardon. Brown-haired and buttoned-down, Reardon had been with the company since its earliest days. He'd started out in affiliate sales in WASEC's Midwest office and eventually became vice president of sales and marketing. He performed well in that position—under his tenure MTV's distribution rose to more than thirty-seven million, while Nickelodeon topped thirty-five million, and VH-1 topped twenty-two million. With

Roganti no longer overseeing ad sales, Tom Freston decided to put Reardon in charge of that area as well, with instructions to whip things into shape.

Reardon didn't waste any time. One day during the fall, he and Freston fired everybody at the top level of the ad staff, all the guys who'd been close to Roganti. Reardon then began searching for replacements. In January, he brought in an executive named Doug Greenlaw to run the day-to-day business of the ad sales department. Slick, polished, and personable, Greenlaw had been overseeing ad sales for the Christian Broadcasting Network.

Over the next few months Reardon and Greenlaw made big changes. They tried to give stability to the whole department. Despite what management had said in the past, and despite whatever troubles the company was now having, they kept stressing that neither MTV nor the other services were flashes-in-the-pan—Nehru jackets. To the contrary, they were tremendous niche-marketing ideas. What's more, Reardon and Greenlaw instilled in the staff a sense of belonging, the sense that ad sales was an important part of this big company, not a ragtag pack out on its own. To that end, Tom Freston started spending more time on the ad sales floor at 1775 Broadway.

Finally, and maybe most important, Reardon and Greenlaw began trying to integrate MTV into the marketing mainstream, something that, in their eyes, Bob Roganti had failed to do. Despite MTV's previous success in ad sales, both men found that many of the relationships between the company and its core clients had begun to deteriorate. Ever since the big ad explosion of 1984 and 1985, advertisers and agencies had sensed an arrogance on the part of many at MTV—service was poor, and there was little room to negotiate over

pg169

prices. While such an approach may have been successful when MTV was red-hot, it wasn't working very well anymore. As a result, Reardon, Greenlaw, and the rest of the second generation worked hard to try to show the ad world that a new day was dawning, that they were going to be more flexible, that they were going to do their best to work with clients.

In six years so much had changed: Cable was legitimate now, and so was rock and roll, so there wasn't much work to be done in pitching the channel's concept. No, the big challenge these days was persuading folks on Madison Avenue and other places that MTV wasn't dying, that it still had some heat with young people.

And by the spring, there was actually some proof that was true.

*   *   *   *   *   *

When the programming crew had met the previous summer and decided that MTV needed to do more long-form programming and produce some shows of its own, Tom Freston had given them the go-ahead for three programs. One was the dance show, *Club MTV*. The second was the music news show, *The Week in Rock*. And the third was, of all things, a game show. There was hardly a consensus among staff members that this was such a nifty idea. While a dance show and a music news show were logical extensions of what MTV had already been doing, trying to come up with its own *Wheel of Fortune* clearly took MTV in a different—and not necessarily appealing—direction. After all, what did a game show have to do with music? What's more, wasn't the game show just about the lowest form of television there was? But Freston insisted he wanted them to do it, if only because of what had happened at Nickelodeon. The year before, the kids' channel began producing its own game show, *Double Dare*, and it had

turned out to be a huge hit. In fact, it was so popular that Freston and Nickelodeon's Gerry Laybourne were considering putting the show into syndication on broadcast television. And if Nickelodeon could do it, why not MTV?

To develop the show, Lee Masters and long-form programming chief Doug Herzog turned to two young writers at MTV, Mike Dugan and Joe Davola. A Brooklyn native with a thick New York accent, Davola had established a name for himself fairly quickly, making documentaries on big-deal rock stars like John Cougar Mellencamp and Bruce Springsteen. He'd even briefly become an on-air personality. In 1986 Davola did a quick spot promoting MTV's coverage of Spring Break. It went over so well that it led to a co-hosting role on the Spring Break telecasts, and that led to "Joe Davola's Spring Break Retrospective," and that led several months later to producing and being on the air in the "Amuck in America" segments. His on-air career culminated at the 1986 Video Music Awards, where he and Alan Hunter presented an award.

Neither Davola nor Mike Dugan was initially very excited about the idea of doing a game show. In fact, when Masters and Herzog told Davola they wanted him to work on the project, he looked at them and said, "You're going to ruin my fucking career." Nevertheless, Davola and Dugan committed themselves to giving it their best shot. Not long after they got the assignment, they, along with Doug Herzog and a bunch of other programming types, rented a hotel room at the New York Hilton for a big brainstorming session, with tons of junk food and a big easel and a pad of paper.

Davola pitched the idea of doing a show about TV trivia. When he was a teenager, he said, he and his buddies back in Brooklyn used to get stoned and drunk and sit around and talk about stupid TV programs. Remember that time on *The Brady Bunch* where Greg hid the goat in his room? Or that time when *Gilligan's Island* did a musical version of Hamlet? Why couldn't they do a game show like that? Everybody liked the idea, and as the thing got batted around, a concept began to take shape: They would do a game show that basically made fun of game shows, with contestants answering questions about pop culture trivia and playing on a board that was a big TV screen, which they'd access with a remote control.

Over the next couple of months, Dugan and Davola developed the concept some more, working out the rules of the game, writing questions, and hiring talent. They considered Danny Bonaduce, the red-headed former kid star who'd been on the seventies show *The Partridge Family*, for the host spot, but ultimately hired comedian Ken Ober, whom they thought could ad-lib better. Just before Thanksgiving they shot a pilot episode of the program, which they were calling *Remote Control*. Then, after reworking some parts of the game, they shot the first episode. It debuted in early December.

The show was a riot. It either parodied or paid homage to just about every stupid thing on TV or in pop culture in general. The set for the program featured photos of game show legends like Wink Martindale and Bert Convy. Contestants were strapped into La-Z-Boy recliners, and at the end of the program the one with the fewest points was descended upon by guys in gorilla suits and pulled through a wall (the producers originally wanted to send people through the roof, but they couldn't obtain a forklift). In the middle of the show there was a snack break, where everybody chowed down on popcorn and pork rinds and cheese puffs. The questions were

ridiculous, as well, incredibly stupid queries about TV, music, and pop culture. Actually, because Davola and Dugan couldn't come up with enough questions, they had to add a couple of other categories. One was called the Laughing Guy, in which an MTV staff member named Steve Trecasse laughed a theme song from a TV show (Trecasse used to do this over the intercom at the office). Another was called Sing Along with Colin, in which contestants had to supply a missing line of a song sung by co-host Colin Quinn, who, naturally, was one of the worst singers in the history of the world. Adam Sandler, the future *Saturday Night Live* cast member, was also on the show, playing a character named Stickpin. At the end of the program, the contestant with the most points moved on to a bonus round, in which he or she sat on a Craftmatic adjustable bed and tried to identify as many videos as possible in thirty seconds.

Reaction to the show was terrific. The very first one got great ratings, and things just got better from there, as MTV began to promote the show more and word spread among the viewers. With its TV and pop culture references, it was the perfect show for a whole generation of TV babies. What's more, with its let's-lampoon-everything attitude, it tapped into the rebellious rock and roll spirit.

By early summer, *Remote Control* was hotter than ever. The channel was playing the show twice a day, once in the early evening (right before reruns of the British sketch comedy show *Monty Python's Flying Circus*) and again later in the night, and the press had started to notice. *People* did a piece on it, and a few months later so did *Rolling Stone*. Best of all, during the second quarter, the combination of heat from *Remote Control* and the other programming changes they'd made had lifted the ratings nearly 20 percent, to .7. Sure, it was a long way from the "Thriller"-inspired numbers of 1983, but to the second generation it looked just fine.

*   *   *   *   *   *

By summer, not only were revenues beginning to climb back up, but the channel's relationships with a number of core advertisers were on the mend. And Tom Freston wasn't about to risk damaging them again.

That rock and roll and corporate America had fallen so lovingly into each other's arms didn't please musician Neil Young. In the summer of 1988 he expressed his displeasure with a slow blues tune called "This Note's for You." The song was a scathing attack on corporate America's coopting of rock and roll, a wicked indictment of Michael Jackson, Eric Clapton, and all the rest of the pop stars who'd made commercials over the past couple of years. "Ain't singing for Pepsi," Young declared in the song, "Ain't singing for Coke/I don't sing for nobody/Makes me look like a joke." The video that Young and director Julien Temple made for the song was even more brutal, mixing shots of Young performing with vicious parodies of a number of those pop star commercials, including one with a Michael Jackson lookalike whose his hair caught on fire.

Would MTV play it? It was a tough decision for Freston. The programming crew wanted to air the clip—they had, in fact, even approved the script of the video before it was shot—but when they saw the finished product, the ad sales people were dead against it, so Freston was going to have to make the final call. What made this doubly difficult for the MTV chief executive officer was the fact that he loved Neil Young—and precisely because Young had never been afraid to say what he thought. But Freston ultimately decided playing the clip would be too risky for the channel. First, because a number

of name-brand products were actually shown in the video, there was the question of trademark infringement. He didn't want MTV getting sued. On top of that, Freston thought that airing the clip would set a horrible precedent. For the past couple of years, the channel had refused to play any video in which a product was prominently displayed. Earlier, a couple of record companies had tried to offset the cost of making videos by placing, for a fee, various name-brand products in their clips. Because MTV had already taken enough heat for being overly commercial, the network banned the practice. Although it was obvious that Neil Young was mocking the products and companies featured in "This Note's for You," not plugging them, Freston believed it was important to stick to the policy. After all, what kind of message would it send to advertisers? Yes, MTV will allow product placement—but only if it slams your products.

That July, executives at the channel informed Young they wouldn't be able to play the video, citing their fear of trademark infringement. But neither Young nor his record company, Reprise, wanted to give up. If trademark infringement was the problem, they said, then they would indemnify MTV for any losses that they might suffer in a lawsuit. The channel again refused, though, this time citing its policy against product placement. Still, Young wasn't about to toss in the towel. Now he offered to remove all the parody commercials from the clip and turn it into a performance video. Once again, the answer was no.

This time, Neil Young responded by writing an open letter to MTV, in which he called the executives at the channel a bunch of "spineless twerps." Naturally, this caught the attention of the press, and over the next several weeks many of the country's major media outlets did stories on the controversy, none of them particularly favorable to MTV. Finally, in early August, Freston realized he'd made a huge mistake and told the programming department they could play the clip—sort of. Rather than putting it into regular rotation, the video was presented as part of a news story on corporate sponsorship of rock and roll.

But not even the ugliness of the Neil Young debacle could detract from the momentum the company was beginning to build up once again. Ad revenues were climbing and *Remote Control* was as hot as ever. There was now no question that traditional shows pulled in better ratings than did an endless stream of videos, and that fall the channel's programming schedule started to reflect that. Over the summer Masters and Abbey Konowitch, a former record company executive who'd recently replaced Sam Kaiser as the head of music programming, had started to package the videos more— putting together blocks of musically similar clips. The most successful of the music shows was one called *Yo! MTV Raps*. Earlier that summer a couple of staff members, Ted Demme and Peter Dougherty, had approached Masters with the idea of doing a show with nothing but clips by rap artists. Masters didn't really think much of the notion at first. While rap was big in the inner cities, the music wasn't yet very popular out in America's suburbs, which was where most of MTV's audience lived. But Masters could see that both Demme and Dougherty were passionate about the idea, and he also figured it would be good for the channel, once accused of racism, to play music that was on the cutting edge. He told the two young producers to put together a one-time special. He was careful not to build up their expectations.

"Listen," he said to them the day before the show went on the air,

"don't worry about the ratings. It's probably going to do a .4 or .5, but don't freak out. Nobody cares. It's here for image purposes."

The show aired that weekend, and when Masters came into the office the following week and saw the ratings, he flipped—the program had earned more than a 2 in the Nielsens. Apparently this second generation of viewers out there across America really loved rap. Masters immediately tracked down Demme and Dougherty—to find out how quickly they could turn their special into a weekly show.

It wasn't only music programs they were adding to the schedule. In the wake of *Remote Control*, everyone inside 1775 Broadway—from Tom Freston down to the lowliest production assistant—had started to see MTV in a different light. No longer was this just a music video channel (FM radio with pictures, as the pioneers used to call it). No, it was now a full-fledged television network, albeit one aimed at teens and young adults. As a result of this new self-image, practically any kind of television show suddenly seemed appropriate, provided it had appeal to the younger generation and could be executed with the proper amount of finger-in-the-eye irreverence and let's-steal-the-moon-landing attitude. Not normal television—that was how they now thought of and publicly positioned themselves. That fall they added a movie show called *The Big Picture*, as well as a nightly talk show called *Mouth to Mouth*. While neither generated the ratings or press attention of *Remote Control*, they both consistently outperformed videos when it came to the Nielsens.

Few of the young kids working at MTV knew his name anymore, but maybe former WASEC chief Jack Schneider had been right after all. Maybe there really was a "compact with the viewer."

★　☆　★　☆　★　☆

First dreamed up in a New York hotel room, *Remote Control*, hosted by Ken Ober, became the catalyst for MTV's renaissance.

Yo! MTV Raps hosts Dr. Dre and Ed Lover. The show became one of MTV's most successful programs in the late 80s and early 90s.

Things weren't going as well for Bob Pittman and his new company, Quantum Media. Many of Pittman's plans for buying other companies and turning himself into a consummate deal maker hadn't worked out. For various reasons, the runs that Quantum made at other companies—ad agency J. Walter Thompson, NBC's radio division, television station group TVX—had failed. Meanwhile, some of Quantum's start-up projects had stumbled, as well. The company's film division never really got off the ground, and QMI Music, the record label that Les Garland had been charged with, was by now, the middle of 1988, all but dead. In fact, several months earlier, Garland had quit. Both he and Pittman cried when he told him he was leaving.

But not all was bleak. *The Morton Downey Jr. Show*, from Quantum's TV production arm, turned out to be a huge hit, although there were certainly plenty of people across the country who couldn't fathom why. The program had premiered the previous year. Some people at New Jersey-based cable superstation WWOR had approached Pittman with an idea: They wanted to do a talk show built around a right-wing host, and they wanted Quantum to produce it. Pittman took the assignment, found Downey working at a radio station in Chicago, and put him on the air. The results were amazing. Downey broke every television rule there was—he smoked on the air, he jumped around, he yelled at and literally got into brawls with his guests—and yet it was hard for people to take their eyes off him. While the show had started out on WWOR, it was now so successful that it went into national broadcast syndication.

The Downey show wasn't Bob Pittman's only success. He had also managed to invade political circles. Earlier in the year, a couple of friends had introduced him to Al Gore, the young Tennessee senator who was running that year for the Democratic presidential nomination. Pittman already knew Gore's wife, Tipper. (As one of the heads of the Parents Music Resource Center, the outfit that was trying to do something about indecent lyrics in rock music, Tipper had come to see Pittman when he was still at MTV.) Al Gore and Pittman met one day and really hit it off. In fact, Pittman later raised money for Gore—and even gave him some advice about the media. The two stayed in touch after Gore ultimately dropped out of the presidential race. And one weekend, Bob and his wife Sandy went down to the Gores' place in Carthage, Tennessee, and did some water skiing. It was really something—this preacher's kid from Brookhaven, Mississippi, hanging out with a presidential candidate. But then again, why not? After all, he and Al were both southerners—and they were both TV babies.

THIRTEEN

THE NEW FRONTIER

By the end of 1988, MTV was back. The falling star stories had vanished from the newspapers, and any notion that the network might be the Nehru jacket of the 1980s had faded away. In fact, fifteen months after the MTV rocket appeared to be in a hopeless tailspin, the company had not only righted itself, but had flown to new heights. Thanks to the heat thrown off by *Remote Control*, Madison Avenue's growing love of cable, and the hard work of Freston, Reardon, and Masters, 1988 earnings from MTV, VH-1, and Nickelodeon hit an all-time high of $59 million.

Although the company was earning more money than ever, the success seemed to have a different flavor this time around. There was little of the hysteria that had existed six and seven years earlier, when the MTV virus first ran rampant throughout America and radio stations were flooded with phone calls. *Remote Control* and the other shows the network had put on were popular, but there wasn't the same sort of passion for the channel that there had once been. To this second generation of viewers, MTV was just one of three or four dozen channels. If something good was on, you watched; if not, you tuned in to something else.

The feeling was different inside MTV, as well. The channel remained a loose, irreverent, exciting place, and clearly most people were happy about the success they were having. But few in the second generation of pioneers seemed surprised or exhilarated by it. And why would they? The company had been up and running and successful when most of the current group arrived. What did they know about hotel rooms that smelled like corned beef?

But Tom Freston and the rest of them were focusing intently on the future. Where could they go next? Like Warner boss Steve Ross five years earlier, Freston and Viacom's Sumner Redstone and Frank Biondi understood that this was no time to rest. They had to take advantage of their success, and where they were going to do it was around the world. They hoped to make MTV the world's first global television network. Ted Turner was trying to do something similar with CNN, but he was largely focusing on hotels that Americans and other Westerners visited internationally. The idea inside 1775 Broadway was different; they wanted to bring MTV to *homes* around the planet.

With the cable frontier in America largely tamed, any further spread of MTV in the States was likely to be slow. As a result, if Freston and the rest wanted the channel to have significant growth, the smartest strategy was to take MTV around the planet. Moreover, Freston him-

every part of the world, and in most cases English was accepted as the official language of rock. Moreover, young people everywhere seemed to like and dislike the same kinds of things.

As Freston was fond of saying, "A sixteen-year-old in Romania and a sixteen-year-old in Des Moines probably have more in common with each other than with their own forty-something parents."

Unfortunately, if international expansion was the goal, things on the new frontier weren't going very well. In Japan and now Australia, where a deal had been struck in early 1987, MTV was only on the air a couple of hours a week, and *MTV Internacional*, a weekly one-hour show that the company was syndicating to TV stations in Latin America, had only been on for a few months, so it was still fairly small.

But even more disappointing was MTV Europe, which in its year and a half on the air had not lived up to expectations. Its situation was similar to that of American

A West Point graduate and former NATO missile base commander, Bill Roedy was an unlikely choice to lead a rock and roll channel. Nonetheless, he made MTV's once-shaky European invasion a success.

self was predisposed to think in global terms. Not only was the trip he'd taken around the world in the early 1970s one of the defining times of his life, but he'd spent a number of years working abroad, importing and exporting clothes from India and Afghanistan. He'd always said that his real dream was to get MTV into India.

MTV, more than any other American cable network, was uniquely qualified for global domination. Whereas other services like CNN and ESPN faced language and cultural barriers, MTV was different. Rock and roll and its message of liberation were popular in nearly

MTV during 1981 and 1982. Things on the programming side were fine; things on the business side weren't. The pan-European ad market was still more of a dream than a reality, and finding distribution for the channel was equally tough. Not only was cable TV still in its infancy in most European countries, but many of the cable operators who had systems up and running said they wouldn't carry the network unless they were paid for it. To solve the distribution problem, the MTV folks had even brought back ad man Dale Pon for a European reprise of the "I Want My MTV!" campaign. But for a variety of reasons, it just didn't work. Even when kids picked up their phones and demanded their MTV—just as American teens had done years before—the European cable operators, unlike their Yankee confreres, weren't budging. I don't care how many runny-nosed kids call me, they told MTV. Pay me or you don't get on.

The European channel had its share of internal turmoil as well—most notably, a shakeup at the very top. Back in September, Mark Booth, the Kansas-born MTV pioneer who was the managing director of MTV Europe, quit to go to work for MTV Europe co-owner Robert Maxwell. When Tom Freston and Viacom's Sumner Redstone and Frank Biondi got wind of what had happened, they could hardly believe it. It was outrageous.

"I don't know about in your country," Redstone told Maxwell, "but in ours, one partner doesn't go stealing the other's employees."

Maxwell, never being one to hold his tongue, essentially told Redstone and the rest of the MTV people to go screw themselves.

To replace Booth as managing director, they hired a former HBO sales and marketing executive Bill Roedy. The trim, balding forty-one-year-old had an unlikely background for the job. He was a graduate of West Point, a Vietnam vet, and had spent three and a half years commanding a NATO nuclear-missile base in northern Italy before leaving the service and going to business school at Harvard. Despite his straight-laced background, Roedy caught Freston's attention, and by early 1989, Roedy was in London trying to turn things around at the struggling European outfit.

After all those years, they finally had an actual battlefield commander on board.

* * * * * *

As the months went by, MTV Networks showed signs of becoming a mature company. First, Tom Freston restructured the company's management, giving each of the corporation's networks its own president. Nickelodeon and Nick at Nite were placed in the hands of Gerry Laybourne, the woman Bob Pittman had put in charge of the channel's programming back in 1984. VH-1 was a tougher nut. The channel they'd launched to fight off Ted Turner back in 1984 was still having trouble defining what it was—and finding an audience. So Freston brought in an outsider named Ed Bennett, who'd been with another division of Viacom. Then there was MTV. Choosing between general manager Lee Masters and ad and affiliate sales chief John Reardon—the two men who'd done so much to engineer MTV's renaissance—certainly wasn't easy. Either one was likely to do a good job running the channel. To make matters tougher, Masters and Reardon were close friends. Freston finally decided to make Reardon president, with Masters as a strong number two person. He thought the channel would benefit more from having a strong businessperson at the top than a strong creative type.

There were other signs of growth and expansion. As an old marketing hand, Freston understood the value of the MTV logo. Consequently, over the past year or so the company had gone all out to capitalize on the MTV trademark. They set up a licensing division, to put the MTV name on appropriate products. The first one was the MTV Skatebike—a combination bicycle and skateboard. The company also got into the concert business, preparing that spring for two upcoming concert tours: the MTV Headbangers' Ball Tour, featuring a slew of heavy-metal acts, and the Club MTV Tour, featuring a number of dance music artists. There was even talk of getting into the theme park business. The company began discussions with Universal Studios about building a place called Rockplex, which would be a combination club, rock and roll museum, theme park, and TV studio from which the MTV veejay segments would be broadcast.

The last bit of expansion that spring came with the announcement of a brand-new channel, an all-comedy network called HA! The idea of creating an all-comedy channel had been around for some time, although the folks at MTV had only gone public with it because HBO recently announced it was starting a comedy network called the Comedy Channel. Since throughout cable's history only one service in each programming niche had survived, practically everyone agreed that only one of these channels was likely to last. Everyone in the company began gearing up for a battle.

But it would be a war with plenty of irony attached to it. Back in the winter, HBO owner Time Inc. and Steve Ross's Warner Communications had announced they were merging. As a result, MTV was now about to go to battle against one of its founding parents.

Even more ironic was the fact that within several months they were going to be pitted—indirectly—against none other than the Keeper of the Vision himself. But over time, Bob Pittman's dream of making QMI a dominant media company started to look less and less realistic, and Steve Ross started talking to him about returning to Warner. While any action would be delayed by the Time Warner merger, that September Pittman came on board at Time Warner as executive advisor to Steve Ross.

To Pittman, it really felt like coming home.

*　*　*　*　*　*

MTV's momentum continued. The programming folks kept putting on new programs (one of the latest was a daily version of *Yo! MTV Raps*), and revenues continued to grow. Things were going so well that they even seemed to have learned something from past mistakes.

In the early part of the year, Madonna signed a multi-million-dollar sponsorship deal with Pepsi. By this point, of course, the singer who had made such a splash at the first MTV Awards was one of the biggest stars in pop music. In a lot of ways, she had even surpassed Michael Jackson as the preeminent video pop star. More than anyone else, she seemed to understand the value of video in establishing image, and over the years she had done any number of interesting clips. This new deal with Pepsi called for the soft-drink maker to debut her newest single, "Like A Prayer," along with portions of that song's video, during a two-minute commercial that would be broadcast internationally on the evening of March 2. The company pulled out all the stops and made the largest one-day ad buy in history to debut the spot. The following day, the entire "Like A Prayer" video would debut on MTV.

The only problem was that a couple of days before the commercial and video were set to premiere, MTV's Lee Masters flew out to California to see the video and meet with Madonna's manager, Freddie DeMann. The clip was pretty outrageous. The whole video was filled with Christian imagery, and some of the scenes showed Madonna singing and dancing in a field of burning crosses and displaying stigmata—wounds that Christians believe Jesus suffered during crucifixion.

"Has Pepsi seen this?" Masters asked.

DeMann hemmed and hawed, Masters would later remember, and he got the impression that not only hadn't Pepsi seen it, but that DeMann and everybody else in Madonna's camp didn't want them to.

"Will you guys play it?" DeMann asked.

"Oh, we'll play it," Masters told him. "We'll have to run it past our standards department, but we'll play it."

The day the Pepsi commercial was scheduled to debut—one day before the video first appeared on MTV—some people at Pepsi called over to 1775 Broadway and asked MTV for a copy of the video. After obtaining permission from Warner Brothers to make a copy of the clip, they sent it over to them via overnight mail. The next day the Pepsi guys called back, and they were going nuts. They didn't want MTV to play the clip.

Tom Freston thought there were only two choices, neither one of which was particularly appealing. If MTV did play the video, Pepsi, one of the channel's biggest advertisers, would likely pull its spots. On the other hand, if MTV didn't play the clip, they were going to be in for the same sort of abuse they'd received when they didn't air Neil Young's "This Note's for You" clip the previous summer. Ultimately, Freston decided to go ahead with it, and that night "Like A Prayer" premiered on the channel. Almost immediately afterward a number of Christian groups protested the clip. Pepsi pulled the "Like A Prayer" commercials that were supposed to run on MTV that weekend, but their relationship with the channel remained intact. However, a month later they severed their ties with Madonna.

The whole controversy showed how powerful the network had now become. A big youth-marketing company like Pepsi had few other places to go if it really wanted to reach its target audience.

And that was the position that the record industry was now in, as well. The recent changes in MTV's programming—putting on shows like *Remote Control* and focusing musically on the hits—hadn't pleased many people in the music business. Not only was there now less time for videos, but fewer of the clips that did get played were by new artists. On top of that, a lot of people in the record industry thought that the MTV staff had become arrogant. Many of them longed for the old days, when Pittman, Garland, Sykes, and Sparrow had been so desperate for programming that they were begging people to make videos.

Nevertheless, the network's power in marketing artists was undeniable. Despite the cutback in clips by lesser-known acts, MTV had a hand in breaking a number of new artists over the past year—New Kids on the Block, Tracy Chapman, and Richard Marx. Consequently, the record industry wasn't about to turn its back on MTV. Labels were working harder than ever to get their clips into rotation. One day that summer, fifty people from Epic Records put on T-shirts and hats reading "Danger Danger"—the name of one of the label's new bands—and marched over to MTV's offices at 1775 Broadway, rode the elevator up to music programming chief Abbey Konowitch's office, and demanded that he immediately screen the band's newest video. And other labels were doing similar things. One day, Elektra Records sent a string quartet over to the network to perform the new single by the group Anderson, Bruford, Wakeman, and Howe.

While they spent a lot of time groveling, those in the record industry did take at least one opportunity to give MTV its comeuppance. Each year, industry insiders voted on the channel's Video Music Awards. And the winner of 1989's best video prize was the clip that

MTV wouldn't play: Neil Young's "This Note's for You."

Young didn't show up to collect the award.

*   *   *   *   *   *

From the day he'd started at MTV Europe, managing director Bill Roedy believed that the key to success was going to be improving the channel's distribution. The history of cable TV in America taught him that those channels that got on first had a much better chance of succeeding than those that came later. He also believed that the product was so unique that just getting it out there into people's living rooms would create tremendous word of mouth. The channel would be its own best advertising. As a result, within a couple of months of his arrival, the whole company became very aggressive about distribution. In addition to doubling their efforts with cable operators, they began to employ different technology to get the MTV signal out all over Europe, including home satellite distribution and traditional broadcasting.

The results were impressive, particularly when it came to Eastern European countries. As Roedy and his co-workers discovered, there was a real thirst in Eastern Europe for things Western, and nothing was more of a window to the West than MTV. The company soon discovered that there were a few small cable systems in Hungary, and after negotiations with the Hungarian government, they managed to get MTV onto them. The process culminated with an official ceremony in Budapest, where Roedy and a number of Hungarian officials gave speeches and made toasts and even exchanged pens, as though they'd just negotiated a peace treaty. As he sat there signing the agreement, the one-time cold warrior had to keep reminding himself that this was only television.

What happened in East Berlin was even better. That fall, Roedy agreed to address a conference of business leaders in the German city, on the condition that MTV Europe be hooked up in the city's hotels. After a long, arduous negotiation, East Berlin officials agreed, and one day in early November, MTV Europe was turned on.

Within an hour, the East German Politburo resigned.

It was just a coincidence, of course. The political sands in Germany and all of Eastern Europe had been shifting for some time. Or was it just a coincidence? Forty-eight hours later the Berlin Wall came crashing down, and as a group of East Germans headed for the West and freedom, they were asked how they knew it was safe to go.

"We saw it on MTV," they said.

With his biting "This Note's for You" video, Neil Young put MTV in an unwinnable position. Either offend advertisers, or look cowardly in front of viewers.

the pipeline

That MTV was helping to knock down the walls of communism was a kick for Tom Freston. More than anyone else at the company, Freston, who had joined WASEC just months after its birth, remembered the earliest days of the channel, when they measured success not by the number of Eastern bloc countries in which they were being seen, but by how many Buggles albums they were helping to sell at Peaches Records. But that was just how much things had changed during the past decade; that was the status they'd now achieved. They were an international ambassador for rock and roll—a youth pipeline.

Freston's own status had never been greater. In an industry filled with raging egomaniacs and insincere syncophants, he had a reputation as a straight shooter, an honest guy who told you how things were without any of the usual bullshit. And two and a half years after he had become the lone king of Sparta, this was finally his company now, just as it had once been Bob Pittman's. Not only had Freston earned the support and respect of Viacom honchos Sumner Redstone and Frank Biondi, but he was genuinely liked and admired by the people who worked for him. The troops appreciated that Freston encouraged an atmosphere of creativity and irreverence.

Throughout 1990, the momentum that had started during the previous years kept up. In programming, they continued to search for ways to connect with their young audience, and in the first few months of that year a whole new batch of shows went on, a few of which were really interesting. One, called *Buzz*, was an attempt at producing an international pop culture show. The show featured a number of ground-breaking, cutting-edge video techniques. Some of them were so cutting edge that they almost weren't watchable, but the show was an inspiration to the creative community within the channel. Another new program, *Unplugged*, in many ways rebelled against the very slickness that MTV and music video had helped to bring about in the music industry. On the show, artists played their songs acoustically. *Unplugged* actually had its roots in a couple of places. First of all, thanks to a new generation of folk singers like Tracy Chapman and Suzanne Vega, acoustic

Meanwhile, the business side of the company seemed to be chugging along wonderfully as well. Distribution for MTV in America now topped fifty million, and ad revenues were zooming through the roof. The key to this success was a more sophisticated way of presenting MTV to potential advertisers. The idea was to sell clients not only on MTV's unique demographic reach, but also on MTV's hipness.

As Tom Freston was fond of saying, "MTV is a lot like *Vogue*." A fashion ad in the stylish pages of *Vogue* made a far different statement than did the same ad in something more mass market, like *TV Guide*. It was the same thing with MTV—some of the channel's style rubbed off on advertisers. Clients were going for the notion; midway through 1990 they were on pace to set another sales record.

Despite all the good news, there were some problems inside the company, not the least of which was the fact that new MTV president John Reardon had

10,000 Maniacs lead singer Natalie Merchant on an episode of *Unplugged*. After appearances by Don Henley and Paul McCartney, the show became one of the hottest venues in the music industry.

music, long out of vogue, was making a comeback. Second, at the most recent Video Music Awards, rocker Jon Bon Jovi had gotten a great response when he performed with an acoustic guitar. So when producers Jim Burns and Bob Small pitched the idea for *Unplugged*, it seemed like a natural thing to do. The program was a wonderful antidote to all the prepackaged contrivance of video. Hosted by singer/songwriter Jules Shear, it had a spontaneous, hootenanny feel— just a few people sitting around playing their guitars. The first show aired in January and featured the band Squeeze and singer Syd Straw.

antagonized people on the channel's creative side. Back in the fall Reardon had fired the top creative guy and his own close friend, Lee Masters. After only a few months it had become clear to Reardon that after they both competed for the top job, there was no longer any room at the channel for both of them. So Reardon, with Tom Freston's backing, had ushered Masters out. To Reardon it was just business, an unfortunate event brought about by circumstances, but Masters didn't see it that way. The two men stopped speaking to one another.

But Reardon's troubles with the creative types went deeper. He cut back on the number of shows in development, and even slashed the payroll. Those in programming really thought Reardon was out of his element. A low-key, conservative midwesterner who'd cut his teeth dealing with the white-belt-wearing members of the cable industry, Reardon simply looked lost in the hipper, faster-paced world of big-time American entertainment. One day, he and music programming head Abbey Konowitch were having lunch with a group of record executives, among them Ahmet Ertugen, the legendary head of Atlantic Records. At one point, Reardon reportedly leaned over to Ertugen and said, "Now what do you do at Atlantic?"

Reardon himself was aware that he had a lot of work to do when it came to understanding the entertainment business. When it came to getting along with the MTV staff, however, he blamed many of his difficulties on Tom Freston. The reason he'd been forced to cut back on program development was that Freston had given him some tough financial goals to meet—and the only way he was going to be able to meet them was by slashing expenses. He also thought Freston frequently undermined his authority with the staff. Because Freston had come up through the ranks, he already had working relationships with many of the folks on the creative side. Consequently, when he wanted or needed something done, he often just called people directly. Though it may have been more efficient, it left Reardon wondering what his job was.

John Reardon wasn't the only problem. By the end of the summer, it was clear that MTV Networks's new comedy channel, HA!, wasn't doing well. Launched that April, its distribution was low and its advertising sales were even lower. The only good news was that

HBO's entry in the comedy wars, the Comedy Channel, was struggling just as much. Talks had actually started between Viacom and Time Warner, and in time the two channels would merge to become Comedy Central.

Overall, the problems of John Reardon and HA! did seem minor compared with the success the company as whole was having. Under Gerry Laybourne, Nickelodeon had matured into a popular and extraordinarily lucrative network. What's more, MTV continued to expand around the world. In September, MTV Brazil, a joint venture between MTV and Abril, a South American publishing company, went on the air, raising the total number of countries where MTV was available to thirty-nine. Even more exciting was what happened in October. That month, MTV Europe chief Bill Roedy and his lieutenants arranged for MTV to be seen one hour each week on Soviet television, allowing them to reach eighty-eight million more people. The reaction of the Soviet kids when they finally saw MTV wasn't much different from that of kids in Tulsa or anywhere else in the American heartland nine years earlier.

As one fourteen-year-old Russian video virus victim put it, "Of course I watch MTV. I wouldn't miss a single show."

* * * * *

Interestingly, the very things that had started all this—the music videos themselves—had never been in worse shape, artistically speaking. Nobody wanted to take any chances for fear that MTV wouldn't play his or her clips. Things got so bad that Tom Freston gave a speech to record executives, calling for more creativity in the videos. And he got it—although not in quite the way he'd been hoping.

MTV: THE MAKING OF A REVOLUTION

By the fall of 1990, Madonna's status as an entertainer and pop culture icon was greater than ever. The controversy over "Like A Prayer" a year and a half earlier increased both her reputation and her success. Indeed, the album *Like A Prayer* had sold more than eight million copies and spawned a number of Top-10 singles. And the Material Girl had continued to push the envelope with her videos, too, going right up to the edge of what was acceptable on MTV. The follow-up to "Like A Prayer" was "Express Yourself" and contained a number of racy scenes, including one in which she was tied to a bed. A few months after that she came out with a video for a new song called "Vogue," in which she wore a sheer blouse that clearly showed her breasts. Surely this must have violated MTV's no-nudity standard, right? As it turned out, it didn't. Ever mindful of the channel's policy on such matters, Madonna had covered her nipples, so despite the fact that viewers thought they were seeing her nude, they really weren't. The singer gave "Vogue" an equally outrageous treatment at the 1990 Video Music Awards. Dressed as Marie Antoinette, with her blond hair piled on top of her head and her bosoms protruding out of her dress, Madonna pranced all over the stage. At one point during the song one of the male dancers even grabbed her breasts.

Having gone right to the edge of the line with her videos on several occasions, Madonna was now ready to cross it. That fall she recorded a new song called "Justify My Love" and flew to Paris to film a video for it. Shot in grainy black and white and set inside a hotel, the clip (directed by Frenchman Jean Baptiste Mondino) depicted what Madonna said were her erotic fantasies—fantasies involveing voyeurism, female and male bisexuality, cross-dressing, and mild sadomasochism.

"It's the interior of a human being's mind," she said.

The instant they saw it, the MTV folks knew they were in trouble. There wasn't just one offensive scene that they might be able to ask her to cut; the whole video pretty much violated the channel's standards regarding nudity and sexuality. It was, again, a case of damned if you do, damned if you don't. If they played the clip, advertisers—and, perhaps more important, cable operators—would absolutely flip. The cable operators would be the ones who really felt the heat if people started canceling their service because of this MTV smut. On the other hand, if they didn't play the clip, they'd not only be passing up a video by one of the biggest stars in the world, but they'd undoubtedly be accused of censorship. Maybe worst of all, they'd lose credibility with their audience. In the eyes of the kids watching, the channel would be perceived in a way that it could never afford to be perceived: parental.

Finally, after a number of meetings about the clip and after hearing out staff members on both sides of the issue, Tom Freston made the call. Despite the damage it was likely to do to its image as the hippest channel on the planet, MTV was going to pass on "Justify My Love."

Almost immediately there was a huge ruckus. Newspapers wrote about it, including the *New York Times* and the *Wall Street Journal*, TV news operations did stories about it, and all over America men and women at office water coolers and boys and girls in school cafeterias were dying to see it. It was the Neil Young "This Note's for You" fiasco all over again—only about a hundred times worse. Madonna was a much bigger star than Neil Young had ever been and her videos were much more anticipated. Consequently, more people really cared about seeing this clip. Whereas Neil Young had become a star

Madonna performing "Vogue" at the 1990 Video Music Awards. Though her appearance caused a stir, it was nothing compared to controversy "Justify My Love" would bring later.

during an earlier era in rock and roll, Madonna was the quintessential star of the 1980s and 1990s. MTV had virtually created her, and now she was rebelling against it. It was incredible.

The whole fiasco culminated with an episode of ABC's *Nightline* in early December, on which the entire video was actually shown (it turned out to be the second-most-watched installment in *Nightline* history). The clip violated ABC's standards about nudity, too, but because this was now a major news story, not just a music video, it didn't matter. When the clip was over, Madonna talked with anchorman Forrest Sawyer, who was substituting that night for regular host Ted Koppel. They chatted about the video, about MTV's decision to ban it, and finally, about the fact that Madonna planned to put "Justify My Love" on videocassette—for the low price of $9.95.

"Madonna," Sawyer said, "it's likely that you're now going to make a lot more money on this than you would have."

Madonna looked unfazed. "Yeah," she said, "so lucky me."

Lucky her indeed. In time "Justify My Love" would sell more than half a million copies. People were actually going out and buying videos —just as Michael Nesmith had predicted a dozen years earlier—thanks to MTV's refusal to play something.

Had Madonna planned this whole thing? Was making a clip that MTV had to ban merely a publicity stunt? Nobody at the network ever knew, although a few had their suspicions, especially since Madonna and her people were able to get the video into stores so quickly. If it hadn't been planned, then Madonna was indeed incredibly lucky. And if it had been planned, you had to admire her marketing savvy. She'd essentially out-MTV-ed MTV.

＊　＊　＊　＊　＊　＊

Madonna wasn't the only one rebelling against the channel. The audience was, too. After hitting a Tom Freston-era peak of .8, the Nielsen numbers began to drop again, and by the first quarter of 1991, they were at .5. It was the lowest rating in the decade-long history of the channel.

There were a lot of explanations for what was happening. To start with, over the past year, thanks to budget constraints, the network had cut back on the number of shows it was putting on and gone back to featuring more videos. Because programs usually outdrew clips, that hurt the numbers. That MTV president John Reardon had clashed so much with the creative people hadn't helped matters, either. Relations finally got so bad that, during the spring, MTV Networks head Tom Freston called Reardon into his office—and fired him. To replace Reardon, Freston called on two people. Creative director Judy McGrath would oversee the programming side of the channel; Sara Levinson, a Viacom transferee who'd been running MTV Networks's new business development division, and who'd supervised much of MTV's international expansion, would oversee the business side of the channel.

Another problem was that pop music had splintered into a number of different genres and styles—rap, heavy metal, alternative—so there was no longer a big fat middle to appeal to, as there had been in 1983, 1984, and 1985, when Michael Jackson, Bruce Springsteen, and Cyndi Lauper had ruled. What's more, there was increasing competition for viewers' attention. In 1977, when Qube had first debuted in Columbus, most people only got a handful of channels. Now, fourteen years later, the average American had twenty-seven program services from which to choose.

Interestingly, neither the low ratings nor young people's apathy toward MTV really seemed to matter anymore. As the months went by and the ratings continued to go down, not one single falling star story had appeared, and revenues just kept rising. How could it be? Sheer size. In America alone, MTV reached more than fifty million homes. Not only did that generate plenty of cash from cable operators, but from an advertising standpoint, it meant that, no matter the ratings, there was no better way of reaching young people.

Then again, maybe none of that was really important. Maybe the reason the channel was now being courted by corporate America was the same reason that so many kids seemed to be losing their passion for it: Nearly ten years after it had gone on the air, this network just wasn't new anymore.

*　　*　　*　　*　　*　　*

That August, MTV celebrated its tenth birthday. The press made a huge deal out of it. For several weeks that summer, it was hard to pick up a major newspaper or magazine or turn on a news broadcast without seeing an anniversary-related story about the channel, noting all the changes it had helped bring about over the previous decade. MTV took a lot of pride in its birthday, too, hosting a huge bash for itself in New York and putting together a sixty-minute birthday special that aired on ABC later in the fall.

Afterward, the network's march around the world continued. That September, they launched yet another international affiliate, MTV Asia. Not only did the new service, which was being formed with a company called Hutchvision, give them distribution in thirty-one more countries, but it also made Tom Freston's dream come true—

the channel was now available in India. And as it turned out, the reaction there was the same as it had been in nearly every other part of the world. Not long after the channel went on the air, Freston got a letter from a young fan.

"I am studying in Bombay," Clayton Rana wrote. "A month ago I bought MTV. And now I am addicted to MTV, so much so that I am neglecting my studies. I would rather listen to more heavy metal. My favorite band is AC/DC."

The network continued to spread behind the Iron Curtain. Several months earlier, MTV Europe boss Bill Roedy had been contacted by Anatoli Lansberg, the president of the Baltic nation of Lithuania. For the past year, Lithuania and the other Baltic countries had been trying to win their independence from the Soviet Union. Back in January, however, while most of the world was preoccupied with the Gulf War, Soviet leader Mikhael Gorbachev had sent Soviet tanks into the country, taking over the state newspaper and TV station, and ultimately killing more than a dozen people. Still, Lansberg and the Lithuanian people had refused to back down. Indeed, when Bill Roedy arrived in Vilnius, Lithuania's capital city, he could hardly believe what he saw. Not only had Lansberg and his lieutenants barricaded themselves inside the House of Parliament, but they'd taken one of the remote trucks from the country's television station and were broadcasting—in direct defiance of Soviet authority—a second signal. And just what did Lansberg desperately want to put on that signal?

You guessed it: Bill Roedy worked out a way for the Lithuanian people to get *their* MTV.

"What was your first rock and roll experience?" one audience member asked. Clinton paused. "O

finally said, with a smile on his face, "going nuts over Elvis Presley." Even better, at least from

perspective, was the pledge that one of the questioners elicited from the Arkansas governor. "My name is Forrest Ray," one

fellow got up and said. "I'm twenty-three, I just graduated from UCLA. It's just great that you're here today talking to us and

in touch with us. But as president, how do you plan to stay in touch with us? I mean, would y

as willing to go back on MTV when you're president and do an interview as you would to be doing your

of the Union address?" Clinton looked at him for a moment, and started to nod. "I'll do that," he said. "I'll come

on MTV as president." The president of the United States on MTV? Those at the network tried not to get too excited

all, the man was twenty points behind in the polls. And the guy who was president didn't seem to want anything to do with the

FIFTEEN

A NEW WORLD ORDER

WINTER 1992 — FALL 1992

The idea to cover the 1992 presidential campaign started with MTV's creative director, Judy McGrath. For a couple of years, largely at McGrath's urging, the channel took part in a public-service ad campaign called Rock the Vote. Started in 1990 by Jeff Ayeroff, the president of Virgin America Records, the campaign's aim was to get more young people registered to vote. To do that, Ayeroff and the other Rock the Vote organizers had enlisted the help of many of the biggest rocks stars around, each of whom made a commercial (some of them fairly outrageous) urging young adults to cast their ballots. MTV had donated a ton of commercial time for the spots, and with an election year coming, the plan was to provide even more. Still, McGrath wondered if there wasn't something else the channel could do to acknowledge the election.

She tossed the ball over to the network's news department. Over several years, MTV News had really grown, both in its size and scope. Though reporting on what various bands were up to was still part of the department's mandate, it had branched out beyond music news and started covering other issues that affected young people. The real turning point in terms of content came at the end of 1989. Since the mid-1980s, MTV had always done a year-end retrospective called *The Year in Rock*, covering all that happened in the music world during the previous twelve months. With the '80s ending, the plan was to do a show recapping everything that had happened musically during the entire decade. As they started putting the program together, though, the notion developed: Why not cover everything that happened in the whole culture? The result was *Decade*, a ninety-minute special about issues ranging from rock and roll to politics to sex to the environment. Though there had been some concern about whether the MTV audience was really interested in such matters and whether the channel should be covering such stuff, the anxiety turned out to be unfounded. Not only were the ratings good, but the program, which despite its serious nature retained the hip MTV style, was so well done that it won a Peabody Award for television excellence. Since then, the news department, under the leadership of Linda Corradina and another staff member, Dave Sirulnick, had kicked into high gear, doing documentaries on sex, racism, and the post-baby boom generation (what many had now started calling the "MTV generation"). In addition, during its daily news reports, they paid attention to more and more non-music issues, such as the Gulf War. And with good reason: Many of the soldiers fighting it were the same age as MTV's viewers.

During the early part of the year, the news crew got together to talk about the presidential race, and after considering a number of possibilities, they came up with an idea: What if they put a reporter on the road and covered the campaign just like a regular news organization? As the idea got batted around, it seemed to have some merit. There were at least a few people in the news department— including a twenty-four-year-old reporter named Tabitha Soren and a young producer named Allison Stewart—who were interested in

politics and who were sure they could handle the assignment. Besides, they thought, covering the campaign seriously might actually appeal to the channel's audience. Contrary to what a lot of older folks assumed, the current generation of young people were interested in political and social issues. Indeed, many of them were quite angry about the state of the nation. The problem was that this generation didn't always see a connection between their concerns and voting. By covering the campaign MTV might be able to convince young people to take part in the process. Finally, there were the benefits for the channel. After years of being perceived in some circles as a network created by Satan himself, doing something pro-social like this, playing this patriotism card, certainly couldn't hurt.

Still, there were risks. The candidates and their campaign organizations might not take MTV seriously. It was one thing to cover an Aerosmith concert or even put together a documentary on sex; it was something else to muscle in next to Peter Jennings or Dan Rather or some other network news hotshot and demand serious answers from the men running to be leader of the free world. Even riskier was the reaction of the audience. MTV's programming could not afford to look like it was homework. What if the kids out there across the country just tuned them out? Worse, what if the news crew covered this campaign in the name of getting young people out to vote, and then the little punks just stayed home?

Despite the risks, they decided that covering the campaign was at least worth a try. And so in early February, Soren and Stewart and a tape crew packed their bags and headed off to New Hampshire to put the MTV stamp on the 1992 presidential race. They were a lot like the pioneers of the channel—filled with passion and excitement, coping with their underdog status and the very real possibility that they were going to elicit "Huhs" and "M-whats" from the people they were covering.

Things in the great state of New Hampshire couldn't have gone better. With the exception of President Bush, who was limiting his appearances, all the candidates were more than willing to talk to MTV. This was partly due to the way the MTV crew approached the candidates. With the camera running, Soren would walk up and say, "Hi, I'm Tabitha Soren from MTV News. We're trying to get more young people to vote. What do you think about . . ." Then she would ask her question. Not only did this approach explain why this unruly pop culture network had immersed itself in presidential politics, but it also put the candidate into a corner. If he didn't talk, he would appear not to care whether young people voted, and that was an attitude that wasn't going to cut it with anyone. But it was more than just the threat of political humiliation that made these guys so chatty. MTV was now so well known as a symbol of the youth culture that the candidates saw it was a way of effectively reaching America's young people, just as the advertisers did. Speaking into Tabitha Soren's microphone, which had a big, clunky MTV logo on it, was tantamount to putting your message right into the pipeline and having it spill out into the homes, hearts, and minds of America's youth. What publicity-hungry politician could pass that up?

When the MTV crew put together their reports, which covered everything from who the candidates were to how hard it was for young people to register to vote, they presented them in the usual fast-paced, ironic, slightly off-center MTV style. Audience reaction was very positive.

Not surprisingly, the network was also getting good publicity for its presidential coverage. When MTV first arrived in New Hampshire and began hounding the candidates just like the rest of the media, the members of the press corps were dumbfounded and responded with a "What the hell are they doing here?" kind of attitude. Eventually, though, the media corps's instincts kicked in and a few of them realized that MTV's coverage of the presidential campaign was nearly as good a story as the campaign itself. Not long after Soren and Stewart and the rest arrived in New Hampshire, the *New York Times* did a piece on MTV's political coverage and put it right there in the middle of Section A, where all the *real* news was.

Because of the positive reaction to the New Hampshire trip, the network decided to continue with campaign coverage. Over the next several months, under the banner "Choose or Lose," Tabitha Soren and her crew stayed on the road, reporting on the presidential campaign. In addition to covering the candidates, they also put together a few educational reports explaining the political process to young people. The question of whether the kids out there in America were understanding this stuff was still open to debate, but you had to admit one thing: It was a hell of a long way from A Flock of Seagulls.

*   *   *   *   *   *

Though MTV's ratings weren't what they once had been, the network's programming continued to generate its share of heat. That spring, the channel launched *The Real World*, "a real-life soap opera" chronicling the lives of a handful of twenty-something folks that MTV put up in a New York loft for several months. The show made a major splash not only with viewers, but with the press, as well.

The acoustic show *Unplugged* had become a lightning rod program, too, although original host Jules Shear had been let go and the show was far less spontaneous than it had been in early 1990. The big turning point came when former Eagle Don Henley did the program, transforming it into a hot venue for big-name acts. After that, Paul McCartney had put out a record of his *Unplugged* appearance, and when it became a hit, artists and record companies began scrambling to get on the show and put out their own *Unplugged* records. Even though it was only two years old, there were already people longing for the show's "good old days."

Despite the success of both The *Real World* and *Unplugged*, it was the Choose or Lose coverage that dominated that spring and summer. And by late spring, when George Bush and Bill Clinton had locked up their parties' nominations, the presidential race really became interesting. There was the wild-card presence of Ross Perot,

during the Depression (although coming from a wealthy family, he was probably more insulated from it than most), had been a naval pilot during the war, and afterward had devoted himself to the twin aims of making money, which he did by starting an oil-drilling business in Texas, and helping his country, which he did by serving in Congress and in the Nixon, Ford, and Reagan administrations.

The forty-five-year-old Clinton, on the other hand (among whose major financial supporters was Bob Pittman), was a quintessential baby boomer. He'd been raised in post-war prosperity (although his own family's means were modest), had been moved by the civil rights struggle, had tried marijuana, had protested the Vietnam war, and had suffered through very public marital difficulties. Unfortunately for Clinton, these latter sins hadn't exactly endeared him to the American public. By the time he won California's Democratic primary in June, most polls had him running

MTV News's Tabitha Soren. The Channel's coverage of the presidential campaign turned the twenty-something reporter into a celebrity in her own right.

who had gone on CNN's *Larry King Live* and proclaimed that if the American people put his name on the ballot, he would run for president. The next thing you knew, pro-Perot groups were popping up all over the country, and by June the man had all but declared himself a third-party candidate.

The battle between Bush and Clinton represented two generations squaring off against one another. And it would have been hard to find two more representative candidates. At sixty-seven, Bush was the quintessential member of the World War II crowd. He'd been raised

third behind Bush and Perot, with fewer than 30 percent of voters saying they were likely to pull the lever for him.

With the field narrowed to three, and with MTV's own political coverage being more well-received than ever, those at the network decided to do something really special. During late spring, the channel extended invitations to the candidates to take part in special election forums, where they could respond to questions and concerns of young voters. The reaction of the candidates? While neither the Bush nor Perot camps seemed interested, the Clinton campaign was intrigued by the offer. And why not? Their man was now so far behind in the polls—and falling farther every day—that they'd begun looking for alternative ways to get his message out. Finally, after negotiations with Tom Freston, Judy McGrath, and others at MTV, they accepted the network's invitation. On June 16, the candidate and his entourage arrived at a studio in Los Angeles to tape the program.

Everyone involved seemed on edge. The MTV execs were nervous because the channel had never done this kind of town meeting program before; young Tabitha Soren, who was co-hosting the forum with CNN's Catherine Crier, was nervous because she'd never done this kind of event, either. Even Clinton looked nervous. It was all so incongruous—eleven years earlier this channel had gone on the air playing practically nothing but music videos; four years earlier it had reinvented and reinvigorated itself with a dopey game show spoof; and now it was playing host to a presidential candidate.

Still, the program came off without a hitch. Clinton stood on a hardwood stage with a funky-looking American flag backdrop behind him and took questions from young audience members, whom MTV had screened ahead of time. Most of the queries were straightforward and intelligent, and Clinton, who seemed to get more and more comfortable as the event went along, answered them all seriously. The event went so well, it was stretched from sixty to ninety minutes to allow for more questions. While most of the forum really did revolve around the issues, at one point the candidate even got to display his rock and roll stripes.

"What was your first rock and roll experience?" one audience member asked.

Clinton paused. "Oh," he finally said, with a smile on his face, "going nuts over Elvis Presley."

Even better, at least from MTV's perspective, was the pledge that one of the questioners elicited from the Arkansas governor.

"My name is Forrest Ray," one young fellow got up and said. "I'm twenty-three, I just graduated from UCLA. It's just great that you're here today talking to us and you're in touch with us. But as president, how do you plan to stay in touch with us? I mean, would you be as willing to go back on MTV when you're president and do an interview as you would to be doing your State of the Union address?"

Clinton looked at him for a moment, and started to nod. "I'll do that," he said. "I'll come back on MTV as president."

The president of the United States on MTV? Those at the network tried not to get too excited. After all, the man was twenty points behind in the polls. And the guy who was president didn't seem to want anything to do with them.

*   *   *   *   *   *

The campaign coverage continued with reports from the Democratic and Republican conventions that summer. The news team reported with typical MTV panache. To help them cover the Democratic convention in New York, they brought in Dave Mustaine from the heavy-metal band Metallica and rapper MC Lite, while at the Republican convention in Houston, singer Ted Nugent and rap star Treach from the group Naughty by Nature were on hand. The reason for the celebrity reporters was twofold: First, the MTV folks thought it would make things more interesting for the audience if musicians did the coverage; second, being media-savvy, they knew it would be a good hook to get publicity.

Not that they needed any more press. After the Clinton forum the media had gone completely crazy. At the conventions, MTV literally had its own press pack—people covering the team while they covered the convention. Tabitha Soren had become a celebrity in her own right. Everyone under thirty at the conventions seemed to want her autograph.

Thanks to the election coverage, in recent months the channel's ad revenues were up significantly, as well. Perhaps more important, the MTV appearance truly seemed to be a turning point for the Clinton campaign. Afterward, the candidate started doing more and more forum-type events, in which he seemed to excel. In fact, by early September, after the two conventions and after Ross Perot had temporarily dropped out of the race, Clinton was ahead in the polls.

And George Bush? Well, back in July he had reiterated his decision not to appear on MTV, saying he wouldn't be going on what he called the "teenybopper network."

* * * * * *

Two months after the Republican convention, Bill Clinton was elected the forty-second president of the United States. In the end it wasn't even that close: Clinton received 43 percent of the vote, Bush received 37 percent, and Ross Perot, who'd jumped back into the race in October, received 19 percent. Clinton's victory margin was even wider in the electoral college.

George Bush finally did make an appearance on the "teenybopper network," as did Ross Perot. The weekend before the election, Tabitha Soren interviewed the president on the back of a train in the middle of Wisconsin. By that point, however, the election was all but over.

And how was turnout among younger voters? It jumped more than 20 percent from 1988, with the majority of young people picking Clinton. While obviously this wasn't all due to MTV, the channel had played a part. Not long afterward a joke began spreading around the music industry. "MTV broke three acts in 1992," people would say. "Pearl Jam, Arrested Development . . . and Bill Clinton."

* * * * * *

By the time Bill Clinton took office that January, it was amazing how much the world had changed since John Lack had first left CBS and ventured out to godforsaken Columbus, Ohio, fourteen years earlier. In many ways the future of television was already here. More than 60 percent of the country's homes now had cable TV. America was closer than ever to becoming the Wired Nation. Moreover, the 1992 presidential race had given cable new credibility. Not only had MTV made its mark on politics, but Larry King's show on CNN had become nearly as influential as the broadcast networks' evening news programs when it came to bringing the candidates to the people.

Rock and roll's place in the world had changed, too. Thanks to Bill Clinton, the music Elvis had made popular was on its way to the White House.

Finally, there was MTV Networks itself. The company that was once known as WASEC was simply unrecognizable from its early days on the cable frontier. There were four programming services in its stable now—MTV, VH-1, Nickelodeon, and Nick at Nite. And in 1992, revenues had exceeded $500 million. Perhaps more important, the war that began in the summer of 1981 finally seemed to be over. In the eleven years since all the pioneers gathered in that bar in Fort Lee, New Jersey, and watched the MTV flag being planted in the moon, the channel had been embraced not only by young people around the world, but also by the record industry, the cable community, Madison Avenue, and now by the president of the United States.

Which was why it seemed so fitting that, shortly after the election, Tom Freston received a fax from Clinton aide Mickey Kantor. It was an invitation to the special economic conference the president-elect was hosting in Little Rock in December. Freston was flattered by the invitation, although he did face a couple of dilemmas: First, the conference was scheduled for the same day as the taping of an *Unplugged* show with Neil Young, and Freston, still a huge Young fan, wanted to go. Second, he felt a little bit uncomfortable that it was he who had been invited, and not Sumner Redstone. But the sixty-nine-year-old Viacom chairman gave Freston his blessing. So in mid-December, Tom Freston packed his bags, flew to Little Rock, and sat at the table with the president-elect and the new pillars of American business, pondering the future of the country.

Meanwhile, back in New York, the bright young brains at MTV began contemplating an equally weighty question: What's a rock and roll network to do when the president of the United States actually *likes* them?

REUNION

Bill Clinton kept his promise to go back on MTV as president. Twice during his first sixteen months in the White House he appeared on the channel—the first time to announce his national service legislation, the second time in a forum on crime. Clinton's second appearance caused a bit of a stir. One of the questioners asked the president what kind of underwear he wore, and Clinton responded honestly. There were a lot of people who didn't think such behavior was very presidential. (In mid-1995, Speaker of the House Newt Gingrich also starred in an MTV forum, though when a wiseacre reporter asked afterward, he declined to specify which type of underwear he preferred.)

As MTV moved into the mid-1990s, its programming maintained the same formula—80 percent videos (now grouped mostly into blocks of musically similar clips) and 20 percent youth lifestyle shows. The majority of those shows were of the here-today, gone-tomorrow variety, but a few captured viewers' imaginations. *The Real World* series was a consistent winner, each year putting a new cast of young people together in a different locale. Meanwhile, *The Jon Stewart Show*, a hip late-night talk program, performed strongly enough that Paramount (which MTV parent Viacom acquired in 1994) took over the show and syndicated it nationally.

But the biggest success of all was *Beavis and Butt-head*, an animated series created by a twenty-nine-year-old Texan named Mike Judge. The show featured two lunkheaded teenagers who dressed in heavy-metal T-shirts, loved stuff that was "cool," hated stuff that "sucked," and spent most of their time sitting on a couch making fun of music videos. The boys first appeared in a short clip on MTV's *Liquid Television* in September of 1992. Recognizing that the characters were cut from the same irreverent but hugely popular cloth as Fox's *The Simpsons* and Nickelodeon's *Ren & Stimpy*—only more so—in November MTV's execs ordered thirty half-hour episodes.

By the following summer, *Beavis and Butt-head* was running twice a day, six days a week, and it had become the hottest thing on the channel since Michael Jackson in 1983. All over America, fans of the show were honing their *Beavis and Butt-head* imitations—"Heh, heh. This sucks," was the most common refrain—while the media were cranking out a new round of rising star stories. *Rolling Stone* put the duo on its cover—twice—and *Time* opined that *Beavis and Butt-head* "may be the bravest show ever run on national television."

taking things a bit far, MTV responded by removing *Beavis and Butt-head* from its early-evening schedule. But even that didn't hurt the show's popularity. By the time the phenomenon had cooled down in late 1994, a Beavis and Butt-head album and a Beavis and Butt-head book had appeared, Beavis and Butt-head T-shirts were everywhere, and even a Beavis and Butt-head movie was in the works.

*   *   *   *   *   *

With Tom Freston at the helm, MTV Networks continued to be a successful financial venture. MTV's ratings fluctuated, but revenues for the channel (which, with the departure of Sara Levinson in the fall of 1994, was now being overseen soley by Judy McGrath), along with those for the entire company, just kept rising. VH-1, the channel that had struggled ever since being launched as a fighter brand back in 1985, finally showed some signs of life. Realizing that most of the kids who watched MTV in the

Nickelodeon stars, Ren & Stimpy. This irreverent duo paved the way for the even more rebellious—or perhaps repulsive MTV stars—Beavis and Butt-head.

Not everyone was so enthused. With the characters' constant scatological references, mind-numbing stupidity, and cruel antics (the original *Beavis and Butt-head* short was entitled "Frog Baseball," and featured the boys blowing up a locust with a firecracker and using a frog for batting practice), many adults considered the program irrefutable evidence that the apocalypse was upon us. The controversy reached a peak when an Ohio woman claimed an episode of the show caused her young son to start an ultimately fatal fire. Though even some of the program's critics thought that charge was

early days had outgrown the channel, the company's execs positioned VH-1 as a service for twenty-five-to-thirty-four-year-olds—a more subdued but still musically hip older sibling to the rambunctious MTV. To lead the channel in its latest incarnation, Tom Freston brought back his old Tulsa traveling buddy, John Sykes.

And the international spread of MTV showed no sign of letting up. In the fall of 1993, MTV Latino went on the air, followed a year and a half later by Taiwan-based MTV Mandarin. By the middle of 1995, with MTV Europe savior Bill Roedy leading all of the company's non-U.S. ventures, nearly one-third of the company's revenues came from its international affiliates. Some predicted that by the turn of the century, that number could climb to one-half.

Would MTV Networks's success last? That was harder to say. Every day new challenges cropped up. In 1994 several record companies announced they were going to start a competing music video channel—the biggest threat since Ted Turner a decade earlier. While anti-trust problems ultimately helped squelch the project, it illustrated the constant tension between the channel and the record industry—despite the good they did each other.

An even greater challenge to MTV was the fact that a whole new frontier seemed to be forming, just as it had in the mid-1970s, when Qube and HBO and the other satellite-delivered networks had first appeared. This time, multi-media technology was the catalyst.

MTV's response to these changes? For a while it had kicked around the idea of splitting itself into three different channels, each dedicated to a different type of music, but the concept was unworkable. Nevertheless, the company was making changes. It developed an on-line presence through America Online and created a new division, MTV Interactive, to develop video games, CD-ROM products, and interactive TV services.

Perhaps most significantly, the company also spun off a division called MTV Productions. The unit was to make shows and movies targeted at youth. Though delivery systems might change, the need for programming targeted at young people wouldn't.

Nor, it seemed, would the youthful spirit inside MTV. Despite its size, the company continued to be a place where young people ruled. It wasn't entrepreneurial any longer—that era had died when the

Beavis and Butt-head, who were originally seen on an installment of MTV's Liquid Television. Did the characters represent the end of civility, or merely the taste of a new generation?

On-line services like CompuServ and America Online were growing in popularity, and experts were predicting that technology would soon make five hundred interactive television channels. Already a whole batch of new networks had popped up or been proposed in anticipation of this new world. Moreover, Bob Pittman had recently started talking about a whole new generation of people out there—computer babies. Just as TV babies had grown up with and been shaped by television, this new crowd was being raised on and influenced by computers.

pioneers left the company in the mid-1980s—but with a constant influx of twenty-something minds, it was still a place that was skeptical of the status quo.

And what of the original pioneers, the people who'd actually created MTV? By the mid-point of the Clinton administration, all but a few of them had left the company and moved on to other pursuits. When asked what impact MTV had had on them, nearly all of them admitted that working at MTV had been the most exciting time in their lives, one they would certainly never forget.

And there was one evening when all of them—or nearly all of them, anyway—reunited. It happened during the summer of 1991, right around the time of MTV's tenth birthday. Although the company was throwing a big bash to celebrate the occasion, Tom Freston thought it would be nice also to have a smaller, more intimate dinner for the channel's founders. He rented a room on the second floor of the Tribeca Grill in lower Manhattan and sent out invitations to the fifty or so people who'd helped build the channel. There were only two important pioneers he didn't invite: Jack Schneider, the former WASEC head who'd once quibbled about Freston's bonus, and Bob Roganti, the former co-king of Sparta.

Nearly everyone showed up. Fred Seibert was there, as were Bob McGroarty, Larry Divney, Sonya Suarez, Andy Orgel, David Hilton, Dale Pon, Sue Steinberg, Robert Morton, Julian Goldberg, Marci Brafman, Carolyn Baker, Gale Sparrow, John Sykes, and Les Garland.

Bob Pittman was there, as well. Pittman continued to move in lofty circles. The preacher's kid was by then president and chief executive officer of Time Warner Enterprises, a division of Time Warner Inc., and was overseeing Six Flags amusement parks; later he would become the chief executive officer of the Century 21 real estate company.

John Lack came to dinner that night, too. The man who'd set everything in motion had certainly had an interesting career. After leaving WASEC in 1982, Lack became president of ACTV, an interactive games channel. Later, after helping to launch ESPN2, he became head of a joint venture between TCI and Acclaim Entertainment.

It was quite a night. Everybody hugged and kissed when they first saw each other, and they all downed plenty of tequila and champagne and other beverages, and maybe even a few other substances. Mostly what they did, though, was catch up on where everyone was and reminisce about all they'd done years earlier. A decade before, they'd all shown up in those ordinary little offices in the middle of midtown Manhattan ready to create something important and change the world. In time, through Rod Stewart hairdos, rising star stories, a video revolution, Ted Turner's attack, an LBO bid, and, of course, the Nehru jacket complex, they'd done just that. If they'd occasionally clashed with one another along the way, you wouldn't have known it that night. The mood was joyous. Later on, it was Les Garland who put it best. "We poured our hearts and our souls into that channel," he said. "Love comes from that."

After a long cocktail hour, everyone sat down at the big round tables that were set up in the room. At each place setting, Tom Freston had put a copy of the very first clip MTV ever played, "Video Killed the Radio Star." Right before dinner was served, Freston got up to say a few words.

"This is a unique club we're all part of, " the MTV chairman said. "Because you can't get into it if you wanted to, and you can't get out of it. We're stuck here. We did it. I know most of the people in this room have probably fired somebody else in this room, and some of you might even hate each other. But we created this thing, and it's really greater than any of us. And it's gonna live on long after everybody in this room is gone."

Freston talked for a few more moments, then said, "I think it's time that we acknowledge somebody we might have forgotten about. Let's really give tribute to the man who invented this thing, John Lack."

Everybody applauded, and Lack got up and said a few words. Then he reached over and handed Freston a bottle of Dom Perignon.

After that, Freston introduced Bob Pittman. The Keeper of the Vision also made a short speech, and then the waiters served dinner and everyone started eating. Except that few people really ate. Everybody kept getting up and going from table to table, drinking and talking to one another.

After dinner, Bob Pittman went over to talk to Robert Morton, who'd stopped Nina Blackwood from choking a decade earlier. When they'd first arrived that evening, Pittman had suggested to Morton that, in the glorious name of rock and roll, they really ought to get a little crazy, break some glasses or something. Now it was time. "Go ahead," Pittman said, "break a glass."

Morton stood up, took aim at one of the room's brick walls, and fired. The glass smashed. For an instant everything stopped. But then somebody else had picked up a glass and smashed it, and somebody else, and then somebody else. Naturally, the waiters came rushing over and told them to cool it. For a minute things did quiet down. But a moment later another glass went flying against the wall, then another, and another. There were broken pieces of glass everywhere.

It went on for a few moments more, until finally one of the managers of the place came in, said enough's enough, and threw everybody out. The next day the *New York Post* ran an item about the party under the headline: "Ten Years Old—And Not a Day Older."

For the pioneers the night didn't end there, however. They were all having so much fun that they piled into cabs and went to a popular place called the Amazon Club, where they laughed and drank and partied all night long, remembering the battles they'd waged and reveling in the world they'd made.

When the sun started to rise, they all went home, trying not to think about the day when their own children would grow up, look at what their parents had created . . . and change everything.

index